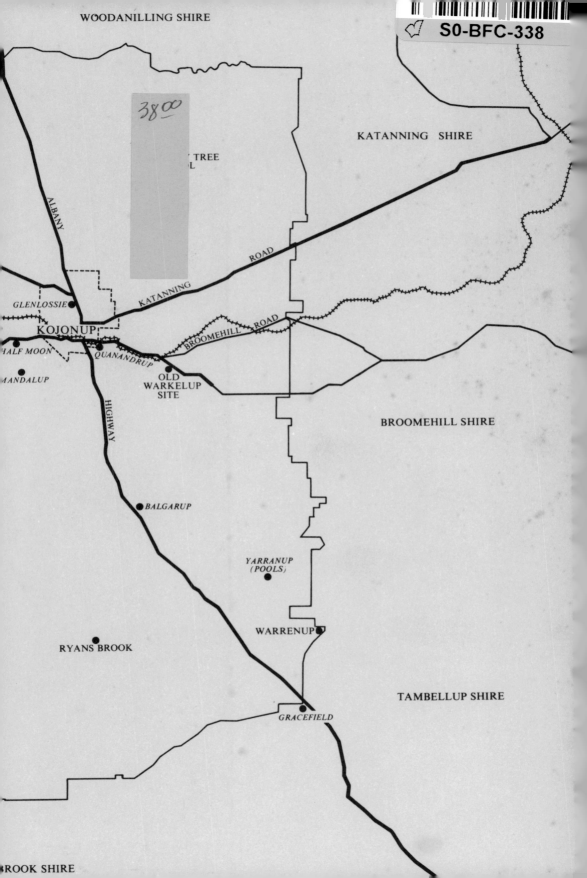

WOODANILLING SHIRE

S0-BFC-338

KATANNING SHIRE

3800

TREE

ALBANY

ROAD

KATANNING

GLENLOSSIE

KOJONUP

BROOMEHILL   ROAD

HALF MOON

QUANANDRUP

MANDALUP

OLD
WARKELUP
SITE

BROOMEHILL SHIRE

HIGHWAY

BALGARUP

YARRANUP
(POOLS)

WARRENUP

TAMBELLUP SHIRE

RYANS BROOK

GRACEFIELD

BROOK SHIRE

FIRST THE SPRING

A HISTORY OF THE SHIRE OF KOJONUP
WESTERN AUSTRALIA

A *kodja* (Aboriginal stone axe) from which
the name 'Kojonup' was probably derived.
The name was given to surveyor Alfred Hillman
by local Aborigines in 1837. The axe measures
13¾ inches in length and is now in the possession
of the Western Australian Museum
(Registration number 9919)

FIRST THE SPRING

A HISTORY OF THE SHIRE OF KOJONUP
WESTERN AUSTRALIA

MERLE BIGNELL

Published for the Kojonup Shire Council by
UNIVERSITY OF WESTERN AUSTRALIA PRESS
1971

First published for the Kojonup Shire Council in 1971 by
University of Western Australia Press
Nedlands, Western Australia

Eastern states of Australia and New Zealand: Melbourne University Press,
Carlton South, Victoria, 3053
Great Britain and Europe: International Scholarly Book Services Inc., London;
U.S.A. and Canada: International Scholarly Book Services Inc.,
Portland, Oregon, 97208.

National Library of Australia Card Service Number
and Standard Book Number 85564-048-0
Library of Congress Catalog Card Number 70-152121

Printed in Western Australia by Alpha Print Pty Ltd,
Perth, Western Australia and bound by Stanley Owen and Sons Pty Ltd,
Alexandria, New South Wales

Registered in Australia for transmission by post as a book

Contents

Illustrations

Foreword

Ours is a young country by world comparisons. Western Australia is only 142 years old and in that time has made tremendous progress. In the year 1971 a number of shires in this state celebrate 100 years of local government. To celebrate our centenary the Kojonup Shire Council commissioned the writing of this book. I feel it serves a dual purpose. It has assembled dates, incidents and stories both sad and humorous to make a convenient reference for future historians. It is also a tribute to the explorers and early settlers who endured countless hardships to open up our district. I recommend it to all book-lovers and students of Australian history.

Kojonup, 1971

L. N. COLLINS
Shire President

Abbreviations

C.S.O.Recs.	Colonial Secretary's Office Records
Kat.H.S.	Katanning Historical Society
K.H.S.	Kojonup Historical Society
K.J.H.S.	Kojonup Junior High School
K.R.B.	Kojonup Road Board
P.R.O.	Public Records Office
R.M.	Resident Magistrate
R.H.S.Vic.	Royal Historical Society of Victoria
R.S.S.A.	Royal Society of South Australia
R.W.A.H.S.	Royal Western Australian Historical Society
Vic. His. Mag.	*Victorian Historical Magazine*: journal and proceedings of the Royal Historical Society of Victoria
W.A.L.Dept.	Western Australian Lands Department

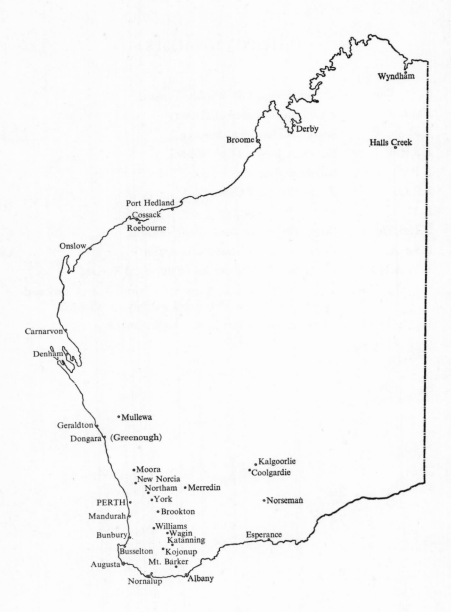

WESTERN AUSTRALIA

I

Living Water

In February 1837, Surveyor Alfred Hillman and party set out from King George Sound, to mark the road to the Swan River by way of York. On the night of Monday 27 February, the party halted at a spot where there was good feed but no water, so that it must have been a great relief to Hillman and his companion Dr Joseph Harris when the next morning, less than two hours after resuming the north-westerly journey, the party met eight Aborigines. The opportunity was taken to inquire where water could be found. On being given generous, exact directions, Hillman altered his course without hesitation, despite the fact that it led through a severely burnt area and along a dry water course. Within 2¼ miles the party was rewarded for its trust by finding 'a spring of beautiful permanent water'.[1] So impressed was the surveyor that he wrote in his field book: 'This would be a good place for a station.'[2]

A full hour was spent enjoying the abundance of water and inspecting the site. The Spring was surrounded by granite outcrops in a slight valley with a rich, deeper valley nearby. Briefly, Hillman made a sketch in his field book of the new commendable water site, along with the name 'Kōjōnup'. It is not known how Hillman meant the phonetic sign 'ō' to be pronounced; whether as in 'boat' or 'rock'. Many old Kojonup identities today claim that, in their childhood, adults always pronounced it as in 'book'.

Without a doubt, Hillman was given the name by the eight Aborigines. More than likely the Aborigines had spent the night at the Spring and when met were travelling in the cool of the morning, as was the custom, to another water spot, hoping on the way to catch some game feeding before the heat of day.

Down through the years of settlement it has been claimed by Kojonup residents that the town's name was derived from the Aboriginal word *kodja*, meaning 'axe', the whole name being translated 'the place of the stone of the axe'.[3]

Another translation was given by the late J. F. Haddleton who was an informed bushman of Katanning. He claimed the name was

1

'Koychnorp', the *koych* meaning 'axe' and the *norp* meaning, perhaps, 'plenty'.[4]

A third derivation has been suggested: there is probably no definite meaning of the name but, although the word was first written 'Kojonup' according to Hillman's understanding of the sound, there is very strong presumptive evidence that it should have been written 'Kojynup' or 'Kogynup', which more closely agrees with the Aboriginal tongue. *Kogyn*, according to this source, is a general term meaning any 'edible bulb', so that *Kogynup* would be 'the place of edible bulbs'.[5]

There is no local folklore to support this interpretation of the name. The weight of opinion seems to be for the association of the district with the *kodja*.

What then was a *kodja*? Although one cannot make any definite statements concerning Aboriginal stone implements of the past, it is thought that there is a distinction between an 'Aboriginal stone axe' and a *kodja*. The former is considered by some to have been made of dark basalt and ground to a sharp edge; whereas the latter is thought to have been originally a flake axe, unground, although the cutting edge was sometimes sharpened by careful chipping.[6]

Both had a wooden handle thrust while hot into a lump of warm tough blackboy gum. The *kodja* of the South-West area of Western Australia generally had one or two stone flakes inserted into the gum on opposite sides of the handle: one sharp for cutting, the other blunt for percussion. In the North-West area of Western Australia, the occasional *kodja* that has been found has had only one stone attached to the handle.

Admittedly, ground stone axes have been found locally by some residents. The explanation could be that they reached these areas through the trade routes which are known to have existed; or that they are experimental efforts of local Aborigines who had come in contact with methods used elsewhere and are therefore examples of a recent level of South-West Aboriginal culture.[7]

As it is generally accepted that the *kodja* was made in most of the South-West area of Western Australia, it is not unreasonable to ask why the Kojonup area in particular should have been termed 'the place of the stone of the axe'. It does not necessarily follow that there is a definite reason. The Aborigines sometimes had quite trivial explanations for place names. Yet, folklore has developed around the theory that the stone for the *kodja* was found in the district. Undoubtedly, there is a great deal of granite around this area, as was described by

2

Hillman when he first visited the Spring; but the same type of stone might be seen at intervals along most of the Albany Highway.

In 1940 the late J. J. Treasure, an old Kojonup resident, stated that the stone for the axe was found on a quartz ridge south of the railway line.[8] It is possible that the Kojonup district possessed a unique stone outcrop which was exceptionally suited to the construction of the *kodja*.

Within five miles south-west of the Spring is a hill of quartzite on the property known as 'Half Moon'. Selby Harris of Boyup Brook, a stone implement enthusiast, classes this site as a 'factory' for stone implements. The stone is technically called 'Kojonup sandstone' and numerous specimens containing leaf fossils have been discovered there. It is a fine hard quartzite which flakes perfectly with a knife-like edge. It is obvious that the site has been used for many years as there are chips of stone inches deep over most of the hill. It is not uncommon to gather, in an afternoon, a dozen pieces of stone that display definite signs of having been chipped meticulously around the edge, from large horse-hoof cores to small flaked scraping implements or spear barbs.

Reports have been received of specimens of this type of stone having been found on known Aboriginal camping sites forty miles south-west of Kojonup and east of Katanning although no similar outcrop is known to exist in these localities. It is possible that the Kojonup sandstone was so prized for implements, and particularly *kodjas*, that the local Aboriginal groups traded it with neighbouring groups and tribes.

On the other hand other amateur anthropologists have suggested that the axe is linked with a legend that existed around the large flat rock on the Spring site, and this is the origin of the name. They claim that there are signs of axe rubbings on the surface, due to hunters rubbing their axes on it in order that the power of the stone would be transferred to their axe. Little evidence supporting this theory is known.

J. F. Haddleton explained that when making a *kodja* it was first necessary to light a fire on a big granite rock, remove it and douse the rock with cold water so that it cracked in great shales. This was broken in pieces about four inches long and the edge sharpened by grinding on another kind of sandstone.[9] Such a method would involve far more effort than working with the Half Moon stone which requires only a solid knock to split it with an almost perfect edge.

The stone of the *kodja* was attached to a hard wooden handle, about seven inches long with one end sharpened to a point. This was of particular importance when using the *kodja* for climbing straight-trunked gum trees to raid beehives, birds' nests or to chase possums. Two *kodjas* were used, one in each hand. With one *kodja* a notch

3

would be cut into the bark, just large enough for a toe-hold, while the pointed end of the other *kodja* would be driven into the trunk to enable the climber to steady himself and to draw himself up. There are many old tree trunks around Kojonup which show evidence of having been climbed in this manner. One is to be found in the bush just north of the Kojonup cemetery. Charlie Elverd (a member of one of Kojonup's oldest families), now in his eighties and a knowledgeable bushman, said that climbing trees in this way required considerable skill and was usually done by young Aboriginal men and never by women or old men. Those who were skilful at it were quite fearless and would climb to enormous heights. When a child he saw a naked Aborigine walking casually from limb to limb on the top of a group of trees forty feet high.

It might never be possible to prove the correlation of Kojonup sandstone, the *kodja*, the Spring and the place name, but it must be admitted that there is circumstantial evidence to signify a possible connection.

The Aborigines assessed distance by the number of camps or sleeps needed to travel from one place to another and naturally these were also associated with watering points. The average distance traversed in a day by a family group was five miles as this was considered the maximum distance that the burden-bearers, the wives, could cover in a day. Camps, although close to water, were not necessarily right at the watering spot. The reasons are logical. Wild game would be familiar with the water site; any unusual noise or smell would frighten them away. To the Aborigine meat was second only to water. Once he had quenched his thirst he had very little use for water but meat was a constant need. Water was not used for cooking and until a liking for the white man's beverage, tea, was acquired, there was little use for any receptacle.

Similarly, firewood was always essential to the camp and had a big bearing on the site chosen. In fact the major factors in choosing a camping spot are thought to be good visibility of any possible approaching enemy; firewood readily available; and water reasonably close at hand so that the transport of game caught at drink was not difficult.[10] It is for these reasons that some old identities are very sceptical that the Spring site was ever used for camping, and their opinion is supported by others who have studied Aboriginal customs and inspected the Spring area. Charlie Elverd states that when he was

4

a child the Aborigines camped at three places, all within about one mile of the Spring: Wilgie Hill (P. Lot 3 [see page 66]), Dorney's Hill (the site of the present Aboriginal Reserve) and the hill on which the Roman Catholic Church is built. Police Occurrence Books[11] mention the camps as being on another hill west of the Spring sited not far from 'Charity Well'. Many stories exist of other camps throughout the district.

By generously explaining to Hillman and his party where water could be obtained, the eight Kojonup Aborigines were following their age-old custom of never withholding from another the knowledge of a water supply, especially in times of drought. To share the Kojonup Spring was the essence of hospitality for this tribal group.

At one time, it was suggested that all those Aborigines living in the area west of a line drawn roughly from Jurien Bay to the southern coast at Esperance were of the one homogeneous group called the Bibbulmun.[12] This contention has not been upheld by more recent anthropologists. Generally, it is agreed that this line divides those Aborigines who practised circumcision (the ones to the east of the line) from those who did not (those to the west of the line).

An attempt was made in 1940 to trace onto a map the known boundaries of those tribes which existed west of this line. In this survey the word 'Bibbulmun' was not used, although the term 'Pi:belmen' was used for a tribe dwelling approximately between the lower Blackwood and Warren Rivers.

On this map the land west of a line joining Katanning, Tambellup, Cranbrook and Tenterden and including the towns Kojonup, Collie, Donnybrook, Greenbushes and Bridgetown, the headwaters of the Warren and Frankland Rivers, the south bank of the Collie River to Collie and thence to the coast and north to Harvey is all classified as being peopled by the tribe termed the 'Kaneang'.[13]

Most boundaries of the area are formed by physiographic and ecological features, for example rivers, oceans, mountains, climate and vegetation, and cut off the drier areas to the east and the bigger, denser timber of the south. There are no large rivers to traverse and the closest mountain range, the Stirling, is beyond the limits. It is interesting to note that the northern boundary corresponds with a change from place names ending in 'up' to names ending in 'ing'.

However, these limits were not rigidly adhered to, especially in the wetter periods of the year when water was not the confining factor of a group's movements. With a plentiful supply of water the tribal groups would travel extensively, intermingling perhaps with nearby tribes and appearing to overlap with them. These would be the times when corroborees were performed, trading done, marriages arranged, visits exchanged to partake of or share in seasonal delicacies, for example fish, bulbs, nuts.

The word 'tribe' was applied to the largest unit of people which had a cultural and social identity and was independent of outsiders for its own perpetuation (although marriages with other tribes were permitted in certain circumstances). A tribe was associated with a certain territory and language but had no over-all authority in economic matters or warfare; such matters were the concern of each local group or family unit within a tribe. Each group was usually attached to a certain locality in the tribal territory. Thus the Kojonup group was within the tribal territory of the Kaneang.

Sometimes it happened that a group at one end of the tribal territory might have more in common with units of a neighbouring, rather than with a unit of its own, tribe situated at the other side of the tribal territory. For example, the group at Kojonup might have been very similar in some respects to the group at Woodanilling, of the tribe Wi:lmen.[14] Boundaries being quite flexible, it was sometimes difficult to know to which tribe certain territories belonged. There was no strict rule that forbade people from moving into adjacent tribal areas, as long as sacred sites were left unmolested. As a rule, a tribe had a common language, but different local dialects could creep in to develop variations in vocabulary in areas widely separated.

The greatest common bond among units of a tribe was above all the feeling of kinship; members regarded one another as relatives and groups of other tribes as outsiders. Kinship was definitely the major integrating element of a tribe.

As has been stated the southern boundary of the Kaneang tribe may be said, for convenience, to be about Tenterden. In view of this it is interesting to read Surveyor Hillman's notes of a journey taken in 1836 to mark the road from Albany towards Perth. (The exploration was discontinued before reaching Kojonup.) The party reached the Gordon River on 13 September and was some distance north (perhaps near Tunney) on the seventeenth, when the surveyor recorded:

Early this morning we were visited by about 50 natives, who apparently had not seen Europeans before. We could not understand a word of their language, they however, proved the most desperate

6

thieves I ever met with. As soon as we got rid of them we formed another depot, and left some of the provisions for our return.[15]

No doubt, Hillman through his work was well acquainted with the King George Sound and Swan River Aborigines and this was possibly his first encounter with the Kaneang tribe which was immediately north of the former, and hence the change of dialect. Three days later he had cause to record further on his new acquaintances. The party had been busy marking the road and had reached a fine loamy valley. Hillman wrote:

> Here we halted for the night and were obliged to remain the next day to enable the men to return to the depot for provisions. In consequence of natives having stolen the last damper and all our knives, forks and spoons while the men were busy with the horses.[16]

Is there any wonder that the Aborigines were attracted to the cutlery when one considers that they were completely dependent on stone for all their tool requirements.

Personal information on the Kaneang tribe has been left by W. H. Graham who made many exploratory trips with friendly district Aborigines in the 1860s. In 1880 he supplied a researcher with information on the tribe which lived at Kojonup and Eticup, and when it was collated it was concluded that the manners of this tribe differed in no respects from those of their neighbours.[17] For instance, class marriages prevailed; children belonged to the tribe of the father; and girls soon after birth were promised in marriage then given to the keeping of their husbands at about nine years of age. Women ownership was usually the reason for most disputes or wars and a man who was found guilty of some offence to another was resigned to such punishment as being speared in the leg.

According to W. H. Graham, in 1859 the Kojonup and Eticup tribal group was thought to have numbered 500, but by 1880 he puts the figure at 200. No reason was given for the great and tragic decrease.

In his journal of 1836 Hillman records that on the party's return journey to Albany several graves were passed. A detailed description of such graves is supplied by W. H. Graham. The body was buried in an oval-shaped hole, about three feet deep, in a sandy area. The corpse was placed in a sitting position, facing east, with the knees doubled up and tied together. The forefinger and thumb of the right hand were also tied together and the thumbnail was burnt off so that the deceased could not dig his way out of the grave. The earth removed was never returned; instead the body was covered with bark, sticks and leaves. The possessions of the deceased were left near the grave but the spears were first broken so they could not be used by the spirit of the dead man. Close by, a fire was made and sometimes a *mia-mia*, whilst surrounding trees might be marked with rings. Charlie Elverd said in his time they would also leave a tin of drinking water. North of the Katanning-Kojonup road, in light soil between Katanning Road and Bignell Road is the site of a once common burial ground of the local tribal group.

On the whole, life for the Aborigines in this district was not severe. Charlie Elverd remembers early local full-blood Aborigines declaring that before the white man they were never hungry; that there was always plenty to eat. This was due to their intimate knowledge and understanding of their territory: the flowering and seeding times of plants, the habits and haunts of animals, the different types of soils and associated vegetation and the geographical features and climatic signs.

The man and woman each had a task in providing for the daily food requirements. On a journey the man would go first, carrying only his spears and *meero* (spearthrower) as he had to be always alert to stalk any animal which came in sight. The woman followed with the children, carrying a *coota* (bag) and with possibly a baby on her back in a kangaroo-skin bag. Albert Elverd (first cousin of Charlie Elverd) recalls the shy way the baby would duck down into the bag, out of sight, if he suspected someone was looking inquisitively at him.

Usually the tribal groups moved around on well-marked tracks from one watering spot to another. It is impossible to say for how many years and by how many pairs of feet some of the oldest of these tracks had been used. One wellknown track led from Perth to Pinjarra, Marrinup, Williams River, Kojonup, Kendenup and Porongorups.[18] It was a fundamental law that no food seen was ever disregarded. There were no storage facilities or means of transport so each day the consumption of food depended upon what was acquired that day. Nuts, seeds and berries would be gathered and consumed as they journeyed. A few might be collected in the *coota* for preparing when camp was made, depending on the time of day it was or the extent of the woman's burden. Two stones were used to bruise the seeds. Thomas Norrish stated that these stones were 'of black flint, one flat and the other round'.[19] The seed from the jam tree (*Acacia acuminata*) was often pestled and sometimes the bark from the roots of a young white gum would be pounded and then chewed incessantly, only the juice being swallowed.

Sometimes these stones would be carried by the woman but often they were left at camping sites for the use of all who came. Food collected by the women and children might still be found in the district. Cranberries (*Astroloma drummondii*) have an orange bell flower and supply green berries the size of a pea. The native lemon (*Sollya fusiformis*) has a green fruit, an inch long. A runner, known locally as *komik*, had a reddish fruit about as thick as a pencil. *Djetta* was an egg-shaped root, brown in colour and sweet and watery to eat. *Carr* was a root that was extremely acrid unless partly cooked. *Jooluk* was red like a carrot but similar to a chilli in taste.[20]

Once many shepherdy bushes (*Pimelea argentea*) grew in the district but they were particularly fragile and were easily knocked over by sheep for roughage. The Aborigines would split the bush at a fork and the collection of small grubs found nestled in the wood would be devoured.

All kinds of bardies, a type of grub (insect larvae), were also much enjoyed. The bardies of the jam tree were considered the best and that of the river gum, the worst. A kind of sawdust at the foot of the blackboy or jam tree indicated the presence of grubs. Blackboy bardies were small and collected together in little heaps easily scooped up in the hand to eat.

The children loved to lick the white scale (*meenah*) which forms on the leaves of the blue gum, also the froth which is found on the red gum in certain years. These together with honey sucked from the banksia cone and the glorious find of a beehive had to satisfy the tribe's sweet tooth. Manna gum, jam gum and prickly gum were popular all-day-suckers. A great favourite, for both its fruit and nut, was the Kojonup peach or, as it is commonly known, the quandong (*Santalum acuminatum*).[21]

Although the man was principally the hunter the catching of the boodie rat (*Bettongia lesueur*, a small kangaroo-like animal with underground nests, now almost disappeared) was left to the woman. On finding a boodie rat's hole the woman would trace the underground passage by tapping carefully with her *wonna* (a blunt-edged stick) and listen for a hollow ring. When she considered she had reached the end of the passage she would exclaim, 'boodie git down!' Then followed frantic digging by all her helpers, at that spot. The skin of this little creature was used for the *coota* and carrying bag for the baby. The *coota* was made with the fur outside, the carrying bag with the fur inside.

To the Aborigines the bush was their garden and they loved and appreciated each seasonal harvest; but it was the spoils of the hunter which they eagerly awaited each day. Meat was cooked although preferred underdone. Sometimes, when the family had not eaten meat for a day or two, the pieces were snatched from the fire when they were hardly hot. The fleshy part of the kangaroo's leg (called the *mart* by the Aborigines), the tail and the little tammars were great favourites.

Thousands of tammars (*Macropus eugenii*) once lived in the district. They congregated in dense thickets of jam tree, she-oak (*Casuarina* sp.), mallet (*Eucalyptus* sp.) or ti-tree (*Melaleuca* sp.). The Aboriginal children and women would rush upon the thickets so that the tammars fled along pads radiating from the area, and the Aboriginal man would be sitting close by ready to hit as many as possible on the head as they passed. This method was soon copied by early settlers and tammar became a favourite and much appreciated addition to the pantry, in lean times.

Another small kangaroo-like animal which was eaten, but is rarely seen today was the *wurrung* (*Onychogalea lunata*), the crescent or nail-tail wallaby. It was brown in colour and always ran with one paw extended. It was once common in many parts of the South-West and eastwards into South Australia, and possibly still exists in desert regions.

Yet, of all the game hunted, the emu was the animal most esteemed for eating. According to Charlie Elverd the meat of this bird is very sweet, almost as if it has been cooked in sugar. The hunter who came into camp with an emu was treated as a hero, but, paradoxically, rarely ate the prize himself. Instead, he watched the others feast upon it. The oil or fat obtained from the emu was greatly valued, particularly by the old Aborigines who rubbed it vigorously all over themselves, massaging it in carefully around the joints.

In summer, emus tended to collect at a site just north-west of Kojonup where some she-oaks grew, whose nuts the emus relished. Nearby was a natural shallow water catchment, formed by a large surface rock with a five inch depression in the centre, and about ten square yards in area. After a summer thunderstorm the emus converged upon this rock to drink. Naturally, the Aborigines knew this and many an emu meal originated there, so much so that the spot was always referred to as 'Emu Rock'.

The brush possum was an easier and more reliable source of protein. The Aborigines could tell by sniffing in a hollow tree if a possum was lurking in the dark. Another more obvious sign, which the settlers soon learned, was the presence of scratched pads on a tree trunk.

To catch a possum hiding in a hollow tree the Aborigines would delve into the depths with a long stick. On contacting the possum the stick would be twisted until it was caught tightly in the possum's fur. It was then possible to extract the possum on the end of the stick. This animal was usually plucked before being roasted. (The fur was spun into lengths by the women.) Because of its offensive smell the ringtail possum was never eaten.

This basic diet was supplemented further by lizards, gilgies (small prawnlike creatures), fish, ducks, parrots, pigeons, bandicoots, birds' eggs and numerous small animals and birds never seen in the district today.

From some of the skins of the animals killed the Aborigines made the few articles of clothing they required. Grease smeared thickly over the body acted as a type of protection from the weather, however during winter further covering was sometimes needed and this was made mainly from the skins of kangaroos. One to three skins were joined together with sinews obtained from the kangaroo's tail. The garment, which was called a *bouka*, would hang from the shoulders to the knee, with the fur worn close to the body for extra warmth. Altogether, the *bouka* was ideally suited to the Aborigines' needs. It was durable, warm and waterproof. Over the years, an old *bouka* became so highly polished and pliable that it appeared to have been tanned expertly. When it rained the wearer merely squatted and was immediately encased in a waterproof shell which shed water like an iron roof (unlike the sodden Government blankets that were, in later years, sometimes turned into a *bouka* by cutting a hole in the middle).

It was quite common to see the Aborigines walking along with a cloud of smoke billowing behind them. This came from a lighted piece of she-oak or jam tree bark which was carried under the *bouka* to enable a fire to be kindled quickly at the next stopping spot. If the bark appeared to be going out it would be held in the wind and waved about until it caught again.

One of the primary uses of the rope spun from the possum fur was the making of a loin band in which *kodjas* and cherished possessions were carried. The wearer seems to have been respected if the *kodja* he carried in his belt was a particularly fine specimen. It has been suggested by one researcher that the *kodja* sometimes had a subtle ornamental and sociological value and not purely a functional role.[22] The Aborigines undoubtedly seemed to prize the *kodja* greatly. Charlie

Elverd can remember Aborigines pestering and bartering extravagantly for a tomahawk whenever they knew a person had one in his possession.

To make their *boukas* the Aborigines required various tools for skinning, trimming the edges of the skins, piercing holes through which the sinews were threaded and scraping the skins. Stone, and sometimes bone, was used for these tasks. At Half Moon and in known camping sites, small hand axes, scrapers and sharp-pointed knife-like implements have been found. The Aborigines would push small stones, found on their travels, into their matted hair and disentangle them when required. This was also an excellent way to carry extra barbs for future spears, the chief killing weapons. These barbs were stuck into tough gum along the side of the spear. When making his spear the hunter gave a great deal of attention to the handle so that the weapon was well balanced and would fly true. Small scraping stones, not much bigger than a man's thumbnail, were ideal for this work.

Another meticulous job done with stone tools was the marking of notches on message sticks. According to W. H. Graham, these were definitely used.[23] The messenger delivering the stick usually explained the meaning. It is thought that from time to time these sticks were sent all over the tribal territories to certain places, generally where groups were known to camp. Kojonup was one of these sites, so too was Tambellup, Boyanup and Dardanup.[24] Some people consider the message stick was an introduction for someone travelling alone, that is, his credentials. The Aborigines were highly suspicious of a lone traveller, who was always suspected of fleeing the law, of being an outcast, or perhaps up to no good.

Charlie Elverd recalls witnessing a corroboree, about 1900, held not far from the Kojonup cemetery. Before the performance the participants painted themselves with the *wilgie*, red ochre, obtained near P. Lot 3, which is known as 'Wilgie Hill'. In 1941, L. V. MacBride was told by the late J. J. Treasure that Aborigines fought many battles on Wilgie Hill.[25]

It is almost impossible to learn at this late stage what were the legends and myths of the local tribe. Certainly there must have been some, as there are many geographical features—large rocks (Bald Rock), soaks, wells—in the district, around which the Aborigines loved to weave a story.

According to elderly F. Lilford of Cranbrook, many years ago an Aborigine, Dinah, the mother of the late, distinctive Ted Smith, told him this legend of the Kojonup district. The country was gripped in drought and the only known water was salty. The health of the parched

Aborigines, birds and animals deteriorated. An eagle-hawk, soaring about the sky and swooping to earth, observed that a fat and shiny crow had a wet beak, wet with fresh water. The eagle-hawk, seething with unparalleled fury, attacked the cunning crow. In so doing his claws split the rocks and the blood of the attacked crow was splattered over the surrounding rocks and earth. So, a fresh water soak is to be found in the Wakhinup area, hidden amid rocks and surrounded by rich, red loam.

One little Aboriginal song recalled by Albert Elverd is of great interest. It was taught to him when a lad, by Frederick Van Zuilecom whose family came to the district in the 1860s. Van Zuilecom was very adept at mimicking the actions and feet stamping which accompanied any Aboriginal performance. This little song seems typical of others collected elsewhere. It is short and about a trifling incident, with no clear concise translation. To be fully appreciated it must be heard, in order to catch the recurrent rhythm and subtle rhyming which echoes the bird's call. As far as Albert Elverd remembers, it is the song of the curlew, calling for food, but without results.

> *Djebbin, Djebbin, Ballard*
> *Tar o Warrin*

The known vocabulary of the Kojonup groups appears similar in many ways to vocabulary lists compiled in other districts. It is interesting to note the similarity between lists collected by G. F. Moore,[26] W. H. Graham,[27] J. E. Hammond[28] and Charlie Elverd, at different periods and in different areas of the state. For instance, such words as *N-Yoonger* (blackman), *twonk* (ears), *koomal* (possum), *waech* (emu), *youger* (kangaroo) and many more are identical.

To conclude this brief look at the occupiers of the Kojonup district before the coming of the white settler, it seems only honourable to record the original names of some of the Aborigines who first befriended the newcomers. Before many years had passed their own names were replaced by common nicknames like Billy, Annie or Jimmy.

W. H. Graham lists Ngaron, Mulya, Peereitch and Ngoganee as the names of men he knew and Birbinan, Wonyeran, Peelan and Yewneran as some women's names.[29]

Daisy Bates claims that when she was in Katanning in the early 1900s the last of the true Kojonup tribe (I presume she means a descendant, according to the kinship laws) was brought to her for medical attention.[30] The girl, a consumptive, was called Ngungalari and had been befriended and reared with refinement in the home of kindly white settlers. A small announcement in the Katanning press on 1 August 1903 almost certainly referred to the same incident.[31] It simply said that Nelly Strongfellow, female Aborigine, twenty years, died from the effects of consumption. The fact that it was printed at all indicates that the editor was aware of the local interest in the plight of the girl and that not all the early settlers were insensitive to the welfare of the Aborigine.

Kojonup*

I'll tell you of its origin as it was told to me—
Those granite outcrops rising in the near vicinity
Were the places where the kooja—the native axe was made
By fixing sturdy handles to a sharpened granite blade.

They tell me natives used to build a campfire on the spot
Till granite rock beneath the fire was rendered piping hot
Then sluiced with water from the spring that trickles to this day
Inducing a contraction for the rock to flake away.

Came the sorting and the shaping and the sharpening with care
The adding of a handle—quite an intricate affair!
Strong sinews of the kangaroo to bind it tight and neat
With manna-gum to strengthen it, the kooja was complete![32]

Ruby A. Penna
(née Bilston)

* Pronounced 'Koojanup', as in 'book'.

REFERENCES

[1] A. Hillman, Field Book 12 (held in W.A.L.Dept.)
[2] *Ibid.*
[3] L. V. MacBride, paper read at Kat.H.S., 1941 (copy in K.H.S.Recs.).
[4] J. F. Haddleton, *Katanning Pioneer* (Perth, 1952), p. 102.
[5] Letter from Surveyor-General's Office, Perth, to K.H.S., 31 May 1968.
[6] R. M. and C. H. Berndt, *The World of the First Australians* (Sydney, 1964), p. 103.
[7] W. D. L. Ride, 'The Edge-Ground Axes of South-West Australia', *The Western Australian Naturalist*, vol. 6, no. 7, 4 December 1958, pp. 162-79.
[8] MacBride.
[9] Haddleton, p. 103.

[10] Berndt and Berndt.

[11] Police Occurrence Books (held in Battye Library, Perth).

[12] D. M. Bates, *Passing of the Aborigines* (London, 1957), p. 59.

[13] B. Tindale, 'A Field Survey', R.S.S.A. *Transactions*, vol. 64, July 1940.

[14] *Ibid.*

[15] A. Hillman, Journal: June-September 1836, p. 586 (W.A.L.Dept.; copy in K.H.S.Recs.).

[16] *Ibid.*

[17] W. H. Graham, 'No. 23—Kojonup and Eticup', in E. M. Curr, *The Australian Race* (Melbourne, 1886), vol. 1.

[18] J. E. Hammond, *Winjan's People*, Paul Hasluck, ed. (Perth, 1934), p. 19.

[19] Thomas Norrish Diary, p. 9 (copy in K.H.S.Recs.).

[20] All information on p. 15 and following pages supplied by Charlie Elverd of Kojonup.

[21] Rica Ericson, *The Drummonds of Hawthornden* (Perth, 1969), p. 164.

[22] Aldo Massola, *On the Western Australian Kodja* (reprint from *Vic. His. Mag.*, 1960).

[23] Curr, p. 349.

[24] Hammond, p. 19.

[25] MacBride.

[26] G. F. Moore, *Diary of Ten Years Eventful Life of an Early Settler in Western Australia* (London, 1884).

[27] Curr.

[28] Hammond.

[29] Curr, p. 348.

[30] Bates, p. 81.

[31] *Great Southern Herald*, 1 August 1903, p. 3.

[32] By kind permission of Mrs Ruby A. Penna, who was born in Kojonup.

2

1829–1838

GRASS HUNGER

An official exploring party under the leadership of Captain Bannister made the original cross-country expedition from Perth to King George Sound eighteen months after the first ship, the *Parmelia,* arrived at the Swan River, in June 1829. Unfortunately, during the last 150 miles of the journey Captain Bannister when commenting on the country did not mention his exact position. A spokesman for the Surveyor-General's Office considers that the party was in the vicinity of Kojonup about 1 January 1831.[1] At this stage, Captain Bannister had written most enthusiastically of the country they were traversing. Between 23 December 1830 and 5 January 1831 he recorded: 'a very great proportion of the tract was land of the finest description fit for the plough, sheep or cattle'.[2] For many years after this, the whole hinterland of Albany, including the Kojonup area, was referred to, officially, as the Plantagenet district.[3]

The land problem (the acquisition of a suitable grant and the development of it) was the prime consideration of the first settlers in the Swan River Colony. Initially, the most desirable land was considered to be around the centre of the settlement, but gradually experienced practical farmers realized that a more profitable selection might be obtained further inland. Such men were the first to perceive that a new type of agriculture (different from that used in their birthplace) was needed for the colony's Mediterranean climate. There was considerable talk of the need for more expeditions to mark out roads into the vast unmapped regions so that settlers could extend their knowledge of agricultural opportunities.[4] The Governor, Sir James Stirling, was just as anxious as his subjects to locate large tracts of arable land: he had been granted 100,000 acres!

In June 1835 he determined that an expedition would have to be made to open the overland communication between the two outposts of settlement, King George Sound and Perth, and to examine the adjacent country. A large party headed by the Governor and Surveyor-General Roe set out in October 1835 to examine the Hotham and Williams Rivers where some of the gentlemen were already interested in establishing stations. From here Stirling and Roe led a smaller party towards the southern coast, but travelled on a line approximately seven miles east of Kojonup. On Stirling's return his opinions of the country traversed were eagerly sought. His report was favourable and one settler wrote to relations in Britain that the Governor's party had seen large tracts of fine grazing country although no sizeable river.[5]

In such a small close-knit community much discourse followed every fresh item of information. Dissatisfaction with the productive possibilities of the coastal plains had developed, and with it a conviction that the most profitable pursuit in the new colony was sheep farming. Twelve months earlier Stirling had written to his brother-in-law, saying that every effort was being made 'to procure sheep, it being evidently the best speculation in this country'.[6] About the same time a colonist wrote to England to say:

> sheep grazing is certainly the most suitable occupation for a new and extensive district requiring as it does, a less proportion of annual expenditure for managing a large capital profitably invested than any other occupation.[7]

These beliefs had been nourished by the glowing reports of the sheep industry in the eastern colonies.

Obviously, there was good sheep country in the interior and individuals were hankering to have grants of land there, but a marked road and conspicuous military protection was considered the first step.

So be it: in May 1836, the Governor ordered Surveyor Alfred Hillman and Lieutenant C. F. Armstrong to leave on the schooner the *Sally Anne* for King George Sound, to establish the line of the future road to Perth and the position of a new military post.[8] As has been seen in the previous chapter, in carrying out these orders Hillman and Armstrong moved into the most south-east part of what is now known as the Kojonup district (possibly as far as Yarranup).

At the same time others were probably familiarizing themselves with the district. Curious adventurers and ambitious individuals accompanied by friendly Aboriginal guides had most likely penetrated the district from various directions. Kangaroo hunters would have been quick off the mark if Hillman and Armstrong's party had been heard to say that they had killed 1755 pounds of kangaroo on their expedition. A newcomer to the colony, Captain T. L. Symers, is thought to have looked 'around the neighbourhood'[9] of Kojonup during his first visit to King George Sound in 1835.

However, it was left to Hillman in February 1837 to print Kojonup officially on the empty interior of the Swan River Colony. Lieutenant Armstrong, with some soldiers, had accompanied Hillman and his party from Albany as far as Warriup (between thirty to thirty-five miles south of Kojonup) where Armstrong and his men remained to set up a military outpost. As has been seen in Chapter 1, Hillman and others, one of whom is known to have been Dr Joseph Harris, continued the journey north and were later directed to the Kojonup Spring by eight Aborigines. Hillman eventually reached Perth, by way of York, on 11 March 1837. Here the report of his trip aroused great interest. He had satisfied the general demand for a marked road between Albany and Perth. This he had done on foot, in sixteen days, a distance of 300 miles.[10] Also, he had discovered some fine sheep land, in particular the Kojonup country. The first to react to this last favourable piece of news was none other than Governor Stirling himself. Hillman was given little time off in return for his accomplishments. At the beginning of April he left Perth to accompany Stirling to Kojonup.

Stirling, although possessing many commendable qualities, has been criticized by some as being inconstant.[11] Furthermore, it has been said that he was not averse to taking advantage of any official information to improve his personal fortunes, and was alert to the mention of any praiseworthy land as a possible site for an establishment for himself. It certainly seems that he reacted with alacrity to Hillman's high praise of the sheep country in the vicinity of the new marked road.

From the comments made in Stirling's journal of the trip, it is possible to follow his train of thought. Just south of Williams on 10 April, he wrote of 'fair sheep land'.[12] On 11 April he commented 'passing through a good level line of country for a road'.[13] That night a halt was made on the Beaufort River where water and signs of good herbage were found, but as it was the end of summer the latter was scarce. The next bivouac was made about 7½ miles north of the Kojonup Spring. There was no water and indifferent land, and one cannot help wondering if poor Hillman was being reprimanded for an over-enthusiastic journal. Nevertheless, the sight of masses of yellow everlastings helped to brighten the landscape and Stirling made a point of recording their startling beauty for posterity.

The next day, 13 April, the party was up early and away just after six. It was a perhaps despondent Stirling who wrote, 'proceeded through a white gum forest presenting occasionally good soil'.[14] Within one and a quarter hours a hopeful note crept into the journal's report: 'country improving gradually'.[15] By 8.10 a.m. he recorded that they were passing through 'a valley of rich red soil falling to the north-west and rather extensive'.[16] A narrow poor ridge had to be ascended before Stirling could give his full approval which must surely be Kojonup's crowning compliment for all times: 'passed into Kojonup Vale over two miles of excellent soil and grass'.[17] At 8.50 a.m. the party reached the Spring. In the afternoon the valley was traced in a north-westerly direction for 3¼ miles but Stirling did not consider the soil greatly improved, although still suitable for cultivation. That night, 13 April 1837, the first Governor of the Swan River Colony, Sir James Stirling, threw down his bedroll and slept by a campfire near the Kojonup Spring.

The next morning the party crossed the valley and working in an east-south-east direction passed over 'soil occasionally encumbered with granite rocks but always good and generally grassy'.[18] It was the word 'grassy' which the vigilant sheep speculators liked to read and Stirling used it whenever possible. By mid-morning the party halted at what Stirling termed 'Hillman's remarkable flat granite rock'.[19] The first rains had been early that year and there was a great deal of welcomed young grass for the weary horses. According to Stirling's calculations the night was spent at a spot thought to be Harris's Rocky Pool,[20] about fourteen miles south of Kojonup and fifteen miles north of Lieutenant Armstrong's military station at Warriup.

At noon the next day the military huts were reached and a day was spent there before returning to the Kojonup Spring from another direction, through excellent grasslands. On the evening of 18 April the Kojonup Spring was once more host to the Crown's first representative in Western Australia. At daylight the company moved off in a direction E.25°N. and on the twenty-first it arrived at Joseph Harris's sheep station on the Williams River.

Two months earlier Joseph Harris (the son of Dr Joseph Harris, see page 1) had obtained the contract to convey provisions from Albany to the military outpost at Warriup, thereupon journeying to his Williams sheep station.[21] Consequently, he would have been very familiar with the country over which Stirling had travelled. In all probability, around the campfire that night impressions and opinions of the new Kojonup district were compared at length. In years to come, on Joseph Harris's death, it was stated in his obituary that during his residence in the Williams district he was appointed Resident Magistrate of the Kojonup district, but never assumed the duties of that office.[22] Was this another of Stirling's rash verbal promises for which some have said he was notorious?

Altogether, Stirling had been favourably impressed with his journey and on reaching Perth talked incessantly of the country's potential. A contemporary wrote abroad:

> The Governor has returned in great spirits from his excursion to the south-east, comprising an examination of country from the Murray River to within 55 miles of King George Sound, having seen a large extent of fine country well watered.[23]

Between the two extreme centres of settlement, there now existed a marked road and official commendation of the adjacent land. The possible consequences and benefits were exciting: the road would enable regular communication, a constant mail service, the overlanding of stock, a drift of travellers and settlers into new areas, plus extended surveys for the fresh crop of land grants that could be expected. However, before such progress materialized it was generally accepted that the Government had to supply military protection for travellers, mail carriers and prospective settlers.

By September 1837 a military outstation, with one officer and seven privates, was formed at the Kojonup Spring.[24] The officer chosen to be in charge was Lieutenant C. F. Armstrong. He and his men were transferred from Warriup to this more northerly outpost. Unfortunately, due to the prevailing concept of class distinction, the names of mere soldiers were rarely mentioned in official reports. So it is that seven of Kojonup's first permanent residents must go down in history, unnamed. They are part of the long list of forgotten men of our past.

A TOWN TO BE

The soldiers who first dwelt in Kojonup were a detachment of the 21st Regiment known as the Royal British Fusiliers. They had arrived at the Swan River settlement from Hobart in 1834.[25] The lot of the British soldier of those times was far from enviable. In most cases he had joined the army (many were actually coerced) because it offered a secure subsistence, slightly better than that of a civilian in industrially developing England. At this period in history conditions for the lower classes were pitiful.

Lieutenant Charles Frederick Armstrong had been commissioned an ensign at Chatham Barracks, England, on 2 March 1832, and became a lieutenant officially on 22 July 1836.[26] In marching north to form their new post the detachment, attired in the regimental dress, must have looked incongruous against the sombre virgin bush. The uniform consisted of a scarlet tunic with blue facings and dark grey trousers with a scarlet stripe down the side.[27]

The soldiers' first duty on arriving at Kojonup would have been to construct a barracks from trees felled nearby. This hut was situated approximately 100 yards south-east of the present stone barracks. Rations of flour, salted meat, pease, salt and rum were brought regularly by a contractor whose visit was keenly anticipated for the news of the outside world as much as for the stores. On the whole, the men enjoyed more freedom than those stationed in the towns. Nevertheless, discipline was maintained and privates were expected to be subservient at all times. To augment and vary their basic rations they were organized to grow vegetables and to hunt for fresh meat. Naturally, as the soldiers' presence became known, they were visited by the local Aborigines from whom they learnt of the likely haunts of kangaroos and other wildlife. Around most military outposts could be found one or two natives permanently camped. Through 'palaver' with these Aborigines the soldiers became conversant with the surrounding countryside, its soil, herbage, water supply, trees and fauna. The proficient dark hunters imparted their traditional skills generously and lonely soldiers could become expert bushmen if they so desired. The life in the colony must have had some attraction because when the 21st Regiment embarked for India in 1839-40 between twenty and thirty men successfully obtained their discharge, remaining in the colony.[28]

The men of this detachment were still stationed at the Kojonup Spring in January 1838 but some time between then and August 1838 they were transferred to the Vasse and the Kojonup outpost was abandoned. (It would seem the Governor's high hopes for the district were premature.) Tragedy struck at the Vasse. On 4 September 1838 the Military Commandant, Major F. C. Irwin, announced that the much esteemed young officer, Lieutenant C. F. Armstrong, had died at the Vasse on 26 August after a short illness brought on by exposure in the bush while on official duty.[29] He was greatly missed: his cheerful laugh and kind and gentlemanly character had won him many friends.

Meanwhile, Armstrong's companion on many occasions, Surveyor Hillman, was preparing to set out on another visit towards the Kojonup Spring, a visit which came close to having the same disastrous end.

Prior to Hillman's departure a puzzling letter was written by the Colonial Secretary to the Military Commandant on 29 October 1838. In brief it stated that the Kojonup post was to be re-established with a party of six men and that it was to be formed about '4 miles further on the line of the road to Albany than it was formerly'.[30]

It is not apparent why the first station at Kojonup was abandoned, and Armstrong and his men sent to the Vasse, nor why it was contemplated locating the Kojonup post elsewhere. The suggestion could have come from Armstrong and his men after they had become more familiar with the district and its water supply; or it could have originated from Joseph Harris, the rations carter, who had come to know the countryside between King George Sound and his Williams station intimately, due to his frequent trips between them.

About four miles east-south-east of the Kojonup Spring was a native well, 'Warkelup', and it almost certainly was the site at which it was proposed to establish the district's new military station. Very soon the name 'Warkelup' became synonymous with the more anglicized name of 'Joseph's Well' on all maps and in official documents, which seems to indicate that the spot was associated with Joseph Harris early in its known history. It is possible that the first soldiers referred to it as Joseph's Well because they learnt of it from the rations carter. Whatever the reasons it is obvious that the town of Kojonup came very close to being founded at Warkelup or Joseph's Well. The order, however, was not pursued further, possibly due to Governor Stirling's imminent departure from the colony and the arrival of the new Governor, John Hutt, in January 1839.

On the other hand, down through history to the present day, Government departments have jealously upheld decisions made by their own officers against opinions of outsiders. This being so it is most unlikely that Surveyor-General Roe would have taken kindly to any attempt to refute a strong recommendation by one of his best surveyors. As will be seen, future almost defensive comments made by Surveyor Hillman seem to support this notion.

In 1838 Hillman appears to have left Perth quite hurriedly and ill-prepared, in the heat of December. He complained in his journal of the extreme difficulty in carrying provisions for himself and three men with only one horse, and that his own.[31] On 12 December 1838, the party consisting of Hillman's assistant (referred to only as 'John'), two unnamed soldiers and Hillman, reached the Beaufort River for the midday meal. Hillman, from his previous journey with Governor Stirling, knew that no other known watering spot existed between there and Kojonup Spring, so great care was taken to fill the 'kegs and kettles' before proceeding.[32] A halt was made at 6.30 p.m. 'in rich and beautiful grazing country but no water'.[33] At 4.15 a.m. the next day the party was on its way, without breakfast, hoping no doubt to cover a sizeable distance before the sun had risen. At 10 a.m. a rest was taken. All the water collected from the Beaufort had been used and a note of alarm crept into Hillman's usually matter-of-fact field book.

> Halted for a rest at 10 a.m.; the men and horse being much distressed for the want of water. Hope in God there is water within a short distance ahead.[34]

Hillman was an experienced surveyor and explorer who was not in the habit of panicking. The situation must have been desperate for him to write in this manner. He knew that they could not be far from the reliable Kojonup Spring and urged the others to keep moving. Within only half a mile of the Spring the parched soldiers could go no further and fell to the ground. Hillman and his assistant, with the horse, pushed onwards and reached the Spring. Once refreshed Hillman sat down to write in his field book:

> Thank Almighty God we arrived at Kojonup Spring at 11.30 a.m., although greatly distressed for the want of water, the two soldiers fell down on the road about a ½ mile back completely exhausted,—I was obliged to leave them, as I knew our lives depended upon proceeding, but if they do not come shortly I shall send the horse out for them, although the poor beast is almost knocked up.[35]

Later he added, 'sent out the horse and John and got the men in by 1.30 p.m. Distance today, 14 miles'.[36]

To recover from this agonizing experience the party relaxed all the next day at the Spring. As well as the plentiful water they had discovered another attraction: fresh vegetables, planted and abandoned by the soldiers of the 21st Regiment—Kojonup's first harvest.

Sitting by the Spring and relishing the 'excellent dish of vegetables'[37] Hillman probably reflected on his military friend Armstrong of whose death he had heard before leaving Perth. Perhaps the harrowing times made him appreciate the Kojonup scenery even more as he wrote, 'the country round the Spring now appears most beautiful, grass of the best description up to our middles'.[38] He reaffirmed his previous recommendation of the Kojonup Spring site in clear, cogent terms, first in his field book, then in his journal and one cannot help asking if this was because a contrary opinion had been mooted.

> The best position for a Townsite is thus bounded ½ a mile North of centre of Kojonup spring—½ a mile South 1 mile West & 1 mile East—thus forming two square miles or 1280 acres.

I have little doubt but that the spring would furnish abundance of water for many persons throughout the year & if not, water may be got by digging in any part.[39]

In his official journal he wrote:

In accordance with my instructions to select a site for a town in this vicinity, I beg to recommend that Kojonup Spring be taken as a centre, and the town laid out in a double square containing two square miles, the greatest length being E. and W. These limits would include good land and abundance of good grass, a permanent supply of good water in the spring, and also plenty of stone for building, and is the most eligible site in the neighbourhood . . . .[40]

(It was another twelve months before the surveyor actually visited Joseph's Well.)

After their day's rest at the Spring and the variation in their limited traveller's diet, the party set off at 4.30 a.m. They had gone sixteen miles before dinner, hoping to find water on the Warriup River but were unsuccessful. Drought conditions seemed to have prevailed. In the afternoon they pushed on to 'the next river',[41] three miles further on, and after searching found water a quarter of a mile to the east. The next morning the group moved on eleven miles, arriving at the Gordon River at 10 a.m. where they remained for the rest of the day.

As the party had left Kojonup Spring they had passed an Aborigine, dead, on the east side of the road. He appeared to have been dead for a fortnight. As Hillman recorded this observation he must have been tempted to add 'there, but for the Grace of God, we also would have been!'

REFERENCES

[1] Letter from Surveyor-General's Office, Perth, to K.H.S., 31 May 1968.

[2] J. S. Battye, *The Cyclopedia of Western Australia* (Adelaide, 1913), p. 6.

[3] F. K. Crowley, *Australia's Western Third* (London, 1960), p. 9.

[4] F. C. Irwin, *State and Position of Western Australia* (London, 1835).

[5] G. F. Moore, *Diary of Two Years Eventful Life of an Early Settler in Western Australia* (London, 1884).

[6] Irwin, p. 65.

[7] Moore, p. 300.

[8] C.S.O.Recs, 8, p. 12 (held in Battye Library, Perth).

[9] Rhoda Glover, 'Captain Symers Trader', p. 128 (M.A. thesis, University of Western Australia, 1952; Battye Library, Perth).

[10] A. Hillman, Field Book 12 (held in W.A.L.Dept.).

[11] W. S. Bunbury and W. P. Morrell, eds., *Early Days in Western Australia, being the Letters and Journal of Lt. H. W. Bunbury* (London, 1930), p. 30.

[12] Sir James Stirling, Journal: April 1837 (W.A.L.Dept.).

[13] *Ibid.*

[14] *Ibid.*

[15] *Ibid.*

[16] *Ibid.*

[17] *Ibid.*

[18] *Ibid.*

[19] *Ibid.*

[20] *Ibid.*

[21] C.S.O.Recs, 8, p. 119.

[22] *West Australian*, 10 December 1889, p. 2.

[23] Moore.

[24] P.R.O. War Office (London) microfilms; information collected and supplied by E. S. Whitely, 1969.

[25] Chris Halls, 'A Short History of the British Regiment in Western Australia 1826-1863', *Sabretache*, vol. 3, no. 3, January 1961.

[26] Personal correspondence from P.R.O., 30 August 1968.

[27] Halls.

[28] P.R.O. War Office microfilms.

[29] Military Headquarters files, 4 September 1838 (Battye Library).

[30] C.S.O.Recs., 12, p. 31.

[31] A. Hillman, Journal: November-December 1838 (W.A.L.Dept.)

[32] A. Hillman, Field Book: 1838 (W.A.L.Dept.).

[33] *Ibid.*

[34] *Ibid.*

[35] *Ibid.*

[36] *Ibid.*

[37] A. Hillman, Journal: November-December 1838.

[38] A. Hillman, Field Book: 1838.

[39] *Ibid.*

[40] Hillman, Journal: November-December 1838.

[41] Hillman, Field Book: 1838, p. 627.

Success and Failure

CURIOSITY

In the early days of expanding industrial trade and colonization an ideal occupation was that of a shipowner. An astute sea-captain could amass a great fortune. When calling into port he was the centre of attention as a knowledgeable link with the outside world. He was accepted by all classes of society for the news he could relate and the special items of the coveted cargo he might bestow on a favourite. In return, he was the recipient of the most interesting local news.

A person in this advantageous position was Thomas Lyal Symers, captain of the *Caledonia*, a barque of 189 tons. As early as June 1835 his supercargo, G. Smith, wrote informing Symers that Sir James Stirling would co-operate in every way to assist the Captain to purchase land at King George Sound.[1] In April 1838 when Symers was in India Sir Richard Spencer wrote advising him, when buying sheep country in the colony, to go inland and acquire 1000-2000 acres for every 200 sheep.[2] Symers heeded all the advice and eventually settled his family permanently at Albany, while he continued his seafaring.

In September 1839, the *Caledonia* was damaged in a storm and required extensive repairs at Fremantle. Being in the hub of the colony Symers busied himself with his land aspirations. He commenced by composing the following letter to the Surveyor-General.[3]

Fremantle.
Oct. 7th 1839.

To the Honourable, the Surveyor-General.

Sir,

I beg you will represent to His Excellency, the Governor, the situation in which I am placed, with regard to the livestock I now possess in the Colony and that which I propose to introduce into it by the earliest opportunity which offers from Van Diemen's Land and Port Phillip, in the hope that the statement of my views may induce His Excellency to grant me facilities for carrying them through as will confer not only considerable individual benefit to myself but will materially advance the interest of the Colony.

The stock of horses and horned cattle which I possess on the Calgan River amounts in value to at least £2000 depastured on land not my own and already requiring more extensive runs than can be found in the neighbourhood or within many miles of King George Sound. In addition to them I own an extensive flock of sheep (amount probably to about 3000 head) at Port Phillip, being the increase from 500 head which I left in charge at Van Diemen's Land five years ago, with instructions to my agent to purchase breeding ewes by every means in his power.

It is my intention to introduce the whole of these into the Colony by King George Sound as soon as I complete my present passage to the Eastern Colonies but feel that my wishes and views are likely to be completely frustrated for want of a suitable station at which to place my stock. Having considerable landed and other property at Albany my inclinations naturally incline to the Sound and in that vicinity I should prefer establishing myself on that account. I have therefore looked around the neighbourhood and find no place better suited to my views than the vicinity of Kojonup which I am however given to understand is not open to the application of purchases in consequence of not having yet been surveyed. Under these circumstances and dreading considerable losses to my stock if I have not a proper run for them I think His Excellency will not object to my making use of the Government land about Kojonup until the same may be opened for location or survey on my guarantee that when the latter is effected I will purchase, at the minimum price of 5/0 per acre about 640 to 1000 acres which shall include all my buildings, stock yards and improvements there and prevent any sacrifice of my present outlay by any other person being enabled to purchase them over my head.

Requesting your early reply,
I remain Sir,
Your Most Obedient Servant,
T. L. Symers.
Commanding Barque Caledonia.

A reply came from the Colonial Secretary stating that the Kojonup neighbourhood was not yet surveyed so was not open to selection in the usual manner, by public auction, but Symers could have 650-1200 acres immediately if he was willing to pay 8s. per acre cash. The alternative would be to wait as the survey of country between Moorilup and Kojonup was to be marked off in blocks of 640 acres for selection by purchase in about six weeks' time.[4]

A further letter within a few days gave the Governor's approval of Symers buying 100 acres in Kojonup, at 8s. per acre cash, without waiting for the survey on the condition that he paid 5s. per acre cash

27

(and not in remission certificates) for any additional land in the area when it was surveyed, plus expending not more than 3s. per acre in some permanent improvements like buildings, yards, wells and fences before the full title was guaranteed. Crown land for pasture would be rented to him at 20s. the 640 acres.[5] Thomas Lyal Symers therefore became the owner of Kojonup location 1 of 100 acres, for £40, the official date being 13 October 1840.[6] He had stolen a march on all the other eager sheep land seekers of the south.

The fact that Symers had cash to meet his commitment would have accounted enormously for the Governor's prompt co-operation in these dealings. The whole colony was suffering from a shortage of actual cash, plus a surplus of saleable land. This situation had developed when early settlers with land grants began under-cutting the Government's minimum land price of 5s. an acre. Remission certificates were frequently used in land transactions because of the scarcity of money.

In addition to purchasing location 1, Symers was also permitted to lease the adjacent deserted Kojonup townsite. For years the aggressive, stubborn Symers carried on a private written war with the Government over the lease price, but finally had to capitulate to its terms.

Meanwhile, Surveyor Hillman could hardly have had time to recover from his last harrowing visit when he was preparing to set out again for Kojonup. It is hard to imagine his relishing the idea. There was no likelihood of midsummer conditions having improved. Despite this, he left Albany on 28 January 1840 and was soon writing enthusiastic reports of the country.[7] Within five days he was relieved to arrive at Kojonup Spring, having suffered greatly from want of water between there and the Gordon River. He made the deserted military hut his headquarters and surveyed from that point.

The inference (by the Colonial Secretary, in 1838) that there was a better site for the town must have been still nettling Hillman because while in the locality he made it his business to locate Joseph's Well, after which he stated, categorically, that the land around, although good, was not equal to Kojonup. He claimed also that it was called 'Annurup' by the Aborigines. Perhaps the surveyor had been fortified with an extra nip of rum that night which caused a slip of the pen, because Joseph's Well was definitely called 'Warkelup' by the Aborigines and is marked accordingly on all old maps. However, Hillman undoubtedly located 'Annurup' (which was another Aboriginal watering point three miles north-east of Warkelup, on the Jackaneedup Creek), since from Joseph's Well he proceeded in the direction of Annurup to a river in pools. This river was on a bearing east-north-east

from Kojonup at a distance of seven miles, and its native name was
'Jejegup'. There was an abundance of excellent water, but, he wrote:

> the land on the banks is of an inferior description, being mostly
> sandy loam, rather thickly timbered. This is supposed to be the
> Beaufort.[8]

That Hillman was aware of the existence of a different opinion regarding the siting of the town is evident by his summing up:

> Having now examined the places most likely to furnish an available
> site for a town and seeing none so good as the land around Kojonup
> Spring, I determined to fix it at that place.[9]

Altogether, Hillman and his party were working in the Kojonup area
for over forty days on this visit but they were not entirely isolated.
Symers had arrived to ensure that location 1 was correctly surveyed.
He had sailed from Fremantle on 29 January 1840 in the repaired
Caledonia. On board was John Gilbert, assistant to the famous naturalist John Gould. The ship remained at Albany two weeks so Gilbert
seized the opportunity to accompany the Captain to his selections at
Kojonup, a journey taking twelve days. On this trip Gilbert discovered
a rare marsupial, a rat kangaroo (*Potorous gilberti*), which unfortunately is probably now extinct.[10] Accompanying Symers and Gilbert
were Messrs Belches, Townsend, W. N. Clark (the Public Notary),
A. Trimmer and three Aborigines.[11]

Having been warned at the Sound that no water was to be obtained
in the thirty-five miles between the Gordon River and Kojonup the
party filled two fifteen gallon casks at the former place before proceeding. Suddenly, not far along the road, one of the accompanying
Aborigines shouted excitedly and pointed to a strange Aborigine high
up in a tree. The fellow was enticed down and after sampling some
offered biscuits led the party to a fine pool of water in the bed of a
river, about one and a half miles on the east side of the road. The
travellers decided to make camp there and were soon joined by many
Aboriginal men, women and children who evidently had never seen
Europeans before. To them the place was known as 'Kinunyup'. Cocka-
toos and pigeons abounded and near one pool towards evening a flock
of pigeons literally darkened the air.

One of the Aborigines, a fine intelligent lad, volunteered to accompany the party to Kojonup. The next morning the boy directed them to
'Yarenup' (*sic*). The country was extremely scenic: fine sheep pasture,
the soil light red and of a loam texture, and the river in pools winding

through it. From here the party proceeded to Kojonup and pitched their tent near the Spring where Hillman was already camped. Of course, the newcomers lost no time in bragging to the Government surveyor that they had discovered an unknown watering spot. However, Hillman confidently recorded: 'I am of the opinion that it will not be found permanent in a dry summer'.[12] (Within a few weeks he was to be proved correct.)

One morning, the Kinunyup Aborigine directed some of the party to the south-south-west. After passing over two or three miles of a rugged ironstone country, all at once they entered on an extensive rich grassy country with a fine pool of water in the middle. It was very park-like. The Aboriginal name was said to be 'Mandalup'. At one spot, near a pool of water, were fifty acres fit for the plough without a tree to check its progress.

The lad told the party that there was more fine grass and water far away to the south-east, called 'Belgarrup' (sic). The explorers hastened back to the Spring, jubilantly, and compared notes with the others who had gone with Hillman to Warkelup and had returned rather disappointed. The next morning it was decided that everyone should start for the promised 'Belgarrup'.

After travelling eight miles over a great deal of excellent land and good feed they reached their destination. The breadth of the river, now in pools, was about thirty yards from bank to bank. The soil was excellent and the grass abundant. Some of the men immediately followed the course of the river towards the west and reached Mandalup. The distance was about twelve miles and the same character of country prevailed. They were compelled reluctantly to leave the place and return to the tents, but expressed themselves highly gratified as when they turned back the same waving grass extended in all directions as far as the eye could see. As W. N. Clark wrote:

> pasturage was discovered sufficient to feed the whole of the sheep now in the colony, were all the flocks driven to that part of this fine district.[13]

Shortly after this the newcomers took leave of Hillman and returned home via 'Yarenup'.

The surveyor was just as enraptured with the country as the settlers and concluded his report by saying:

> My time would not allow me to examine the country on the left bank of Balgarup River, but on the right bank, I have no hesitation

in stating that from 30-40000 acres of land, fully as good, if not better than Kojonup, may be selected available for sheep farming. The alluvial flats on the river would afford sufficient land for agriculture.[14]

News of the wonderful land just discovered travelled fast and far, so much so that people were warned to wait for the official anouncement before believing it all. On 23 May 1840 the land open for selection was advertised. It included:

> a tract of 13 miles of excellent country on the Kojonup River established 3 miles S.E. and 10 miles N.W. from a conspicuous land mark on the right bank of that stream placed 6½ miles S. from the Kojonup Spring; as also the whole of the country around the Kojonup townsite as far as it may be selected in contiguous locations.[15]

On 9 September 1840 the Government held a public sale of Kojonup locations 3, 4, 5, 8, 10, 11, 12, 13, 14, 15, 16, 17, 18, 19, 20, 21 and 22.[16] By 11 January 1842 the sale of locations 5 and 6 (an area of 6000 acres) had been officially concluded. They had been bought for £1500 by a gentleman of the stock exchange in London, Louis Samson, uncle of the then Fremantle merchant, Lionel Samson. At the same time the title for locations 15, 16, 17 and 18 amounting to 2560 acres, was transferred to Perth surgeon, William Horatio Sholl, for £640.[17] Obviously, the speculators had their ears pricked for all favourable reports.

POISON

The news had spread abroad that sheep were in demand and fetching high prices in the Swan River Colony. Formerly, the trip around the tempestuous Cape Leeuwin had deterred traders from transporting stock to the Swan River, but the blazing of the overland track had now eliminated this hazard. In November 1839 the pioneers of the Williams district, Dr Harris and his son Joseph, acquired a flock of sheep at King George Sound and drove them overland to their Williams station.[18] They did not lose a single sheep, even though they did not always stay close to the road but detoured to known watering points to the east. On a second trip the Harris family lost about 3 per cent of the sheep, but this was negligible compared with the losses encountered on a sea voyage. In addition, the sheep arrived at their destination quicker, and in better condition, with less cost. Joseph Harris appeared to have originated a profitable droving business for himself.

31

Another person who was quick to see a profitable proposition in this route was Edward John Eyre. At the age of twenty-five this future explorer, with Lieutenant Alfred Mundy and Edward Bate Scott, arrived at King George Sound on the barque *Cleveland* at the end of February 1840, and ferried ashore 1000 ewes, 450 lambs and 70 head of cattle, with the intention of driving them overland to the Swan River to sell.[19]

It was one of the worst months of the year for such a task. Eyre's party was warned that from the earliest days of the settlement of York there had been reports of a puzzling plant from which feeding stock died. This plant was known to grow in the vicinity of the Williams River, but south of this river was considered free of it. Unfortunately, Eyre's flocks were to prove otherwise. Just seven miles south of Kojonup the stock became affected and some died. By the time the expedition reached York 150 to 200 sheep and some cattle had died from eating the unknown poison plants. On the journey numerous experiments were performed to try to diagnose the trouble, but to no avail. Eyre showed great insight into the problem and made accurate notes of his observations of the suffering animals. The surviving stock was sold at good prices.

Some of the sheep had been purchased by Albany settlers, previous to Eyre's departure from the Sound. One of these buyers was Thomas Lyal Symers. His flock was mainly maiden ewes, in a very weak condition, badly affected with scab. It was decided not to drive them immediately to the newly-acquired Kojonup pastures but to hold them along with some horses and cattle at 'Meergannup', a watering spot just north of Mt Barker, until they improved or seasonal conditions were more propitious for their removal. Accompanying Symers' men was the garrulous W. N. Clark who, for a time, showed a great interest in Kojonup.

In June the Symers party pulled up roots and headed for their previous watering spot, Kinunyup, but they discovered Hillman's prediction to be correct. The stream was dry. They explored for water two miles north and east and in so doing located P. Belches' flock, already depastured on 'very superior runs of considerable extent'[20] with George Maxwell in charge. The country was so extensive the party decided to make another halt at a spring with the name of 'Warriemup', about eight or ten miles short of the Balgarup River. It was a wise choice as the stock soon improved considerably. The area was 'completely a pastoral country composed of gentle hills sloping into valleys covered with grass and having a water course in the centre'.[21] Nearby were two other rich valleys, 'Peeneeup' and 'Mooteeup'. Belches was not the only one who had lost no time in depasturing sheep on these lush lands; some sheep belonging to Tapson were in the area, and Souper of York had a mixed flock of approximately 700 feeding close by.

At the end of July the Symers party moved on to their Balgarup River selection. W. N. Clark wrote:

> We are 8 miles S.S.E. of Kojonup and I have marked a road between the two stations so that no person can mistake his way. The nearest point of the Swan River Road is about 2 miles at the back of our place in a N.E. direction.
> I have been twice at Kojonup under the escort of natives and have remarked that the country between the two places is good. Three large valleys with brooks of water particularly attracted my attention. They are called "Belbarribup", "Wandunup" and "Corunup", all ending in ups. The latter place is particularly fine and within two miles of Kojonup townsite, travelling from Belgarup [sic].
> Since writing the above I have had some conversation with Mr George Maxwell, late overseer to Mr Belches, and he informs me that about 12 miles east by south of Peeneenup he, after we left him on our route to Belgarup [sic] discovered a fresh water river there in very large pools; on several of which there were immense covies of water fowl. The land to the east of the river he describes as very fine. He was accompanied by two natives and he states that numbers of other aborigines were seen in this new district but that they invariably fled at his approach.[22]

At the same time as this expedition was in progress another astute sea-captain was dropping anchor in King George Sound. He was Captain John Hassell. The year before, when visiting Albany, he had purchased the 'Kendenup' property, north of Mt Barker. He had now returned with sheep, cattle and horses which he swam ashore, to establish a settlement there.[23] In the interim he kept a watchful eye on the development of the Kojonup district.

Stock continued to be greatly in demand. When Eyre was struggling towards York with his pitiful flock, Symers was negotiating the following sanguine transaction[24] with one of his numerous harbour acquaintances, William Rolfe Steel, proprietor of the Royal Hotel, Fremantle. Steel was one of the many townspeople who wanted a share of the promising pastoral industry.

5th March 1840.

Sir,
    In consequence of an arrangement made and entered into between you and me, on this day, I have delivered to you Four

Hundred and Fifty-Seven MO. lamb ewes marked with a Wadd Cutter on the left ear.

The sheep are to be at your risk and expense from this day and to be properly fed and attended to by you or your Servants. Your remuneration to be one third of the produce thereof whether male or female, as the same shall be divided by myself or a person or persons appointed by me. Such division to be made within four months after the birth of each lamb and not sooner.

If I should require to remove the Sheep at any time, *then* I bind myself to pay you or your Representative a sum not exceeding Twenty Pounds per Annum for every One Hundred Ewes and hereby reserve to myself the full liberty of doing so at any moment, on paying you the aforesaid sum. The Wool of the said sheep and their increase is to be sheared, clipped, washed, properly packed and sent to Albany by you, one third therof to belong to you and your representatives, and the remainder to me and mine, subject to my direction. Any rams that I may purchase are to be my sole property, and to be removed along with the flock, if I choose to do so. Any sheep of yours are to be marked to distinguish them from mine.

I am Sir,
Your obedient humble Servant
Wm R. Steel

I hereby accept the above offer to fulfil my part of the agreement.
T. L. Symers.

Witnessed by, Wm Nairne Clark, Notary Public
H. E. Johnston

Steel's meticulous foresight was destined to fail. As for Symers, this agreement was to result in disaster—just another of many calamities he was to endure about this time. In South Australia he had become involved in a protracted nautical court-case which demanded his full personal attention. In the meantime his wife, Mary Symers, a gracious, well-born lady, was in charge of his Western Australian interests.

One of the duties she performed on her husband's behalf was to welcome William Sounness to the colony on the ship *Advocate*, in August 1840,[25] and to arrange for him to go to her husband's Kojonup holdings, as a shepherd. Sounness would barely have had time to become accustomed to local conditions and practices when he was embroiled in a calamity which was to have lasting far-flung consequences for the district to which he had migrated.

In September, Mary Symers received the following letter[26] from the overseer, J. Craigie, on her husband's Balgarup property.

Balgarup
5 September 1840.

Mrs Symers,

I received your note by Mr Souper. I arrived safe with the cart but sorrow to inform you of the great loss with the sheep. They have taken the disease that Mr Belches sheep had. They had an attack a week before I arrived, 25 dead all of Mr Steels. Yesterday we had another attack. I had been at Kojonup for the purpose of arranging to take them there. Upon arriving home the sheep were lying dead in all directions and running mad all bleeding, 29 dead, 26 of Mr Steele, 2 Captain Symers, 1 of my own. This is plain proof that Balgarup will not do for sheep. The cattle and horses is thriving remarkably well. Mr Steel has sent for his sheep by Dr Harris. I think of putting the others in charge of Mr Sounness Shepherd at Kojonup. However I shall be into the settlement in the course of ten days or fortnight.

Your Obt Servant
J. Craigie.

This was the death-song of the embryonic pastoral industry of Kojonup. Hereafter, a stigma clung to the name. The word 'poison' was associated with its lush countryside for almost a century. News of the tragedy spread throughout the colony. If Mary Symers felt unequal to the task of combatting this new disaster which had befallen the family she gave no sign of it. She was capably and unobtrusively assisted by her brother, H. E. Johnstone. The colonial botanist James Drummond, as well as a visiting German botanist Ludwig Preiss, were anxious to investigate the causes of the sudden sheep deaths and Mrs Symers, in the absence of her husband, offered every facility to them 'to prosecute their researches'.[27] They accompanied H. E. Johnstone, W. N. Clark and J. Craigie to Balgarup on 25 October 1840. For five days they journeyed, investigating and discussing the vegetation as they went. The two rival plant-collectors disagreed on the cause of the sheep fatalities. Drummond maintained the culprit was the *Lobelia* species but the superior Preiss considered this plant was harmless. 'At Balgarup the first experiment was conducted with the lobelia, which had no effect on the sheep at all.'[28] A second test was made with another pea-flowered plant suspected by Joseph Harris, 'but Drummond having lost his argument'[29] departed for the recently re-opened military post at Kojonup on his homeward journey to Hawthornden near Toodyay. Here he found a scarcity of rations and was unable to obtain the promised supplies. He therefore had to abandon plans to deviate to Mt Williams, and instead 'took the direct route to the Williams, unaware that the sheep in the second experiment died suddenly'.[30]

35

On reaching Harris's station Drummond and the host fed a healthy goat with some of the pea-flower species, crushed to a fine powder. Within fourteen hours it was dead. When the colonial botanist published a report on this experiment (and history has proved him correct) Preiss denounced his findings and arrogantly claimed that the prickly nature of the plant caused 'an acute irritation of the animals' stomachs . . . and drank, with bravado, a wineglass full of an infusion of the leaves' to prove his point.[31] To get to the bottom of the whole perplexing problem the Agricultural Society conducted a series of experiments at Guildford, attended by Drummond and the Harrises. These experiments proved conclusively that certain of the colony's plants were poisonous to stock. Drummond's description of the plant which he suspected and with which he experimented fits one of the now known York Road poisons.[32]

It seems enquiries about the poison were being made from all likely sources. W. N. Clark seems to have undertaken the task of chief informer of the Balgarup area, but unfortunately his reports are rambling and his facts and figures questionable. He was a great talker and by his own admission was sometimes inattentive on some of his excursions. He wrote in November 1840 to the Colonial Secretary, regarding a trip to the east taken earlier by Drummond and Preiss, that the river referred to by George Maxwell (see page 33) was the Gordon or the 'Pakeerup'. As to the Beaufort, he states that the native name for it was 'Yeu-annerup'; the native word for a river in pools was 'Bele'. In his opinion:

> The value of the Balgarup District consists in the richness of the red loam soil, well adapted for wheat and the number of large valleys with brooks of water that run into it from the N. and S.W. Mr Harris and I struck into one so large that we actually mistook it for the Balgarup River until we were undeceived. We saw several pools of fresh water in the valley which runs into the Balgarup about 3 miles W. of the house. We fell in with it on our return and being engaged in talking insensibly struck up the right bank until the mistake was found out by reference to the compass. None of the Burtonia was seen in this valley. There are two other large valleys between this and Kojonup intersecting the district N. and S. which afford capital back runs for sheep and healthy pasture watered by central brooks. I think I mentioned in one of my previous letters that we are 9 miles S.S.E. of Kojonup. On our journey to the settlement we come on the Swan River and King George Sound Roads near Kinnunup, passing through a fine country to the south of Yarenup. The road from Kojonup to Balgarup to King George Sound is much nearer than the old road and intersects a fine country.[33]

1 Alfred Hillman, from a
miniature (1830)

2 Distribution of Kaneang
tribe

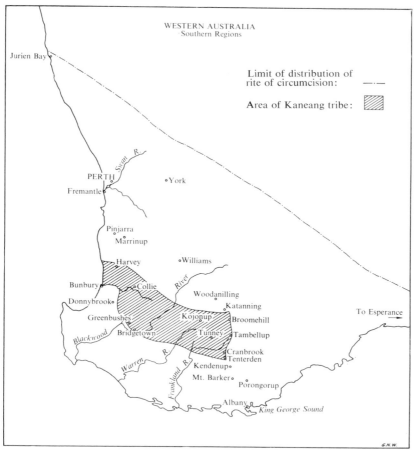

WESTERN AUSTRALIA
Southern Regions

Jurien Bay

Limit of distribution of
rite of circumcision:

Area of Kaneang tribe:

Swan R.

PERTH
Fremantle
York

Pinjarra
Marrinup

Harvey
Williams

Bunbury
Collie
River
Woodanilling
Donnybrook
Katanning
Greenbushes
Kojonup
Broomehill
Bridgetown
Tunney
Tambellup
Blackwood
Cranbrook
Tenterden
Warren R.
Kendenup
Frankland R.
Mt. Barker
Porongorup

Albany
King George Sound

To Esperance

G.N.W.

3 Mandalup (1970). Similar park-like country attracted Kojonup's first pastoral speculators in the late 1830s

4 'Harris's Rock Pool' (p. 19)

From this letter it is obvious that Symers' establishment was still in existence on 6 November 1840. The owner had always favoured the breeding of cattle and horses on his properties and when two cows in good condition died, J. Craigie went to the port to consult his employer. It was felt that swift action was urgently required. As the suspected plants grew along the track all the way from Balgarup to the Gordon River, a distance of twenty-two miles, the problems seemed insurmountable. Then an ingenious scheme was devised. The surviving sheep and cattle were muzzled for the journey through the poison-infested area and then driven to the safer pastures around Albany.

All this news of the ominous presence of poison at Kojonup spread abroad. The colony's newspapers gave full coverage to it, week by week. A newcomer to Albany wrote to England on 8 November 1840:

> There have been some dreadful losses among the sheep. Out of one flock of 400 which was being driven overland from here to the Swan, all died but 30. It is believed from the effect of some poisonous herb. A short time ago ewes sold in Perth for £5 per head.[34]

Drummond reported in the *Perth Gazette* on 5 December 1840 that Steel and Belches had met with heavy losses from the poison plant. The following week in the same newspaper he voiced another criticism of the Kojonup district which was becoming more prevalent: 'Kojonup, in my opinion, will prove too dry for a summer station for flocks and herds'.[35]

Clark's answer to this was that it could easily be remedied as it was at Balgarup: 'we have dug a well and at the depth of 8 feet procure pure spring water sufficient to supply the establishment in the dry months of the year if the pools in the river fail'.[36]

However as summer approached, the scarcity of surface water with the increased flocks in the district was fast proving to be another acute anxiety for the Kojonup pioneers. The whole wretched situation was summed up as follows, on 19 December 1840:

> Some rumors [*sic*] have reached us this week of a nature calculated seriously to effect the value of landed property at Kojonup, a portion of the Colony hitherto pronounced to be one of the finest districts for depasturing sheep. The report we allude to is, that the establishment formed there by Capt. Symers has been broken up—that others, who have visited the district with a view to settling there have abandoned it—and, that, recently many sheep have died from want of water, as well as from eating the fatal plant described by Mr Drummond in our late numbers.[37]

In the same issue, one veteran supporter of Kojonup, Dr Joseph Harris, rushed into print in defence of the district. He wrote:

> I have heard that Capt. Symers' establishment at Belgarup [sic] is broken up; but although such a reason is given as want of water, by persons ignorant of the matter, I assert that it is not on that account they have been removed, and you may be assured, Mr Editor, that the district is not in danger of being abandoned. . . . In adducing these remarks, hastily drawn up, I am actuated by a desire to relieve the numerous owners of land at Kojonup and Belgarup from the fears entertained from the representations of hasty observers—the country is occupied, and will continue to be when it will be found to be one of the best districts in the Colony, although not exempted from the usual accidents occurring in settling a new colony.[38]

This same article seems to offer further proof that Joseph's Well was named by Dr Joseph Harris or his son, and they had suggested that the townsite be removed to that watering point. For instance, he wrote in the article:

> As to the water, I have always been of the opinion that the townsite spring is insufficient for the wants of a large population, and the few inhabitants now on the spot have been inconvenienced by the quantity of sheep now depasturing there, and which have been allowed to exhaust the water. There are other springs in the immediate neighbourhood, sufficient for wants of a household, but not for stock.[39]

Conversely, Clark pointed out, on 6 January 1841, that the heavy sheep losses met with by Tapson had been due more to over-driving than anything else. They had been made to cover twenty miles a day. In February 1841, it was being said that the prospects might not be as gloomy as was previously thought. Sutherland (location 3) had just returned from inspecting his holding and the general feeling was that water was to be obtained by digging and the poison evil could 'in a great degree, if not altogether, be avoided'.[40]

Sometime during these turbulent months the military resumed residence in the hut barracks at the Kojonup Spring. The soldiers were of the 51st Regiment from Hobart, and had come to replace the 21st Regiment which was moving to service in India. An officer of the 51st was George Egerton-Warburton who in August 1840 walked to Perth 'a distance of 300 miles carrying a load for the greater part of the way and sleeping in the open air for fifteen nights'.[41] He had hoped to be appointed to the Survey Department but this was not possible (nor desirable to him when he learnt of the meagre salary) and in October he returned to Albany by ship and was placed 'in command of two outposts, the further 100 miles distant which I am expected to visit'.[42] As Dr Harris had written, Kojonup was certainly not being abandoned. The military was to be closely connected with it continuously for almost three decades. In January 1841 it was stated that 1600 sheep and a number of horses and cattle were already in the district and others were preparing to follow.[43]

Yet T. L. Symers' influence in the area was waning. He seemed to be on the road to ruin. As soon as his ship touched at Fremantle his former business partner, W. R. Steel, demanded £430 compensation for the sheep he had lost at Balgarup. Further troubles and expenses were demanding Symers' attention in Adelaide and Sydney. He was unable to meet the commitments for his Balgarup holdings and on 28 April 1841, the Colonial Secretary's Office publicized that on 1 June it would be auctioned.

It was described as:

> Kojonup location No. 2 comprising twelve hundred and eighty acres in the form of a double square, adjoining the S.E. side of the reserve of Balgarup townsite, and extending due N.E. from Balgarup River, with a width of 80 chains. This land has been in the occupation of Mr J. L. Symers [sic] by whom several improvements have been effected, comprising buildings, stock yards, well and cultivation.[44]

However, owing to the lack of money in the colony and the recent bad rumours of the district it was some time before the land was officially re-allocated.

Henceforth, the frustrated Symers concentrated on his other land holdings closer to Albany, although his initial purchase was still in his possession in 1855.[45] He was perhaps Kojonup's first visionary, who through factors beyond his control was forced to withdraw and leave to others the opportunity to commence developing the Kojonup district to its full potential.

REFERENCES

[1] Rhoda Glover, 'Captain Symers Trader', p. 120 (M.A. thesis, University of Western Australia, 1952; held in Battye Library, Perth).

[2] *Ibid.*

[3] C.S.O.Recs., 2, 7 October 1839 (Battye Library).

[4] *Ibid.* 17 October 1839.

[5] *Ibid.* 28 October 1839.

[6] W.A.L.Dept.Recs. of original landholders (copy in K.H.S.Recs.).

[7] A. Hillman, Journal: February-March 1840 (copy in K.H.S.Recs.).

[8] *Ibid.*

[9] *Ibid.*

[10] D. L. Serventy and H. M. Whittell, *Birds of Western Australia* (Perth, 1967), p. 35.

[11] Facts about this trip from Albany on pages 29 and 30 are in a letter from W. N. Clark, in C.S.O.Recs., 90, 15 March 1840.

[12] Hillman, Journal: February-March 1840.

[13] C.S.O.Recs., 90, 15 March 1840.

[14] Hillman, Journal: February-March 1840.

[15] *Perth Gazette*, 23 May 1840, p. 2.

[16] *Perth Gazette*, 4 July 1840, p. 4.

[17] W.A.L.Dept.Recs. of original landholders.

[18] Rica Ericson, *The Drummonds of Hawthornden* (Perth, 1969), p. 55.

[19] Malcolm Uren and Robert Stephen, *Waterless Horizons* (Melbourne, 1942), p. 94.

[20] Letter from W. N. Clark in *Perth Gazette*, 24 October 1840, p. 4.

[21] *Ibid.*

[22] *Ibid.*

[23] Personal correspondence from C. L. Hassell, 2 October 1969.

[24] Symers collection of letters (copy in possession of Rhoda Glover).

[25] Glover, p. 189.

[26] Symers letters.

[27] Glover, p. 190.

[28] Ericson, p. 58.

[29] *Ibid.*

[30] *Ibid.*

[31] *Ibid.*, p. 59.

[32] T. E. H. Aplin, 'York Road Poison and Box Poison', *Journal* of the Department of Agriculture, vol. 8, no. 5, May 1967.

[33] Letter from W. N. Clarke to Col.Sec., 6 November 1840, in Exploration Diaries 1836-46, vol. 3 (Battye Library).

[34] Letter from G. Egerton-Warburton, 8 November 1840 (copy in possession of D. Crabbe).

[35] *Perth Gazette*, 12 December 1840, p. 2.

[36] Exploration Diaries.

[37] *Perth Gazette*, 19 December 1840, p. 2.

[38] *Ibid.*

[39] *Ibid.*

[40] *Inquirer*, 10 February 1841, p. 4.

[41] Letter from G. Egerton-Warburton, 8 November 1840.

[42] *Ibid.*

[43] *Perth Gazette*, 27 January 1841, p. 3.

[44] *Government Gazette*, 8 April 1841, p. 3.

[45] Glover, p. 229.

4

A Stronghold

THE LULL

The pastoral bubble had burst but not before some speculators had been caught red-handed. Legal recording of land transfers was frequently protracted so that official dates of land sales are not particularly indicative of the first application. When Dr Harris had written of 'numerous owners of land at Kojonup and Belgarup'[1] he was referring to people such as Henry Charles Sutherland, Collector of Revenue of the Colony of Western Australia who was to become the official owner of Kojonup location 3 (1200 acres) in 1846, for £300. In the same year locations 7 and 8 (6500 acres) were transferred to George Walpole Leake, a member of the first Legislative Council, for £1625; and location 19 (522 acres) on the Balgarup River, for £313 4s. 0d. was allocated to Jonah Smith Wells, a member of the stock exchange in London.[2] Whether these investors regretted their hasty actions soon after is not known but there is no evidence that they took any active interest in their holdings.

Much of the incentive for pastoral speculation in the colony had developed from the tales of the lucrative profits made in the wool industry in eastern Australia, during the 1830s. The coming of the 1840s brought a slump in the price of wool and this together with a labour problem and the lack of actual money heralded hard times for the Swan River Colony.

In 1840, £40 was allocated to improve the road from King George Sound to Kojonup.[3] The following year, the monthly mail between Albany to Perth via Kojonup and Bunbury was carried by Mary Symers' brother, H. E. Johnstone, who instead of using the usual spring cart, rode fast horses which he changed at Kojonup.[4] In the same period Joseph Harris was the mailman between Guildford and King George Sound.[5] The beam of light or the smoke of the fire at the Kojonup military hut must have many times been a welcoming sight to them.

Initially, the hut was occupied by seven men and the pay list for the period from October to December 1840 mentions Corporal Chadwick, Privates R. Cowell, J. Davies, W. Eaton, G. Overhand, G. Stevens and J. Woodfall.[6] Private Cowell could not have been satisfied with the life as the officer-in-charge G. Egerton-Warburton wrote from Albany on 11 December 1840:

> I lost a man the other day at a Detachment 100 miles from here. I rode out there to enquire into the particulars and endeavour to get a native on his track but without success. It is astonishing how soon a man gets lost in the bush and sometimes being confused wanders for days without getting a quarter mile from the same spot. But I think this man must have deserted for the trees were so well marked that he could not have lost his way.[7]

Cowell was shown on the pay list as missing from 7 November.[8] Later, in 1842, Private Overhand and a Private Worthing were caught deserting and were court-martialled. The sentence was three months in prison with twenty-eight days in solitary confinement, the remainder with hard labour.[9] Another instance of the strict discipline parcelled out to the troops of the time was the order issued after a soldier committed suicide at another station. The reason was given as the 'pernicious effects of drinking intoxicating liquor'[10] and a long harangue was drawn up and orders issued that it was 'to be read to the troops, at every station in the Command on three successive parades'.[11]

In January 1842 there were five soldiers stationed at Kojonup.[12] In December of that year the Commanding Officer, Major F. C. Irwin, visited all the military posts between York and King George Sound[13] and in the following January the numbers at Kojonup had been increased to one sergeant, Lance-Sergeant Davies and five men. In January 1844 and January 1845 it was further increased to one sergeant and ten men.[14]

Yet, Captain John Hassell (see page 33) wrote to J. R. Phillips, the Resident Magistrate of Albany, on 14 June 1843, that the Kojonup district had 'been entirely deserted and all confidence lost as to its value, to the prejudice of the colony at large'.[15] If others were prepared to boycott the district because of its adverse publicity Hassell had sufficient confidence in his own judgement to write:

> I feel great good is to be done there, and provided His Excellency the Governor will hold out sufficient inducement I will commence an establishment the next ensuing year with 1000 sheep in two flocks.[16]

Shortly afterwards he wrote again to the Resident Magistrate stating that he considered that the Kojonup district had been vacated without sufficient cause and to support this opinion requested that 5000 acres of his Kendenup freehold land be transferred for a block of 5000 acres, on which he would put 1000 sheep, to be chosen within fifteen miles of the Kojonup military station. The reply was that land ownership was not transferable from one district to another.[17]

In September 1843 one of Kojonup's admirers (possibly Dr Harris) was defending it in print:

> The spring at Kojonup contains abundance of water. It was made known to a party, including the writer, when in distress for want of water, by some natives, who had never before seen white people, and approached with caution; but they were friendly and have always continued to be so since. The country is beautiful to a great extent around. Many thousands of acres have been purchased, no settlers however at present located, chiefly owing to fear of the poison plant of which there is some to be found on a few of the grants; others are entirely free . . . .[18]

Only the week before the same writer had written that at Kojonup was a military station 'with an excellent barrack'.[19] At some time the writer, like many transient adventurers, had probably been relieved to glimpse the little hut barrack on the hill above the Spring. For the resident soldiers the tedium of isolation was broken by spasmodic visits from a variety of travellers who had usually planned to spend a night at the outpost for protection and companionship. As well as the mailman and the military personnel there were surveyors, merchants passing through to Albany, shepherds, wandering sandalwood cutters, would-be settlers and curious Aborigines. Over the years the little building had taken quite a battering from weather, time and occupation.

Only six months after the writer to the press had mentioned Kojonup's excellent barracks the following order was issued by Major Irwin, Commanding Officer of the troops in the colony:

> The hut Barracks at Kojonup having been found on inspection to be unfit for the occupation of the troops and incapable of further repairs the Commandant have approved of another being erected on a new site in the vicinity by the soldiers of the detachment on a plan which will be transmitted to Lieutenant Warburton, 51st Regiment commanding in the district.[20]

Work on the new barracks would have interfered with the soldiers' leisurely life. Instead of mostly trapping and hunting they would be kept busy manhandling hefty granite blocks from the valley to construct the solid well-proportioned little building which still stands like a sentinel on its elevated site overlooking Kojonup town. In those days it was shingled, with no linings and only earthen floors.

In 1845 the first shipment of sandalwood was exported from Albany to Asian countries. Little, if any, came from the Kojonup district. J. R. Phillips, the Resident Magistrate, Albany, writing in relation to Kojonup said:

> On this side of the colony the wood is so scattered that I do not conceive . . . that it would answer anyone to take out a license for a given number of acres.[21]

The occasional wandering sandalwood cutter who had discovered fresh thickets of the trees, unknown watering points, favourite haunts of wild game or fertile tracts of land, would have been a popular overnight guest at the barracks. Similarly, botanist James Drummond, who visited again in 1846 (see page 35) would have been closely interrogated for such facts. On this visit he was accompanied by an absorbed assistant, George Maxwell, the one-time overseer of Belche's flocks, in 1840.[22]

Meanwhile, Captain Hassell persisted in his attempts to secure land in the Kojonup district. He was experiencing some difficulty owing to the prevailing land sale condition which prevented land from being sold until surveyed. On 12 May 1846 the Magistrate Phillips forwarded to the Surveyor-General two applications for Kojonup land made by Hassell. Six months later the Colonial Secretary requested Hassell to contact Assistant-Surveyor A. C. Gregory, at Kojonup, and point out to him the desired locality. Six months is more than ample time to change one's mind and when Hassell communicated with Gregory, instead of requesting the survey of the land for which he had originally applied (ten miles south-east of Kojonup), he fixed on several other spots, including one near the notorious Joseph's Well. Gregory would not mark the positions until Hassell had contacted the Surveyor-General's Office. When no further orders were received and other detailed work had been completed Gregory departed leaving a very impatient and frustrated Hassell. According to a letter the Surveyor-General was to write in explanation, it was not the fault of the Government that the land was not marked out twelve months ago![23] So much for the proverbial British red tape! During this visit to Kojonup Gregory drew up the earliest known map to feature the barracks and the Spring.

Eventually, Hassell was permitted to arrange with Gregory for a private survey of the country he wanted. This included land around

Joseph's Well; land within seventeen to eighteen miles of the Kojonup Spring; and land ten miles south-east of the Kojonup Spring, on the Balgarup River.[24] The usual procedure for the active pastoralist was to purchase 160 acres of land near a reliable water-point as that entitled the purchaser to the use of unsold Crown land for ten miles around. The art of making a selection consisted of picking out 'a good block of 160 acres with land around it sufficiently good for a back run but not so good as to tempt purchasers'.[25] The rapidly expanding pastoral empire of Captain John Hassell was achieved along these principles. Where one sea-captain had failed another seemed determined to succeed.

In 1846 there were included in the Albany list of persons qualified to serve on juries the names of two labourers, John Gale and the ubiquitous George Maxwell whose place of residence was given as Kojonup.[26] Possibly they were then employed as shepherds at Hassell's location.

In short, when the year 1846 drew to a close Kojonup was a district of large grants with passive absentee land-owners, one resolute non-resident pastoralist, an occasional shepherd, wandering travellers, sandalwood cutters, hunters and Aborigines and a military outpost manned by a handful of desolate soldiers.

RICHARD NORRISH ARRIVES

Towards the end of 1846 and the beginning of 1847, thousands of miles from Kojonup military orders were issued which were to have a continuing effect on that district, up to the present day. As a result of these orders, in January 1847 a detachment of the 96th Regiment of Foot arrived at Albany from Van Diemen's Land, on the ship *Java*.[27] The detachment consisted of Captain R. Bush, Lieutenant McGill, two ensigns, Assistant-Surgeon de Lisle, five sergeants, two corporals, one lance-corporal, two drummers, more than ninety privates, eleven women and twenty-four children.[28]

A day after the arrival of the *Java* a corporal and seven privates were ordered to proceed to Kojonup to relieve the detachment of the 51st Regiment which was to leave for service in India. The corporal-in-charge was Richard Norrish and the privates were probably Crispin George Atkinson, John Baker, Joseph Bateman, William Best, Elijah Blyth, Samuel Blyth and John Bowra.[29] Richard Norrish had been born in the parish of St Luke near the town of Chelsea, in Middlesex, thirty-five years before, and had enlisted at the age of eighteen.[30]

Before leaving for Kojonup he settled his wife and children in Albany as best he could. However, Honora Norrish had no wish to be separated from her husband now, after accompanying him halfway around the world. Within two weeks it was arranged that she and the children would accompany the rations contractor, John Young and his son David, to the isolated post ninety miles inland. Unfortunately, the carts were loaded to capacity and twelve-year-old Richard Norrish, junior, and ten-year-old Thomas Norrish, were forced to walk most of the way alongside the teams, for the journey of six days. Mrs Norrish was a great curiosity to the local Aborigines, most of whom had never before seen a white woman.

To an adventurous, keen-eyed lad like Thomas Norrish, the new life was a great education. As the men had to parade only once a week, a great deal of time was spent kangaroo hunting, for the sale of the skins greatly augmented the soldiers' meagre pay. Whenever possible the young Norrish boys went along too. At night there was the thrill of sitting around a flickering fire set in one of the barracks' immense stone fireplaces, listening to the yarns spun by the soldiers: stories of past battles, the cruel era of Van Diemen's Land and of boyhood days in the old country. Instead of formal school lessons the Norrish children were instructed by their new dusky playmates in the strange customs, language, skills and bush lore of the Aborigines.

But there were also times of fear. At dawn on their first Easter Sunday, the man on duty awoke Corporal Norrish to report that the building was surrounded by natives. Thomas Norrish recalls in his diary:

> On my father and the men turning out they found the house completely surrounded, there being about 300 natives and everyone seemed to be carrying fire beside their spears. When they got within about 100 yards they all squatted down for some time. Then three men walked up to the house where there were two natives sitting that were staying with the men, kangaroo hunting. After a few minutes the three new natives began to talk and sing very loud and the two natives sitting there seemed very much afraid. Where the natives were standing was about three paces from the corner of the verandah. My father sprang off the verandah to where the natives stood, with his musket in his right hand and with his left he caught the stoutest native by the beard. Then the natives gave a great shout and took to their heels. The man my father held trembled very much and then sat down. Then my father let him go and told him to be off. Whether he understood or not he soon took to his heels. After the natives had cleared off, the other two told us they had come that morning with the intention of killing

two other natives who usually stayed with the soldiers but were absent. They must have been determined to kill those two natives whose names were *Bimbert* and his brother who was called *George* by the soldiers, for only a week or two afterwards they made another call, but in the evening this time when they caught the man Bimbert and his brother's woman with her boy about eighteen months old on her back and his own woman. When the natives came up to them they were about 300 yards from the house. On hearing the natives shouting the men ran down but Bimbert had five spears through him and his brother's woman had thirteen spears through her. One spear pinned the boy on her back to her and he also had one spear through his hips and one through his arm. When the natives saw the white men getting close they ran away for a distance and then collected together as if considering to return and finish their work but just then the man called George came on the scene from a different direction and when he saw his brother lying on the ground and his own woman and child, he threw off his *boka* then gave a terrible yell and ran down to the other natives who began to scamper in all directions but he was soon among the crowd when a lot of those who had at first run away ran back again. The whites thought there would soon be an end of him and ran to his assistance but by the time they got there the natives again began to run away. They found that George had speared three men and would have soon put an end to them if the whites had not come to their rescue but it was no easy matter to keep George from killing them as he was like a madman. At last he was got away from them by making him understand that his brother and his woman were not dead but the whites could not get the spears out. The worst was the spear that pinned his son to his mother's back. It was thought impossible for either of them to recover but they did and Bimbert lived till 1898 when he died a very white-haired old man.[31]

Another atrocity inflicted by the local Aborigines on their own kind, about this time, was the killing of a woman and her two little girls as they led a 'Yankee' hut keeper from the barracks to the Hassell's sheep station at Joseph's Well, called 'Warkelup'. Thomas Norrish accompanied the soldiers when they investigated the case. The coming of the white man was possibly beginning to have grave effects on the traditional laws of the original inhabitants.

Perhaps one of the saddest incidents in the early history of Kojonup occurred in 1847. At the time James Cooper had the contract to convey the rations to the troops. He felt compelled to report a particularly wicked act of persecution of an Aborigine in Kojonup, adding that while such acts of violence were committed on the Aborigines he did not consider it safe for him to travel on the road. Immediately, the

Resident Magistrate at Albany investigated the incident and found the allegations only too true. In reporting to the Colonial Secretary he wrote:

> It is my painful duty to report to you as gross an act of brutality committed on a native at Kojonup by two shepherds as I ever heard of.[32]

Richard Norrish, being in charge of the detachment at Kojonup, wrote a report giving full details.[33]

Kojonup
1st September 1847.

I certify that on the 4th July that Eagan, Mr Hassel's shepherd and a man named, Martin, came to Kojonup about 8 o'clock p.m. and went to the native huts and took a native named Bandit or Black Joe. Eagan when he came to the Barracks owns to giving him 5 dozen whip cuts made of raw hide and then they made him go to Warkelup with him. And the native on his return stated the next day Eagan and Gale flogged him again all over and on the Testacles which were in a very sad state and stabbed him with a fork. The native when in Barracks took a fork and said it was one like that. They then cut all the hair off his head and off his face. I kept him here for 10 or 12 days until he was able to go away with some of the natives. The native returned hereabout a week ago and is much better. All of the men of the Detachment can state the same if required.

I am Sir, Your Obed Servt
Richard Norrish;
Corp' 96th Reg
Commander of Detachment.

Martin, who was a visitor at Warkelup, later gave a sworn statement of the whole affair. He explained that Hassell's shepherds at Warkelup, Gale and Eagan, believed that Bandit was responsible for stealing some of their sheep and were trying to force a confession from him. Martin's first-hand information painted a picture even more vile. Two soldiers at the barracks, Bowring and Bateman, were prepared to confirm the second statement if required to do so. Gale and Eagan were eventually arrested and committed for trial for stabbing with intent to inflict grievous bodily harm.

With the growing traffic the old road to Albany deteriorated and the mailmen were continuously delayed .This was intolerable to the news-hungry settlers and complaints were numerous. In August 1848, in answer to their demands, the soldiers at Kojonup were ordered to form working parties to open a new and easier route, thereby setting an enduring precedent for linking the history of the little settlement at Kojonup with the history of the Albany Road.[34] The new and easier route chosen is thought to be that recommended by W. N. Clark in November 1840, passing through the Balgarup settlement. It is basically the same route followed today.

The Norrish family lived in the barracks for approximately twenty-three months when all the 96th Regiment were relieved and transferred to Perth. It was with a fund of happy memories that Richard Norrish, his wife and children, departed from their first home in Western Australia for the capital.

Prior to this, in October 1848, Surveyor-General Roe, with assistants Gregory and Ridley, Privates Buck and Lee of the 96th Regiment and some Aborigines left York to lead an expedition to the south coast as far east as Esperance Bay. On 19 January 1849, on their return journey, they arrived at a squatter's hut at 'Carralup' (*sic*) and as there was excellent water nearby they made a camp. Shortly after:

> two men belonging to Mr Hassell's establishment arrived at the hut with a cart to carry away some of their things to Warkelup (4 or 5 miles S.E. of Kojonup) preparatory to starting from that place with a large number of Mr Hassell's sheep for a place called Jeeramungup. . . . These men speak of much good country hereabouts within 20 or 30 miles, but cursed with the poison plant . . . .[35]

wrote Roe.

The explorers were delighted to make contact with the world again and plied the men with questions. They were astonished to learn that Governor Fitzgerald had been speared by a native on a recent visit to the Murchison.

The next day they proceeded south-west along a beaten track, crossing another branch of the Beaufort, 'Galcuttup' (*sic*), to Warkelup or Joseph's Well. Here they found Hassell's overseer busily preparing 'to remove his flock also to the Fitzgerald, the country around having been extensively burnt by the natives and the grass nearly all destroyed for the season'.[36] Roe estimated that there were 700 sheep to be moved. They had been watered at the Warkelup spring which supplied sufficient water, continuously, to fill two ponds. He commented:

> It has however a sweetish flavour and in a short time will probably become as brackish as the spring at Kojonup.[37]

On the site he observed 'a small boarded cottage with a thatched roof'.[38]

After lunch the surveyors moved off towards Kojonup and arrived at the barracks

> at 2-45 and found all well with the party of 8 including Corp Bagley in charge.
> Here we heard a confirmation of the previous rumour at Carrylup that the Gov. (Capt Fitzgerald) had been speared in the knee by some troublesome natives north of Champion Bay, and also that Col. Irwin the Cmdt had passed through the post for King George Sound yesterday, and the postman for Perth only this day at 11 o'clock.
> The military party obligingly came forward to assist in taking our horses to the camping place we might fix on, or to render any assistance in their power.
> Here we discharged our two natives, Charley and Donkey who we soon found knew very little of the country.[39]

On Sunday 21 January the visitors remained at Kojonup and the Surveyor-General 'performed Divine Service' to the party, 'according to the custom invariably followed throughout the journey whenever circumstances permitted'.[40] On Monday they set off along the Post road to Bunbury. They found sufficient quantities of both grass and water but even so the horses 'continually cropt from many bushes on their way, and from none more eagerly than the poisonous plant'.[41]

Like Roe, other settlers were being convinced by such incidents that the plant was not so noxious to horses as to sheep and cattle and were being persuaded that the country of Kojonup had many desirable features that more than compensated for the possible poison risk.

RICHARD NORRISH RETURNS

In Perth Richard Norrish learnt that the 96th Regiment was shortly to be sent to India where Britain required reinforcements to combat local outbreaks of hostility. After much consideration, particularly in relation to his eight dependants, Richard Norrish claimed his discharge from the army in order, as the official discharge paper states, 'to become a settler in Western Australia'.[42] The date on the discharge certificate was 5 July 1851 and at the foot of it was a section for comments on the soldier's character. It could be discarded if no comment was thought desirable. For more than eighteen years loyal service, the British Army (a past master of the understatement) exerted itself to compose a three-word compliment on Richard Norrish's character: 'Has been good'![43]

For a while Norrish worked for a private contractor, Solomon Cook, cutting timber for the Canning Bridge. Then, one icy winter morning, a slippery beam fell across his back: the resulting injury was to trouble him for the rest of his life. Civilian life was vastly different from army life, and city life involved many stresses and very little independence. The thoughts of all the family turned frequently to the happy days spent at Kojonup. In the end, Richard Norrish concluded that more opportunities awaited his large family back in the familiar Kojonup bush.

Still very troubled with his back, he loaded up his cart, and with two horses to pull them the family set out for the south through York, Stanton Springs and Williams. The exact date of their departure is unknown but it is thought to be some time in 1849 (prior to the official date on the discharge certificate).

Within three weeks they arrived at the Kojonup barracks where they renewed old friendships with both white and black. The latter, in their usual unsophisticated, generous way flocked around, keen to assist their old friends to establish themselves. The soldiers of the 99th Regiment, now stationed there, supplied a most welcome and convenient piece of news which proved to be a godsend. From them the Norrishes learnt that John Hassell had given up the old sheep station at Warkelup, and had taken his sheep away. Thomas Norrish recalls:

> On hearing this my father started for Warkelup and took possession of the shepherd's hut. There was a running spring on the place known then by the name of Joseph's Well. It was brackish but that did not matter to us we had lived on the same kind of water in Kojonup before. Now the time had come for us to consider what we were to do to get a living. Here we were in what could well be called the wild bush, a family of nine, five boys, two girls and our parents. What we had to start with was, 17/6 cash after our journey, two mares, one cart and three dogs on which we depended to catch kangaroos for our own use and the skins to provide us with what else we required. We also had two spades, three grub hoes and two sickles.[44]

Once his family was reasonably settled Richard Norrish set off for Albany to replenish the depleted stores and to try to raise enough finance to purchase ten acres of land at Joseph's Well. A previous acquaintance agreed to lend him £10 on condition £20 was returned within two years. and James Cooper agreed to supply rations in return for kangaroo skins. He had brought with him the skins the family had acquired on their journey south, plus some the friendly Aborigines had insisted the family have. An old Day Book of the Ship Inn, Albany shows entries made for R. Norrish, December 1849, for goods supplied, and substantiates the claim that he was back in the south during that year.[45]

Meanwhile, the oldest two boys were busy cutting grass for hay. It was mostly canary grass which grew very rank on the old sheep camps. This provided for the horses and the cow that was bought in the second year.

> The piece of land selected was not very heavily timbered so we began at once to grub a little of the land ready to dig when the rains came, as the land was very hard till then. When the rains came, which was about the end of April, we lost no time but were grubbing with hoes and sometimes digging with spades till we had about two acres and having got one bag of wheat we sowed it on the two acres. When it came up it was very thick and before it ripened part of it lay down but however we had a very good crop which provided us with seed for next year and a little for bread.[46]

This is the first known cereal crop to be harvested in Kojonup. By September 1852 statistical records show that Norrish had four acres under crop: two of wheat and two of barley. The total for Albany's thirteen farmers was 109 acres of wheat and 96 acres of barley.[47]

With such limited resources it was essential for the family to augment their income in a variety of ways. In August 1850 Richard Norrish was successful in obtaining the contract to carry the mail between Albany and Kojonup. A Mr Jackson carried it from Kojonup to Bunbury and from there it went to Perth. About the same time Norrish also obtained a contract to deliver the provisions to Kojonup military station at 1d. per pound. This paid very well as it enabled him to back-load when he carted skins to sell at Albany.

Every spare minute was spent in accumulating skins. Soon the likely spots close to their home had been shot out so young Thomas, who loved the sport, decided to go further afield to a large watering point, 'Kilacardup', about five miles distant. He was accompanied by some of his old Aboriginal friends. The event as told by Thomas gives an insight into the Aboriginal law of the time.

> After we had been there a few days and I had built myself a hut with one half of the front closed in, I was sitting on my bunk behind the closed up part having just finished my dinner after the morning hunt when one of the natives sitting round the fire exclaimed in a rather loud voice as if he were startled, the word 'Cullungpan' the name of the native I had heard a lot about. I also knew that a great

5   The barracks, with pepper trees (p. 178); it is now preserved as a museum by the Kojonup Historical Society with a garden of favourite plants of early settlers. The Spring is about 100 yards to the left

6   Early water supply, Kojonup. Hollow-log troughs were for summer watering of stock

7 Pensioner cottage built by McDonnell on P. Lot 2 in the 1850s; Charlie Elverd has lived in it since birth in 1888

8 Sergeant John Tunney of the Enrolled Pensioner Force in his uniform; the only photograph of a Pensioner guard known to exist

many of the natives were in dread of him. On looking out I saw what I thought was a very strong built man, very black, an unusual thing to see among the natives about here as they mostly inclined towards copper colour. Another thing I noticed was that instead of standing some yards away for a few minutes as was their custom, he walked boldly up to the other men and sat down close beside them. Where I sat on my bunk I had a good view of him which chance I made good use of. After sitting a short time, he used the word *knetinung* a name they had given to the white men. I must state here that I thoroughly understood all he said and could also speak nearly as well myself as a native but this man was not aware of it, though all the other natives did, as we always spoke in their language. When he made use of this name, all the others covered their heads with their bokas. After they did that Cullungpan began to sing putting his intentions into the words of the song and increasing his voice till he had got it to a very high pitch which was a usual thing to do when urging others to do what was wanted. For a moment on hearing his words, a feeling of dread crept over me but it soon passed off and I proceeded to act as I knew that he soon would if I did not. I had a double-barreled gun on the bunk beside me, one barrel loaded with ball. As he could not see me I very quickly and quietly loaded the other barrel with ball and just as he was gesticulating and at the same time raising his voice, I leaped from the hut and placed the muzzle of the gun to his head, telling him it was I who would take his life, not he taking mine. It is hard for me to picture the look of that native and the sudden change that came over him, from one of great excitement to one of fear and trembling. After he had gone the others said they were glad I had taken the action I did for he would have soon acted, but they all said they would not have assisted him but dared not hinder him as he was sure to have killed some of them. I had often been told before of the number of natives this man had killed and the great dread he was held in by most of them. Strange to say he came back a few months afterwards and would insist on staying with me and he did this for about ten years, only leaving for short intervals and was a good native for hunting and shepherding after we got sheep.[48]

A legendary characteristic of the typical Australian is said to be his resourcefulness in times of need. This image has evolved from tales of amazing improvisation by pioneers when unprepared for emergencies or experiencing hard times. Richard Norrish and his family were often forced to extemporize. For example, on the first trip made by the Richard Norrishes, senior and junior, to bring rations for the military station at Kojonup, the axle of the cart broke about twenty-four miles from Joseph's Well. Richard junior rushed home on horseback while his father unloaded the cart. Returning with the few tools he had

53

collected from home, Richard junior chopped down a jam tree and from it fashioned an axle to fit the box of the wheel, making a hole for the one-inch pin with a gimlet and his knife. When next in Albany the old iron axle was welded but on the return journey it broke a second time. Fortunately, they had thought to keep the homemade wooden axle so once more it was fitted into place where it remained for some time until Richard senior was able to have a new axle made by black-smith Walker of Bunbury, carrying it home on horseback by balancing it in front of the saddle.

Gradually the Norrish family built up their little farm at Warkelup, with a setting of duck eggs, a cow, a few geese, fowls, a donkey, a wheat crop and a vegetable garden. The family tried to be as self-supporting as possible. From the kangaroo tails moccasins were made, thereby not spoiling the skins that were to be sold. Boots were made from leather of their own rearing and tanning. Trousers and jumpers were made from coarse dungaree.

Even so, there were some commodities for which they could find no perfect substitute and for which they craved. One was tea! Wasted barley was sometimes used as a substitute. (It was termed 'shingow'.) When in the bush and desperate for a refreshing billy of tea native ti-tree leaves would be used or even burnt bread. (This was termed 'burnt Tommy'.) Another item of diet which they often missed was flour and its precious product, bread. Once, in 1853, there was no flour to be bought in all Albany and Richard Norrish had to return to his expectant family with only a cask of weevily biscuits and a small cask of oatmeal. Another time, when the family had been without tea for a considerable time Mrs Norrish, on a rare visit to Albany, went every-where to purchase some but without success. Finally Mrs John Hassell, the wife of their neighbouring land-holder, kindly sold her some for 3s. a pound, which was very cheap, in those days.

It was a hard and lonely life the Norrish family had chosen. There were some compensations but many deprivations and anxieties, both imagined and real. Over one hundred years after their return to Kojonup, Honora Norrish's grandson, octogenarian George Norrish, recalled many visits to Warkelup as a little boy. He vividly remembered his grandmother sitting on a stool outside her little cottage, with her late husband's gun across her knee, attentively watching the gate leading to the yard, as if ever on the alert for danger. Nearby stood a wooden rainwater barrel and the visiting grandchildren coaxed their grandmother for a drink from her barrel of special water 'which had come from heaven and never touched the ground'.[49] To this early pioneer, who for years had relied on a brackish well, pure water was another highly valued beverage!

ARRIVALS AND DEPARTURES

John Hassell continued to vacillate about where he would have his permanent sheep leases. In November 1848, he applied for a depasturing licence for 4000 acres at Joseph's Well, the spring being the centre. Two months later he discovered another desirable site, at 'Youghanup', twenty miles north-east of Kojonup and he applied for a depasturing licence there of 4000 acres. Uncertain of the reliability of the watering point he inquired whether he would be permitted to transfer to another location if Youghanup failed to have permanent water. The latter licence was still not finalized when the water at both it and Joseph's Well proved insufficient for Hassell's needs and he applied for both sites to be transferred for 8000 acres of unknown country, 100 miles east of Kojonup called 'Jerramungup'.[50] One marvels at Hassell's prodigious energy, intellect, stamina and far-sightedness in his endeavours to settle himself substantially in the colony, but there can be no denying he must have been a dreadful headache for the Surveyor-General's Office.

Since the Youghanup licence had not been finalized it was possible for it to be transferred to Jerramungup, but the Warkelup depasturing licence was not transferable and Hassell re-established a station there. However, Norrish had been quick off the mark and had purchased twenty acres at the site, thus acquiring the honour of possessing Kojonup location 2, as well as location 20, both ten acres, and Hassell is recorded as being allocated locations 14 and 13 (the latter incorporating the actual well) in the year 1857.[51]

Meanwhile, the soldiers stationed at the barracks continued to welcome visitors. On Saturday 8 March 1851, there arrived from Albany the intrepid traveller, Archdeacon Wollaston, on his second Archidiaconal tour of the colony, accompanied by J. Herbert, who was farming about 40 miles from Albany, and Mr Wittenoom, junior. The next day being Sunday, the worthy clergyman seized the opportunity to have a church parade for the isolated detachment, at which he preached on the duties of the Christian soldier'.[52] On his return journey, on 18 May 1851, he once more stayed at Kojonup and was pleased to learn the latest news of Albany from the residents. He celebrated the Sabbath with the troops with evening prayers and exhortation.

Just as the Archdeacon liked to catch up on fresh reports of his hometown, so too did his two native companions wish to talk with their own kind and hear all the latest chit-chat. It was the Archdeacon's custom to allow the horses to graze with their tethers on, watched by his Aboriginal employees, until evening when the animals were tied up. Such dull tasks were completely forgotten by the two Aborigines amidst the boisterous interchange with their friends. Soon, a horse from York took it into its head to make for home, and the others naturally followed.

The next morning to compensate for their negligence, the Aborigines tracked the horses to the Beaufort, twenty miles north, where they found the frayed tether ropes. Wollaston, impatient to be on his way, as he knew his wife would be expecting him, was not impressed by their tracking skill. He searched around for means to continue his journey without further excessive waste of time. As a result, the following day (probably at the suggestion of the soldiers) he sent a messenger to 'Norris's [sic] farm'[53] offering a reward if they could recover his ponies. Considering their straitened circumstances it is not surprising that Richard Norrish arrived at the barracks, post-haste, with two horses. He lent one to the fractious Archdeacon and started off immediately with the other and Wollaston's two natives, in pursuit of the runaways.

Leaving the bulk of his traps to follow in Trimmer's cart (the ration contractor at the time), Wollaston set off for home. It did not take long for this expert equestrian to realize that Norrish's old nag was no charging steed. He nicknamed him 'Dobbin' and declared that he had never ridden such a thing before. At Kendenup he borrowed an old spur to try to hasten the poor beast along the track.

In time the lost ponies were found safe and sound at Stanton Springs, 101 miles from Kojonup, and forwarded to their owner. He, in turn, rested Dobbin for a couple of days and then sent him back to Warkelup, knowing only too well how necessary the horse would be to the family's daily routine.

From this small local incident it is obvious that the important changes which had existed in Western Australia for almost twelve months had not yet substantially affected the little settlement at Kojonup. This situation was not to continue for very much longer. Already, movements were under way for the materialization of the town of Kojonup.

REFERENCES

1 *Perth Gazette*, 19 December 1840, p. 3.

[2] W.A.L.Dept.Recs. of original Kojonup landholders (copy in K.H.S.Recs.).

[3] *Perth Gazette*, 11 April 1840, p. 2.

[4] Rhoda Glover, 'Captain Symers Trader', p. 185 (M.A. thesis, University of Western Australia, 1952; held in Battye Library, Perth).

[5] *Government Gazette*, 30 April 1841, p. 3.

[6] E. S. and G. S. Whiteley, 'The Military Establishment in Western Australia 1829-1863', p. 64 (unbound, 1970; Battye Library).

[7] Letter from G. Egerton-Warburton, 11 December 1840 (copy in possession of D. Crabbe, Kojonup).

[8] Whiteley and Whiteley, p. 64.

[9] *Ibid.*, p. 23.

[10] *Ibid.*, p. 25.

[11] *Ibid.*

[12] Card index under Kojonup Barracks (Battye Library), from information collected and supplied by E. S. Whiteley from P.R.O.War Office (London) microfilms.

[13] Whiteley and Whiteley, p. 42.

[14] Card index under Kojonup Barracks; Lieut.-Sgt. Davies mentioned in Whiteley and Whiteley, p. 24.

[15] C.S.O.Recs., 119, 14 June 1843.

[16] *Ibid.*

[17] Personal correspondence from C. L. Hassell, 2 October 1969.

[18] *Perth Gazette*, 28 September 1844, p. 2.

[19] *Ibid.* 21 September 1844, p. 2.

[20] War Office Recs., 1845 (Reel 28, Battye Library).

[21] C.S.O.Recs., 164, 26 April 1867.

[22] Rica Ericson, *The Drummonds of Hawthornden* (Perth, 1969), p. 113.

[23] C.S.O.Recs., 149, 9 October 1846, memo, Hassell's application.

[24] C.S.O.Recs., 149, 7 and 12 November 1846, memo, J. S. Roe.

[25] Warburton Letters, 2 July 1842 (copy in possession of D. Crabbe, Kojonup).

[26] C.S.O.Recs., 149, Jury list, 1846.

[27] Thomas Norrish Diary, p. 1 (copy in K.H.S.Recs.).

[28] Whiteley and Whiteley.

[29] *Ibid.* p. 64.

[30] Original discharge paper of Richard Norrish (Battye Library).

[31] Thomas Norrish Diary, p. 1.

[32] C.S.O.Recs., 164, 24 September 1847.

[33] *Ibid.* 1 September 1847.

[34] J. R. Wollaston, *Albany Journals 1848-1856* (Perth, 1955), p. 55.

[35] J. S. Roe, Field Book 7, 19 January 1849 (held in W.A.L.Dept.).

[36] *Ibid.* 20 January 1849.

[37] *Ibid.*

[38] *Ibid.*

[39] *Ibid.*

[40] *Ibid.* 21 January 1849.

[41] *Ibid.*

[42] Discharge paper of Richard Norrish.

[43] *Ibid.*

[44] Thomas Norrish Diary, p. 4.

[45] Day Book of Ship Inn, Albany (in possession of Rhoda Glover).

[46] Thomas Norrish Diary, p. 5.

[47] C.S.O.Recs., 248, statistics for September 1852.

[48] Thomas Norrish Diary, p. 6.

[49] Personal conversation with George Norrish, senior, 1968.

[50] Personal correspondence from C. L. Hassell, 2 October 1969.
[51] W.A.L.Dept.Recs. of original Kojonup landholders.
[52] Wollaston, p. 114.
[53] *Ibid.* p. 134.

5

||||||||||||||||||||||||||||||||||||||||||||||||||||||||||||||||||||||||||||||||||||||||||||||||||||||||||||||||||||||||||||||||||||||||||||||||||||||||||||||||||||||||||||||||||||

Transportation

NEW AND OLD ARRIVALS

Richard Norrish lacked ready cash but at least he had a large, permanent, reliable and enthusiastic workforce. Few settlers in Western Australia before 1850 possessed both finance and a labour supply. Many had neither. Although the colony was not likely to be abandoned, its potential had little chance of realization unless more labour and money was attracted. There were public works and roads to be built. More outlets for surplus products, and more incentives, were required for the settlers to make the most of the grants with which many had been saddled and which they had no hope of surrendering without irretrievable monetary loss. Gradually, despite their dislike of the idea of convicts living among them, many prominent settlers became convinced that the introduction of convicts to the colony from Britain was the only practical solution. The decision was by no means unanimous. G. Egerton-Warburton wrote in February 1849:

> Anything rather than convict labour, though some foolish colonists here wish for it. I sincerely pray they never obtain it.[1]

The hopeless state of affairs was soon evident to the new Governor, Captain Charles Fitzgerald, and in March 1849 he sent a despatch to the Secretary of State for the Colonies detailing the situation: depressed sandalwood sales, lower sheep values, higher freight charges, higher shearing costs and shepherds' wages, in addition to the withdrawal of investment capital and the departure of some of the population for South Australia.[2]

The Imperial Government decided on a two-fold solution. They would ease the accommodation pressure in British gaols and at the same time assist the struggling colony by supplying a free labour force and thereby indirectly benefiting the colony in a variety of other ways.

Once the decision was made very little time was lost. On 1 June 1850, the initial batch of seventy-five convicts arrived at Fremantle on the *Scindian* and with them began an entirely new chapter in Western Australia's history. Accompanying the convicts were 'fifty pensioner guards with their wives and families, as well as a small staff of officials headed by the Comptroller General'.[3] The convicts were 'all men of good conduct, too near their ticket-of-leave to want to escape'.[4]

It was some considerable time before the effects of the arrival of the first shiploads of convicts and their guards and kin were felt in the remote parts of the colony, such as Kojonup. Immediate essential works around the port of Fremantle and the capital, Perth, absorbed most of them. The supply from England was irregular, in fact during 1853 there was a general scare that transportation had ceased. It was not until October 1851 that the first Pensioner detachments were sent to Albany and Kojonup, the latter being regarded as the most isolated detachment of Pensioners, at that time.[5]

Two months before this, Richard Norrish's mail contract had expired and he was anxious to renew it at the same rate of £30 per annum. He was recommended, officially, by the Albany Resident Magistrate, as always having been 'very punctual and careful'.[6] Unfortunately, his application failed and the contract went to another ex-private of the 96th Regiment, Nathaniel Newstead, who was appointed mailman by Governor Fitzgerald and promised a grant of ten acres of land, under the same conditions as it was granted to the Pensioner guards.[7] As a result, Newstead erected a cottage in Kojonup near the native well, 'Quin Quin', and settled there.

However, the first journey south by the new mailman was dogged with misfortune. An official complaint was written on 23 October because the mail was many days overdue. The next day a very woebegone Newstead arrived in Albany minus the mailbags. A rambling explanation followed. Mailman Jackson, another ex-private of the 96th, had handed over the bags at Kojonup on 12 October. Newstead proceeded with the journey but in the morning his horse took fright after he had loaded it with the mailbags, broke its rope and bolted. Newstead was forced to walk all the way back to Kojonup, searching and enlisting the assistance of anyone he met: natives, Trimmer, the corporal at the barracks, Jackson and Norrish. The Resident Magistrate offered a reward of a bag of flour or £2 to anyone who found the lost bags.[8]

Not until 16 November were they delivered, and by none other than the previous contractor, Richard Norrish. He, 'having heard the natives had found the mail on Saturday, 8th Inst. prevailed on them to bring it to him'.[9] The bags were all opened but Norrish offered to try to recover any missing letters. As he had brought the natives who had found the bags with him and had fed them all that time, Norrish claimed and was granted the reward.

The Resident Magistrate and Norrish discussed the latter's failure in obtaining the mail contract. It appears that Norrish had inferred, unknowingly, to those at Headquarters that he would decline the renewal. On the contrary, he had incurred a great deal of expense in purchasing a saddle and horse under the impression he would be allowed to continue. The upshot was that Norrish was reimbursed with £5 on the direct order of the Governor.[10] Furthermore, when the contract for the Kojonup-Bunbury run was vacant Newstead was approached with the proposal to run that mail so Norrish could recommence the Albany section. However, Newstead preferred his original contract as he was comparatively ignorant of the other road, particularly the fording of the Blackwood River, whereas Norrish was acquainted equally with both.[11]

Meanwhile, Kojonup had not been altogether stagnating. The area had become extremely well known as a favourite feeding ground of kangaroos and had attracted two or three individuals who procured 'by means of the natives and large packs of dogs, vast quantities of kangaroo skins which from time to time they shipped from King George Sound'.[12] These people could have been discharged soldiers, or their descendants, over whom Kojonup had in the past cast its magnetic spell. (A list of dogs licensed in the Plantagenet area, for the first four months of 1852, showed one person having twenty-four dogs and another twelve.)[13]

When three convicts managed to escape from Bunbury, in 1852, there was wide conjecture as to where they could hide out. It was suggested in one of the newspapers that 'the kangaroo hunting parties at Kojonup might harbour them'.[14] Policeman Scott and men traced the runaways as far east as Kojonup, but were refused supplies by the 'party in charge'[15] there and were forced to return to Bunbury. Eventually, the convicts were recaptured but it was felt that the details were strangely stifled.

Soon the increase in trade, production and population which followed the commencement of transportation enabled a regular and direct mail service with Britain, by means of steam, to be established. Mrs G. Egerton-Warburton wrote to England on 15 October 1852:

I begin this letter today with a kind of satisfactory feeling as to the certainty of its reaching you with speed and safety. How much

61

nearer steam communication will bring us and then too the frequency and regularity of mails every two months. The novelty of steamers arriving is beginning to wear off. The third one is now in the harbour.[16]

The first custodians of the steam mails to convey it speedily from the ship at Albany to Perth, were policeman Thomas Chipper and the versatile George Maxwell.[17] Chipper carried the mail from Albany to Kojonup where it was transferred to the waiting Maxwell. The latter settled for a while at Kojonup, erecting a small building for accommodation at his own expense. This was taken over by Robert Toovey when he obtained the mail contract in August 1854.[18] These contracts were in addition to the regular monthly mails.

Originally, Maxwell made his journey by way of York, but towards the end of 1852 a new route via Kelmscott was under consideration. During the latter part of 1852 this line of road had been plotted by A. Gregory of the Survey Department and inspected by a newcomer, Lieutenant W. Crossman of the Royal Sappers and Miners. The Lieutenant concluded his report of 19 January 1853, by recommending the Kelmscott line as it brought King George Sound thirty miles closer to Perth than the York line and forty miles closer than the Bunbury route.[19] Within a month he had second thoughts about the Bunbury line and was considering a more direct track south-west from the Blackwood crossing. He actually wrote this suggestion to Perth from a camp at Kojonup.[20] Fortunately for the existence of Kojonup this second recommendation was not heeded.

Crossman, a discerning and progressive engineer, wrote in his comprehensive report of the Kelmscott route:

After crossing the Arthur we ascended a grassy range of hills with ironstone on the Summit; the ascent was easy; we then descended into the Beaufort Plains; a large extent of country here must be flooded in winter and a long causeway will be required. The distance between the Arthur and Beaufort is about 6 miles and on the whole a good road can be made. On the Beaufort the feed is but indifferent. After crossing this river we directed our course to Kojenup but found that the road would have to run over such loose sandy country, that we struck into the York road, at the southern part of what are called the Beaufort Plains and about 15 miles from Kojenup. The road hence to Kojenup runs in one or two places over steep ironstone ridges, but these I imagine can be avoided, there is feed and water in a gully 7 miles from Kojenup; the road from this gully to Kojenup is very good, and runs over a grassy country. . . . At Kojenup there is some very good land, and the feed is very good;

a good crop of hay might be got off the townsite every year, there is however a scarcity of fresh water, the springs are also very brackish; however if tanks were dug, I have no doubt an ample supply of fresh water could be ensured throughout the whole year; and I would beg to recommend that the detachment of Enrolled Pensioners stationed there be employed on the work. There is now at a place called Quin Quin on the Sound road, ½ mile from the Barracks, a tank where fresh water can be got most part of the summer, but it is not large enough to ensure a supply throughout the whole year; this I would recommend to be enlarged, deepened and well fenced round to keep wild horses and cattle from it. There is also another place about a ¼ of a mile N.W. of the Barracks which it would be well to have enlarged and kept clear. . . . After leaving Kojenup the road for the first five miles is not very good and much more direct, level and firm line can be made by keeping down a valley a little to the Westward of the present road; from the 6 to the 18 mile gulleys from Kojenup the road is very good and hard, it is in some places at present very soft in winter, but this can be easily remedied. The clearing is very light, the timber being white gum and the soil gritty (ironstone). Small causeways are required across gulleys 16 and 18 from Kojenup.

There is water to the Eastward of the Road in a small well 15 miles from Kojenup, this requires enlarging and clearing; at 17 and 18 miles from Kojenup there is water but very brackish, the feed is also scanty.[21]

The Bunbury road discussed by Crossman seems to coincide with the present 'Collie Road'. In describing it he says:

It hits the Blackwood at a place where the feed is very good. Between this and the crossing place one or two causeways will be required across some lowlands which seems to be below the level of high floods. Between the Blackwood and the 18 mile Gully (from Kojenup) the country is rather steep and sandy and it does not seem that the steep hills on the present line can be well avoided. Between the 18 mile Gully and Kojenup the road is very good and there is always water in the 18 and 7 mile gullies. This road runs into the present York and Kojenup road about a mile and a quarter N. of the Barracks.[22]

Not long after this report was received survey parties and work parties began to establish the foundations of the present Albany Highway, beginning from the Perth end.

THE PENSIONERS

On 11 February 1853 Archdeacon Wollaston sent a bag of crushed barley to Kojonup by a cart taking stores, and followed two days later with the postman, as he considered it imprudent to travel alone (presumably because of the number of convicts abroad). He recorded in his journal that Kojonup 'is now occupied by Enrolled Pensioners instead of the regular military'.[23]

The Archdeacon was distinctly of the gentry class and a devout, but biased, adherent of the Church of England. His way of thinking was usually a complex combination of these two hereditary factors, and the opinions formed were not always correct. One of his greatest misconceptions concerned these Pensioners who accompanied the convicts as guards on the long sea journey from England and supervised them for a period on their arrival in the colony. In return for this service they were induced 'to become a steady and useful class of colonist'[24] by the allocation to them of small grants of land. In Kojonup it was generally ten acres.

They were known as the Enrolled Pensioner Force as they were men recruited from the ranks of retired British soldiers, of which there were great numbers remaining from the huge defence force amassed early in the nineteenth century by the fast-growing British Empire, to protect and operate its expanding territories.

Although life was hard in the British Army (flogging was common) at least it was an ordered existence, with a certain peculiar security. When discharged the soldier discovered that life as a civilian in new industrial Britain was in many ways far worse with wretched working conditions for those who were fortunate enough to find work, and an almost complete dislocation of the old social life due to the growth of big industrial centres. To make matters worse, in 1840 and 1842 there were a series of bad harvests and bitter winters. In England 'one person in eleven was thought to be a pauper'.[25] In Ireland conditions were shockingly pitiful, even before the Irish famine when the potato crop, upon which the Irish peasant almost wholly existed, failed. That many of these discharged soldiers jumped at the chance to return to army discipline and to face a long hazardous sea voyage and a dubious life in a strange land, is not surprising. Such a decision must have been made by Pensioner Robert Loton and his wife who were, in years to come, to play leading parts in the establishment of Kojonup civil affairs. Loton was discharged from the 58th Regiment, in Dublin, on 22 February 1842.[26]

Archdeacon Wollaston rashly condemned these Pensioners, in 1853, as 'worn-out soldiers, for the most part utterly unfitted for agricultural employment'.[27] On the contrary, many were men in the prime of life, prepared to grasp an opportunity to build for their families a better life than existed in their birthplace. The Pensioner Sergeant John Tunney was forty-three, married with five children, the first of whom had been born in Sydney, the next three at various military stations in India, and the last in Ireland. Tunney had served twenty-two years in the army prior to his discharge but within four years he had joined the Pensioner Force to migrate to Western Australia as a Pensioner guard.

The methodical Wollaston had become accustomed to visit the military station and be greeted with due deference by submissive members of the regular force. There was now a different kettle of fish! Instead of a handful of meek privates, keeping a respectful distance, the loyal Church of England cleric found the main room of the barracks in an uproar: it was occupied by three Roman Catholic Irish families —men, women and children—with only three beds between them, a roaring fire and a haze of smoke, cooking odours and alcoholic fumes. He approved of the corporal-in-charge, describing him as 'a very civil well-conducted man',[28] but declined the offer of his room for the night as to reach it he had to pass through the overcrowded living room. He preferred to have his tent pitched under a nearby haystack where he slept uninterruptedly.

Wollaston was not the only one to be impressed with Corporal Hamilton. In 1851 a police force had been formed in the colony and the Superintendent of Police was wide awake for high-principled recruits and was not averse to poaching them from other quarters. On 19 August 1853 he wrote to the Commanding Officer, Major Bruce, high-handedly informing him that the Governor had directed him to appoint Hamilton as constable at Kojonup, concluding the letter by saying: 'I will bring him on duty from the first of next month. His pay is to be 1d. per diem'.[29] Bruce found such intervention into the sovereignty of the army insufferable and moved swiftly to express his indignation, and to show just who was still boss. 'Moreover Corporal Hamilton is on the eve of being relieved, his time having long since expired',[30] he replied, closing the subject.

Another Pensioner who was present at this visit by Wollaston was Ambrose Forsythe. He had a two-month-old daughter who had not been baptised. As the Forsythes were members of his church Wollaston performed the service and Margaret Forsythe became the first Anglican known to be baptised in Kojonup, on 13 February 1853.[31]

The occupation of the barracks by the families of the Pensioners would have only been a temporary arrangement, until they could be allocated their grants and have some kind of dwelling constructed. As the Pensioners could be called on to keep order in an emergency it was imperative for their ten acre grants to be in close proximity to the barracks. Luckily the soil about the barracks, due to Alfred Hillman's careful townsite selection, was highly suited to farmlets, as one or two of the keen Pensioners discovered when they began breaking the ground of their grants in late 1852.[32]

The grants were recorded with the prefix 'P', designating 'Pensioner'. The first six lots were located immediately north of the barracks, P.1 being adjacent to that reserve. The two lots first officially recorded were P.1 and P.2 granted respectively to Timothy Sullivan, formerly a private of the 48th Regiment of Foot, and William McDonnell, formerly a private of the 88th Regiment of Foot, on 20 November 1852. Officially, Ambrose Forsythe was not granted his ten acres, P.5, until 1862, almost ten years after he arrived in the district. Michael Reilly was originally granted P.3, William Noonan (ex-54th Regiment) P.4 and Thomas Caffrey (ex-88th Regiment) P.6.[33]

In August 1854 the Kojonup Pensioners had a visit from their Commanding Officer, Major Bruce. Those present at the time of his visit were Corporal J. Robinson[34] (who apparently had relieved Hamilton), Privates Sullivan, Forsythe, McDonnell and Noonan. The Major reported that he found them:

> efficient in discipline,—the arms, clothing, appointments and ammunition being in good order and the men expert in handling their arms.[35]

Archdeacon Wollaston had not been the only one to criticize the Enrolled Pensioner Force and Bruce was extremely sensitive to such criticisms; his correspondence files display his fierce loyalty to his men whenever justly possible. His visit to Kojonup was a great reassurance to him and he was determined to broadcast the success stories he found there, in retaliation to the numerous condemnatory remarks which were continually cropping up elsewhere in the colony.

> Every individual of the party afforded indications of industry but Privates Forsythe, McDonnell and Sullivan who have been longest here have not only cleared and fenced their respective allotment but have actually managed to erect for themselves cottages which would stand a favourable comparison with any construction for Pensioners either in the York or Toodyay Districts. These cottages are substantially built stone dwellings, roofed with strong bound timber and are well thatched as to be perfectly water tight of which heavy rain there occasionally falling gave me ocular proof. They consist respectively of two rooms, each room being fourteen feet by thirteen feet.

The frame work and doors although perhaps not as neatly executed as if by hands of a professed carpenter are equally serviceable.

Upon asking the Pensioners how they managed to accomplish the erection of such excellent dwellings they informed me that they took advantage of travelling ticket-of-leave men and conditional-pardon men passing Kojonup, from time to time, and induced them to remain a few days and assist in the work. The iron work and nails they were obliged to get out from Albany by mail carrier whose charges for such carriage formed no small item in the expenses.[36]

In return for the three Pensioners' resourceful diligence the Major recommended that each receive the sanctioned sum of £15 towards the cost of the cottages. As well as constructing their own dwellings he was impressed with their agricultural achievements and ambitious for their future.

I am happy to add that each of the three men adverted to has a couple of acres of wheat in the ground and that the crops appeared to be thriving luxuriantly. They would have had much more, but that they were obliged to perform all their work with the spade. The seed being finally covered by means of a rudely constructed harrow, which was pulled over the ground by the united power of men and women.

Considering the position of Kojonup, in relation to the great Southern Road, the Pensioners will never experience a difficulty in disposing of their produce. The requirements of the mail contract alone would absorb a large proportion, whilst travellers will be only too glad to obtain corn and even flour from their hand mills, at any price.—Privates Forsythe and McDonald had each nearly an acre of wheat last year, for which they obtained 14/- a bushell and they could have disposed often times the same quantity if they had it. Judging from the wheat fields, as well as from a large vegetable garden upon which the Corporal chiefly bestows his labour, I consider the soil at Kojonup to be equal if not superior, to any I have seen elsewhere in the Colony.[37]

Major Bruce was primarily a military man and his judgement of what constituted arable land was narrow to the extreme and probably based on the good advice of supposedly knowledgeable acquaintances. From his following remarks it is obvious that the rumours of the extensive growth of the dreaded poison plants had already reached the ears of the Pensioners. It has been claimed that such exaggerated tales were in some ways the reason that many of the Pensioners and their descendants did not rapidly expand their farming practices.

Indeed the luxuriant grass which clothes the country within the area of five or six miles all round the Pensioner locations, fully attests the superiority of the soil.

Beyond that radius all is repulsive and barren. Although by making a paddock the Pensioners may keep cows, yet the prevalence of the poison is destructive to ruminating animals, and must preclude such stock being permitted to range at large.

I have recommended the men to try and obtain a plough, harrow and a couple of brood mares, and have intimated my readiness to assist them with an advance of funds in the event of such a purchase offering. There is no part of the Colony more adapted to horse breeding than the grass and wellwatered district of Kojonup whilst the surrounding bareness forms as effectual an enclosure as a Park waste.[38]

Despite what Bruce wrote he was pleased to acquire 3200 acres (location 4) in the district. It was, however, within the 'five or six miles' he quotes as being the most superior country. A few years later he applied for more land (location 41) to bring his holdings onto the Balgarup River. (It is possible that Bruce employed some of the Pensioners on this property when off-duty, and it was partly for news of these projects that he was always so anxious to receive his Kojonup mail.)

Numbers of kangaroos were still to be seen in the district, despite the inroads made by many hunters in the past and the Pensioners were never without fresh meat, according to their spokesman Major Bruce. In fact he includes in his report his own particular tip in cooking the game: 'from experience I can say that cooked with a small quantity of salt pork this meat is exceedingly palatable'.[39] The Major's delight with the progress of his detachment of Pensioners at Kojonup is well illustrated in the tale he relates of Private Forsythe. It is hardly the tale one expects to read in a military report.

As another instance of the laudable spirit of exertion manifest at this isolated post which is in reality an oasis surrounded by dreary tracts of the most barren soil, I would mention that Private Forsythe, having saved up some money, obtained permission to proceed to the Bunbury district for the purpose of buying a couple of cows.

Having made his selection of two cows and paid £12 for them the poor man had only got them half the way home when they became furious in consequence of bad feed and breaking away from him returned to their acre.

The person from whom he bought the cows would neither return the money nor assist him, even upon the offer of payment to get them to Kojonup, consequently, for some days, he was in dismay upon the subject. At length, Norris, the Bunbury mail carrier, consented, for consideration of £6 to lash the cows by the horns to

the back of his mail cart and thus to drag them as far as the Black-wood River from whence Forsythe and one of his Comrades with a supply of corn will take charge of them for the remaining thirty miles in order to preserve them from the poison with which the country between the Blackwood and Kojonup abounds.
The success of this arrangement has yet to be proved as the attempt will be made by Norris in his return from Bunbury at the end of the present month.
I mention the above circumstances to show that the Pension body is not without men able and willing to help themselves amidst the difficulties which beset a settler in this Colony and in no part of it more than in such a remote and isolated place as Kojonup.[40]

In time the Pensioners grew fruit trees, and a fig and an almond planted by Pensioners Reilly and Loton respectively still flourish. The station of six Pensioners had in 1856 'about thirty-five acres under crop amongst them—looking remarkably well'.[41] By 1857 William Noonan had nearly completed his cottage and applied for the usual £15.[42]

Noonan's wife, Eleanor, was a fearless, far-sighted woman. An official description of her in 1862 said: 'the woman is a hard-working, indus-trious female—with a large family which she is struggling to main-tain.'[43] She had not left her beloved Ireland for nought and was determined to gain by the transplant. To her, advancement went hand in hand with schooling and as this was not available at Kojonup she decided that when the 1855 school year began her twelve-year-old, Bridget, should be enrolled at a school in Fremantle run by some Roman Catholic Sisters, who were fast becoming recognized as the leading educationists of the colony, for Protestant as well as Catholic girls. But it was one thing to make such a decision and another to carry it into effect when Fremantle was over 160 miles away and no transport was within the means of the Noonans. Undaunted, Eleanor decided that she and Bridget were quite capable of walking the distance.

It was learnt that Toovey's mail cart, escorted by Constable McGuire, would be passing through Kojonup from Albany about this time. By arranging for their belongings to be carried in the cart, and by Bridget and herself setting off long before the carter each morning, Eleanor estimated that they would be able to cover the miles (about twenty-four to thirty-five) between the official daily halting stations, although they would have to be prepared to turn in long after the men on some nights. These bold plans for the departure of Kojonup's first boarding-away student were rare enough, but the trip was to become even more exceptional by the events that followed.

It happened that on board the cart was a prisoner whom the police were forwarding to Perth. Through some oversight the constable had not been informed that the man was considered mentally unbalanced. The first stop was made at the Beaufort where McGuire handed over the mail and the prisoner to Constable Knibbs. In doing so he briefly warned Knibbs to be wary of the prisoner as he had attempted to seize a pistol from a holster, at the Gordon River stop-over.

When the mail cart reached the Williams River, Toovey dismounted and went with Knibbs for water, leaving the prisoner, Stevens, alone with the fire-arms.

> While the two men were at the watering place they heard Stevens crying out after them and asking where they were. Upon this they returned to the cart, the policeman somewhat in advance of his companion. As soon as he came in sight of Stevens, the latter told him to kneel down, as he was going to shoot him: Knibbs continued to approach nearer to Stevens, and when within a little distance of him, he was shot through the heart and died instantaneously. Toovey, who was close behind the policeman, seeing what had happened, and fully aware that the maniac had other loaded fire-arms at his command, very prudently made off through the bush, and came up to Grainger's station for assistance. However, as Toovey was making his escape, Stevens sent a shot after him and he heard the ball distinctly whiz close to him. As soon as Toovey fell in with Grainger they both stole with great caution through the bush to the spot where the cart was left. Unperceived, they came up within a very short distance of where Stevens was, and saw him very near the cart, in which they could also see the fire-arms deposited. Upon his perceiving the two men making towards the cart he attempted to seize a gun; but fortunately Toovey was too close for him to effect this, and knocked him down with an axe handle. He was subsequently secured, although with some difficulty, and left in charge of Grainger while Toovey went back to the Beaufort to inform the wife of the unfortunate man who had been shot, of her bereavement. The body of the policeman was brought along the road as far as the Bannister, where it was found necessary to bury it.[44]

It is claimed that on Mrs Noonan's return journey (which she made alone and completely on foot) she found on reaching the Bannister that the shallow grave had been partly uncovered by wild dogs. She made time to fetch stones to place on the grave to secure it from further depredation. This same grave can be seen today, close to the Albany Highway, near the Bannister. It is said that Mrs Noonan made this journey more than once, to put her children to school.

As for the poor widow, a month later the Superintendent of Police appealed to His Excellency, the Governor, for some Government charity. She was close to her confinement and was left totally destitute.[45]

The next month there were strange doings at the Kojonup barracks. The women bustled around full of importance and the men were not wanted in their stronghold. Sometime during the day of 10 April, the shrill cry of a new-born baby drifted through the little windows of the sturdy stone fortress: a woman had given birth to what is thought to be the first white child born in Kojonup. She was Mary (later known as Elizabeth), the daughter of Corporal John and Mary Robinson.[46] It was not until 6 October 1859 that the birth of a white boy is recorded: James Nathaniel, the son of Mary Anne and George Birchall, a plasterer.[47]

Some indication of the extent of Kojonup's population is gleaned from the list of the Roman Catholic parishioners in 1858. The names recorded were: John and Mary Robinson, Elizabeth (2), Alice (1); Thomas and Mary Caffray (sic); William and Eleanor Noonan, Bridget (15), William (10), Margaret (8); William and Mary McDonald (sic); Timothy and Ann Sullivan; Honora Norris (sic), Mother, Richard (22), Thomas (19), Josiah (16), George (14), Anna Maria (12), John (10), Matilda Mary (7); James Rock; Marianne Smith, Mother, William (11), Jane (9), Ellen (4), John (1); Edward and Eliza Barron, Ellen (2), Jane (1).[48] (In the district about this time were policemen of the surnames Barron and Smith.)

Subsequently, other Pensioners were allocated ten acre grants in Kojonup: James Watt, Robert Loton, Daniel Shinners (sic) and W. Weir.[49] Also, some Pensioners and their families (such as the zealous Mrs Noonan) purchased additional land to expand their farming activities. Yet, some Pensioners who are known to have been in Kojonup do not seem to have been granted any land at all in the district.

No longer did the barracks stand in solitary splendour above the Spring. An approaching traveller could see at a glance a dozen or more little buildings dotting the surrounding hill slopes. Outlying settlers, shepherds, contractors, flock owners, mailmen and regular travellers soon came to know the newcomers and a community feeling gradually developed. From the settlement of the Pensioners around the barracks in October 1851, the nucleus of the town of Kojonup evolved. For those who had come to the colony to escape from destitution in their homeland, being possessors of ten acres of arable land was an undreamed-of achievement, but it was difficult for them to become big farmers, overnight, without considerable capital. Nevertheless, a new generation was well established when the 1860s began and the prospects for it, although not rosy, were possibly more promising than they would have been in the homeland.

THE CONVICTS

All told 9668 convicts, all men, arrived in the colony between 1850 and 1868. They were a mixed lot, guilty of offences ranging from 'stealing during the Irish famine to robbery, assault, rape, murder and sedition'.[50] Most were unfortunate products of the social hardships of industrial Britain. As was often said by old colonists 'there were many in that ought to be out and many out that ought to be in'.

Albany's first contact with the convicts was in November 1851 when a hiring depot was formed, in the town, with seventy-two ticket-of-leave men.[51] The shortest sentence of a convict was seven years. After a period of good behaviour a convict could graduate from Government employment, as a probationer, to a ticket-of-leave man. This label brought with it a considerable amount of freedom for the convict. He was actually able to choose his own employer and be paid wages. More than half of the original ticket-of-leave men at Albany were hired by settlers as shepherds and farmhands. Such men, with continued good records, could be granted conditional pardons before the expiration of their sentence.

When work began on the formation of the Perth to Albany road the adjacent districts and their scattered inhabitants came into closer and more general contact with the convicts. For the engineer-in-charge, Lieutenant W. Crossman, the main object was to get the whole line opened as quickly as possible. Under him were Assistant-Superintendent A. Gregory, in charge of the ticket-of-leave men whose task was to clear the line, and Vincent, the gaoler, in charge of the colonial prisoners who erected the bridges along the route.

Work on the road was very hard, especially in the warm weather when water was not plentiful, even though wells had been previously constructed at intervals along the route. Often the men had to walk long distances to and from their work. Their camps were frequently being changed causing further discomfiture. Despite the primitive working conditions the line advanced steadily. In October 1853 the work gangs were encamped at the thirty-nine mile peg from Perth and before the middle of 1855 the entire road had been roughly encompassed. On their return journey the gangs did additional work such as improving the drainage and formation of the road.

For this onerous work the men received rations and a wage which was four times higher than at other depots.[52] The rates ranged usually from 6½d. to 1s. 4d. per day, depending on the type of work being done.[53] Keeping up the supply of fresh meat to men who were doing exhausting physical labour was a constant problem. Mostly it was kangaroo meat. The work was also extremely hard on the men's clothing and replacements had to be paid for out of their wages, as did extras such as additional sugar and their one permitted solace, tobacco.

These were the conditions when trouble flared up at the Arthur River camp, towards the end of 1853. Lieutenant Crossman investigated the complaints in a commendable, clear-thinking, just manner. The disturbance could almost be said to be one of the first strikes in Western Australian history. In fact, Crossman used this very word in his report when he stated that three particular men 'had endeavoured to excite others to strike work'.[54]

Outwardly, the discontent had arisen mainly from the working conditions: tainted kangaroo meat, ill-health and the high cost of extras due to the isolation and cartage rates. However, Crossman was quick to see that much of the trouble stemmed from too long a time in the bush, for some of the men. A few had been with the party for six months. He recommended that while the depot was in unsettled districts no man should be forced to stay longer than four months.

Thirty-six of the best men (including carters and cooks) expressed no desire to leave the road gang and these nameless men probably moved on to form that stretch of the Albany road which ran through the Kojonup district. Crossman recommended that 2d. extra per day be allowed to those who had been there more than three months. Another proposition he put forward was that the practice of permitting a work official to sell extra necessities to the men be disallowed, to prevent any grumblings of corruption. This suggestion must have been followed, to the benefit of the Norrish family.

Up until now the family had been able to augment their income by the sale of kangaroo skins. But in March 1852 an export duty of 1s. had been placed on all skins so that the price had fallen disastrously. Then the family heard that the convicts were clearing the Perth-Albany road, about thirty miles from them and it might be possible for them to obtain a contract to supply rations to the work party. Young Thomas visited the workers and offered to deliver casks of American flour to them for 10s. above the cost price, which was £5. They accepted the offer and also agreed to pay a fair price for all other items, after an examination of an Albany price list.[55]

It was in ways such as this that settlers throughout the colony directly benefitted from the coming of the convicts. With the extra money acquired they were able to make ends meet and branch out into other ventures. For instance, about this time Richard Norrish met a man on the road with twenty-five ewes which he had been given in lieu of wages. (This was quite customary.) Richard Norrish bought the small flock on the spot and so began the family's long association with the wool industry. From these ewes they had the good fortune to obtain 100 per cent lambing, the first year. The shepherding of the flock was put in the charge of the third son, Joseph, while the fourth boy, George, tended the cattle.

Nathaniel Newstead was another who directly benefitted from the work parties along the Albany road. In April 1862, he supplied No. 5 party, in charge of the warder Constable Jackaman, with 601 pounds of hay and ten bushels of barley and later an additional load of hay.[56]

This particular party was experiencing considerable trouble. From the report of the disturbance some first-hand details of the life led by the prisoners working between the 160 and 165 mile pegs, may be deduced. The party consisted of probation prisoners, that is those with some years to serve before gaining their ticket-of-leave. The men worked in groups under a Probation Constable (a prisoner who could read and write and had proved to be of good conduct). He received an increased daily wage, according to his period of service, and if the authorities found him totally satisfactory he could receive a premature remission. The Probation Constable seems to have been in direct contact with the workers' day to day requirements, whereas the warder's responsibility lay in overseeing the progress, detailing the schedule, scouting for water and organizing the rations for both beasts and men.

Conditions had improved since the first line had been cut. The life was not nearly so isolated. There were more stations along the road and a steady flow of travellers in both directions. Now the vital task was to traverse the initial track, consolidating its foundations with stones and filling the ruts. The atmosphere was more relaxed and discipline was less severe. True, the No. 5 party was supplied with 'poor tents, the wet comming right through and wetting the men's beds and clothes in their bags'.[57] Also, when there was no convenient watering point the men had to walk 3¾ miles to and from their camp, and still break thirty loads of stone carted by the warder and a prisoner, as well as 'repair fifteen yards long and five yards wide and ninety yards of cart ruts'[58] for the day.

Still, in the thirty days covered by the report the warder allowed them six full days and three half days off work, either to wash clothes, to observe the Sabbath or simply because it was raining too heavily for work. On such holidays permission was sometimes given for hunting sorties. Living close to the land observant men became conversant with the ways of the native animals and devised ingenious methods of capturing them for pets as well as for a supplementary food.

Discontent with the way their rations were being issued caused an outbreak of complaints amongst the men of the No. 5 party. It was the warder's habit to give the Probation Constable sufficient supplies to last the men for a week. Instructions were given for the rations to be locked in a box and weighed out daily to the cook. According to Phillip Furlong, the acting Police Sergeant of Kojonup,[59] the Probation Constable of No. 5 party handed the key to the cook, thereby renouncing all responsibilities for the management of the rations. Furthermore, he had supplied himself and a crony with excess flour. In defending himself, he claimed that he had merely taken two days' supply to make one large damper and to reserve some for dumplings. Due to this mismanagement the party ended up one day's rations short. The dispassionate comment of the Superintendent regarding this calamity was: 'the men will make it up by living on kangaroo for the day'.[60]

Other accusations made against the convict constable were: 'he never turns his party out';[61] the proper advances of tobacco were not being received; he allowed some privileged prisoners to 'traffic' (that is, mend clothes for payment); and that he and two companions once went absent without leave for a whole night. On this occasion 'P.C. Elverd traversed the bush for about ten hours in search of them'.[62] On his return at 11 a.m., the accused claimed he had been given permission to go kangarooing but was unable to return as one of his associates was suffering with the intriguing affliction, 'moonblind', and 'he had to stay in the bush with him'.[63]

In his report of the whole incident the warder, Constable Jackaman, explained that the man had been a good prison constable but was quite unfit for the increased responsibility required outside.[64] In addition, being of limited intelligence he was dependent on other more literate prisoners to do tasks assigned to his charge. He regretted his misdeeds and had been returned to Perth. Another more suitable, hardworking prisoner who had been regularly assisting Jackaman, was placed in charge and was recommended for the position of Probation Constable.

When returning such prisoners to Perth the custom was that they would be accompanied by a policeman and at night the policeman would chain them to a tree and lie down beside them. When making a request for some kind of shelter the superintendent explained, 'it was all very well' during the summer but 'not just the thing in winter'.[65]

Just as the early soldiers had become attached to the three areas where they had been stationed, so too did the convict road gangers. They were on the whole well behaved and no complaints during the twelve months ending 19 June 1863 had been made against any of them by residents along the road, according to an official commentary. In fact, all who were 'worth their salt'[66] obtained employment 'from persons residing on the road, immediately they were released as ticket-of-leave men'.[67]

Towards the end of the century it was possible to find an occasional lonely old lag squatting at some watering hole and passing his last days trapping. Many left the colony altogether. Between 1863 and 1893, 801 departed from the port of Albany. There was some cohabitation with Aboriginal women and a few fortunate men found a settler's daughter who cared not if the man she loved was bond or free. Those so favoured were able to make good and merge into the community and it was only the very malevolent colonist who would point a finger at him and sneer: 'He did not choose to come out here.'

REFERENCES

[1] Letter from G. Egerton-Warburton, 25 February 1849 (copy in possession of D. Crabbe, Kojonup).

[2] Alexandra Hasluck, *Unwilling Emigrants* (Melbourne, 1959), p. 30.

[3] *Ibid.* p. 32.

[4] *Ibid.* p. 34.

[5] C.S.O.Recs., 273, 22 April 1853.

[6] C.S.O.Recs., 218, 18 August 1851.

[7] C.S.O.Recs., 372, 24 November 1857.

[8] C.S.O.Recs., 218, 24 October 1851.

[9] C.S.O.Recs., 218, 17 November 1851.

[10] C.S.O.Recs., 248, 12 October 1852.

[11] C.S.O.Recs., 248, 18 July 1852.

[12] *Perth Gazette*, 23 July 1852, p. 3.

[13] C.S.O.Recs., 248, June 1852.

[14] *Perth Gazette*, 23 July 1852, p. 3.

[15] *Perth Gazette*, 16 July 1852.

[16] Letters from G. Egerton-Warburton, 15 October 1852 (copy in possession of D. Crabbe, Kojonup).

[17] C.S.O.Recs., 248, 20 August 1852.

[18] C.S.O.Recs., 372, 3 April 1857.

[19] Lieut. W. Crossman, Letterbooks, 19 January 1853, p. 11 (1543A microfilm, held in Battye Library, Perth).

[20] *Ibid.* 10 February 1853.

[21] *Ibid.* 19 January 1853, pp. 5, 6, 7, 8.

[22] *Ibid.* p. 4.

[23] J. R. Wollaston, *Albany Journals 1848-1856* (Perth, 1955), 13 February 1953.

[24] C.S.O.Recs., 273, 22 April 1853.

[25] J. A. R. Marriott, *England Since Waterloo* (London, 1954), p. 33.

[26] P.R.O. letter in possession of Merle Bignell, 10 November 1967.

[27] Wollaston, 11 February 1853.

[28] *Ibid.*

[29] C.S.O.Recs., 273, 19 August 1853.

[30] *Ibid.* 22 August 1853.

[31] Baptismal Recs., Church of England, Albany.

[32] Crossman, p. 7.

[33] W.A.L.Dept.Recs. of land grants to Kojonup Pensioners (copy in K.H.S.Recs.).

[34] The descendants of Robinson possess two silver medals awarded to Robinson for his participation in campaigns in India before coming to Australia with the Enrolled Pensioner Force. Previously he had been in the 9th Regiment and in 1842 had taken part in a punitive expedition at Cabul, to avenge the treacherous murders of the British Envoy; in 1845 he had been at Mookdee, Ferozeshah and Sobraon against the Sikh Army. Others of the Pensioners must have had similarly bloody war records, but little evidence remains.

[35] C.S.O.Recs., 303, 9 September 1854.

[36] *Ibid.*

[37] *Ibid.*

[38] *Ibid.*

[39] *Ibid.*

[40] *Ibid.*

[41] Bishop Hale Diary, p. 12 (309A, Battye Library).

[42] C.S.O.Recs., 383, 7 April 1857.

[43] C.S.O.Recs., 513, 7 November 1862.

[44] *Inquirer*, 21 February 1855, p. 2; other details from *West Australian*, 5 October 1937, p. 25.

[45] C.S.O.Recs., 335, 24 March 1855.

[46] Baptismal Recs., Roman Catholic Church, Albany, supplied by D. Bulbeck.

[47] Baptismal Recs., Church of England, Albany.

[48] Recs., Roman Catholic Church, Albany, supplied by D. Bulbeck.

[49] W.A.L.Dept. Recs. of land grants to Kojonup Pensioners.

[50] K. F. Crowley, *Australia's Western Third* (London, 1960), p. 38.

[51] Crossman, 3 June 1852.

[52] *Ibid.* 20 January 1854.

[53] *Ibid.* 1 November 1854.

[54] *Ibid.* 20 January 1854.

[55] Thomas Norrish Diary, p. 9.

[56] C.S.O.Recs., 505, 24 April 1862 and 3 May 1862.

[57] *Ibid.* 17 May 1862.

[58] *Ibid.* 13 May 1862.

[59] *Ibid.* 24 May 1862.

[60] *Ibid.*

[61] *Ibid.* Wilson's report, 3 June 1862.

[62] *Ibid.*

[63] *Ibid.* ..

[64] C.S.O.Recs., 505, 3 June 1862.
[65] C.S.O.Recs., 525, 25 February 1863.
[66] *Ibid.* 19 June 1863.
[67] *Ibid.*

6

The Changing Scene

SPICE OF LIFE

While the newcomers were becoming acquainted with their new environment the old settlers were busily engaged in their own activities. John Hassell placed a shepherd, Anthony Walton, his wife Elizabeth and their children on his block at Warkelup, where by 1856 he had built up his flocks to 3000.[1] Three years earlier Hassell was said to have a total of 14,000 sheep in the colony.[2] However, he was not without his problems. All but two mobs (those grazing on his Kojonup holdings) were severely affected with scab. This was becoming a serious problem in the colony's sheep industry and in 1857 statutory control of scab in sheep was introduced.

Another old colonist who still had confidence in the Kojonup grasslands was the York businessman, J. Monger. He was grazing a large flock on the Beaufort River and in 1853 T. Barrett, an Albany storekeeper, had purchased 500 wethers from him.[3]

Near Kojonup, Elijah Quarterman (sic) was running 1900 sheep, all in one mob and in excellent order. This flock he grazed between there and Beverley, the journey taking three weeks.[4]

Considering the fate of the previous would-be sheep owners in the district, and conclusive evidence that the great tracts of grassy country concealed scattered poison plants from the uneducated or unobservant, one marvels at the optimism of this second wave of Kojonup flock owners. Their success seems to have depended on taking the risk, accepting the occasional deaths and relying on the vigilance of their shepherds. Good shepherds who were knowledgeable bushmen were paid well and were very much in demand. Those new to the life were advised by oldtimers to carry specimens of the various poison plants to compare with suspected plants.

In return for this exacting service flock owners often had to turn a blind eye to the private lives of their shepherds. It was a lonely life and the company of Aboriginal women was frequently sought to compensate for the isolation. To mercenary flock owners this was a lesser evil than that of imbibing hard spirits which left the shepherd incapable of heeding his flock's movements.

The Norrish family was growing up and must have greatly appreciated the increased company in their little neck of the wood. The Waltons were not much older than the two oldest Norrish boys and their little daughters were about the same age as Matilda Mary and Anna Maria Norrish. These small girls must have spent many happy hours together, in between doing their share of their families' numerous manual tasks. But tragedy was never very far away.

In January 1856 Wollaston set out on his fifth and last Archidiaconal tour. On reaching Kojonup he found more changes. Cottages had been erected since his last visit. To his dismay, of the six families settled at the little hamlet, five were Roman Catholics and only one (the self-effacing Forsythe family) was Protestant. In the afternoon of Sunday 6 January, the Archdeacon dutifully said prayers in their humble little cottage and then hurried on to the Beaufort Bridge.

On his return on 14 March a jaded Wollaston merely stopped a night, replenished his corn bags as previously arranged, and was ready the next morning to move to the next stopping place. Then a message was passed on to him of the death of a little girl, Fanny, only five years two months old, the daughter of Anthony and Elizabeth Walton. At the father's request the conscientious Wollaston detoured four miles to read the burial service over the little grave, dug just six days earlier. Two weeks later Wollaston returned to Kojonup to bury another of Walton's children, Rose Ellen, aged eight years. He recorded in his journal that in both cases the cause of death had been croup and a third child was grievously ill. Kojonup had experienced its first epidemic, small but lethal.

Rose Ellen Walton's burial service was to be the last said by Wollaston. Her burial register number in the Albany Church of England's records is 45 and number 46 is that of James Ramsden Wollaston.

Whether or not the third sick child mentioned by Wollaston was one of the little Norrish girls is unknown but Honora Norrish must have watched over them anxiously, for fear of any sign of the fatal illness. The lonely days that followed were formidable for the broken-hearted Elizabeth Walton. In her sorrow she was gently comforted by the Norrish girls, particularly Anna. Perhaps, eight months later, members of the two families went together to worship at the church service celebrated in the barracks by the first Church of England bishop of the colony, Matthew Hale.[5] Sectarian feelings were put aside for such an illustrious dignitary as a bishop-designate and twenty people formed the congregation, including some Roman Catholics. At that time, Mrs Richard Norrish was a Roman Catholic but not her English-born husband. This occasion was probably the first major social event of the embryo town. What a pity the Bishop did not give any inkling in his diary, of what those twenty people did after the service. Certainly, they would have taken the opportunity to exchange news of families, livestock and crops; but did they adjourn to a cottage for a lingering 'cup that cheers'?

About this time an Aborigine relayed to the Norrishes a disgusting tale of treachery. It seems that Elijah Quartermaine had made his southern headquarters at Yowangup, the watering point which had previously interested John Hassell, twenty miles north-east of War-kelup. Quartermaine had left a hut keeper there named Isaacs. One day a tramp arrived at the hut and the old man offered the customary hospitality, being only too pleased of the company. Before his departure for Albany, Isaacs gave the tramp some rations. Late that night the old hut keeper was awakened by someone moving around the hut. It was the tramp, returned to rob the lonely old man of what few valuables he possessed. According to the Aborigine the tracks of a white man were clearly marked on the old sandalwood road heading in the direction of Warkelup. This horrifying tale spread rapidly amongst the Kojonup settlers.

A few days later another shepherd, named Ryan, who was camped five miles from the Norrishes, came in great haste to say that the same tramp had called at his place. Ryan had given him a meal and had left him resting at his hut whilst he had gone, supposedly, to tend his flock. Instead, he had hurried to Warkelup to warn the family and to obtain some moral support. The tramp who carried a large sheath-knife in his belt was no stranger to Ryan. He knew him well for an untrustworthy scoundrel.

The Norrishes were alarmed but felt duty-bound to see justice done. Richard Norrish, trained for many years to uphold the law fearlessly, was ill; but his sons were of the same bold-spirited breed. It was decided that Thomas and Josiah Norrish and Anthony Walton would go to Ryan's hut that night after Ryan had returned with his sheep. With thoroughness they laid their plans. Ryan was to tie his dog to the leeward and after the evening meal to sit, yarning, on his bunk facing the hut's entrance, allowing the tramp to have the box opposite him, so that his back was to the door. At a signal from Thomas Norrish, Ryan was to leap on the stranger and pin him to the ground.

At dusk the three upholders of the law left the safe circle of their families and travelled the five miles to Ryan's camp. The Norrish boys, being highly skilled hunters, were able to creep noiselessly to the opening of the hut while Walton stayed back in the shadows ready to assist. Peering into the hut Thomas saw the scene set, as planned. He raised his hand in the doorway and in an instant Ryan leapt forward and grasped the tramp around the body. The man struggled violently, biting, kicking and muttering threats at his captors as he vainly endeavoured to reach his sheath-knife. Soon the lads had secured his hands behind his back and to recover from the excitement the usual billy of tea was brewed. The captive would have none of it but sat nearby, sullenly threatening to have his revenge at a later date.[6]

Knowing their families would be anxiously waiting, the three adventurers departed with their prisoner to trudge the five miles home. Eventually, he was taken in custody to Perth where he was tried for robbery and sent to gaol for two years. It is not difficult to imagine the praise heaped upon the heroes nor the number of times the residents of the little settlement retold this brave adventure around their firesides.

Camaraderie was very evident in the early days, but nevertheless a calculating wariness was necessary to combat the notorious self-interest of some settlers. One year the Norrish family were forced to sell their wool to an Albany merchant for 7d. a pound. They later learnt that another settler received 1s. 6d. per pound for his wool. The Albany storekeeper on being questioned insisted that he had lost money on the Norrish deal. This was proved untrue. According to a price catalogue it had realized 1s. 8d. As a result, for three years the family carted their wool the whole tedious way to York where Monger advanced them 1s. 4d. a pound and later forwarded them a further 2d. after commission and sundry expenses had been subtracted.[7] These improved prices for wool were a reflection of the boom in the wheat and wool industries experienced after transportation began. This boom was to stimulate much more interest in these districts.

MEN OF SUBSTANCE

Before 1860 the property first chosen by the unfortunate T. L. Symers, and universally known as 'Balgarup', was acquired by Joseph Spencer, a son of the renowned Sir Richard Spencer, first Resident Magistrate of Albany. Since their family's arrival in the colony in 1833 the Spencer boys had come to know the Albany hinterlands like the palms of their hands. In addition, they had become keen horsemen, fair shots and eager hunters.

From the very beginning their parents' home was a focal point for the social life of King George Sound. On it converged all the latest colonial news and the most important travellers. In these surroundings the young Spencers were fired with a spirit of adventure and restlessness, and were later indulged by a doting widowed mother. Like many ambitious sons of propertied settlers they were drawn to the virgin bush in the hope of making their fortunes in wool, as they had heard others had done in early times in New South Wales.

At the same time, dogged perseverance and a liking for solitude were not in their make-up. Balgarup, situated on the mail route and visited by all north-south travellers, was the ideal property for Joseph Spencer. From this vantage point he expanded his holdings. In 1859 he was officially registered as buying location 3, known as 'Sutherlands'.[8] On maps drawn up in 1862 he was shown as owning location 30 of 100 acres west of the barracks, on which was growing a wheat crop. In 1862 there existed on his Balgarup locations 23 and 29 a dwelling, a large garden, six other buildings, a well, various yards and the chimney of the thwarted Symers' original house, marked as a survey point. Locations 28, 39, 42, 46 (totalling 132 acres) contained a dwelling, a wheat field, pig pens and another building.[9] Sometime before 1866 Spencer leased 640 acres at 'Mooradup Pool', where the township of Muradup is today.[10] All these sites were first-class and there can be no doubt that his judgement of ideal country was seldom at fault.

A friend of Joseph Spencer and a frequent visitor to his Balgarup property in the early 1860s was W. H. Graham. Graham had arrived in the colony as a lad, about 1852, to join his uncle George Cheyne and his cousins the Moirs. At the end of 1861 Graham had officially bought Kojonup locations 43 and 44, on the Nanamillup and Wadjekanup creeks near the little settlement of Eticup, approximately twenty-two miles east of Kojonup; yet it is obvious from his diary[11] that his establishment at Nanamillup was in existence prior to 1860. The original grazing lease in this area was granted to Albany merchant John McKail in 1852. A permanently resident neighbour of Graham was a naturalized Dutchman, Solomon Drolf, one time sandalwooder, kangaroo hunter and shepherd, who owned Kojonup locations 24 and 27, totalling 42 acres, which contained the actual 'Ettakup Pool'. This was about two miles from Graham's. Edward Spencer, oldest of the living Spencer men then, also had a holding nearby of 125 acres, which he and other members of his family visited from time to time.

Inertia and loneliness seem never to have been part of the lives of those at Eticup. Hardly a week passed that travellers did not visit or a member of the settlement did not set out for some distant spot. Often when travelling to Balgarup Graham took a route through his out-station, Wadjekanup, and probably the watering point known today as Graham's Well. In the years 1860 and 1861 he employed a large staff and more than likely most were ticket-of-leave men although he never mentions the fact in his diary. All, both black and white, he appears to have treated with absolute fairness and cordiality.

The 1860s began in the district with incessant rain from a violent thunderstorm. Graham travelled to Balgarup on 3 January, to grind some grain with Joseph Spencer's mill, but after two days of damp conditions he had only three bushels of ground flour. He returned to Eticup where he found the stacks of barley and wheat all badly soaked. The next few days he and his workers were kept busy turning the stacks, collecting roofing thatch from the nearby river and making hurdles and battens. In between chores he found time to return the sieve he had borrowed from Solomon Drolf.

On the nineteenth he again travelled to Balgarup, apparently to meet mailman Toovey, and stayed the night, helping 'Joey' to thresh the next day before returning to Eticup on the twenty-first.

On 5 March he started out once more for Balgarup. This time he slept a night at Wadjekanup on the way. For two days he and Joseph Spencer were grinding wheat. By working all day and sifting by moon-light Graham was able to return to Eticup on the ninth with '1500 on the cart'.[12]

Anxious to meet the mail he returned to Balgarup on 19 March as he was expecting the replacement of a universal joint for his threshing machine. The mail passed but brought no universal joint and a frus-trated Graham returned to Eticup empty-handed.

A week later he was on the track again. This time it was an errand of mercy—to collect a winnowing machine for Solomon Drolf. He not only delivered the machine to him but went over the next day 'to see the machine put to right'.[13]

On Saturday 21 April he again journeyed to Balgarup and was sur-prised to find Joseph Spencer absent. As the Balgarup employees expected his return the next day, Graham waited. It could not have been a very pleasant wait. The larder was bare and on the Sunday Graham wrote in his diary 'Mr Joseph not arrived. Very hungry for meat and went to look for a possum'.[14] During Monday the mailman, Jim Webb, arrived with two sawyers to work at Balgarup but the owner

9 'Warkelup' *c.* 1913; Richard Norrish established his farm here in 1849

10 'Balgarup'; note haystack and old wool press at right

11 Elverd's Hotel (p. 108); note shingled roof and water barrel at right

12 Kojonup Inn (p. 108), with Spring Street post office at left; note lamp post with brackets

13 Royal Hotel (p. 150), with Samuel Bagg on horse; note fancy trim on gutterings, also post and rail fence where early sheep sales were held

still did not appear. On Tuesday Graham gave the Balgarup workman, Hughes, a hand to cart some firewood. Apparently he was more patient than the sawyers. They gave up waiting for the master of Balgarup on Wednesday, and set off for King George Sound—not before one of them had sold a gun to Graham for £2. By this time the latter also had grown weary of waiting and the monotonous diet. In true Scottish fashion he 'boiled a bit of wheat'[15] for his dinner and started for Eticup.

The following Sunday he was back at Balgarup, pleased to find Spencer at last at home. This time, instead of returning to Eticup on his usual track, he went into Kojonup to see an H. Hill and arranged to meet him at Balgarup when he came over for a machine on 8 May. Later he called to see Pensioner Noonan. Unfortunately, Graham rarely records his reasons for such visits.

Then followed almost a month of confusing activity. Before returning to Balgarup on 8 May he discovered he was out of wheat and had to ride over to Solomon to ask if he might borrow three bags to take to the mill. Agreement being reached he had to return the next day to collect them. From there he visited one of his shepherds to select a killer sheep to take with him, not wishing for a meatless diet again. On reaching Balgarup he spent a day sieving flour, then with Joseph Spencer returned to Eticup with the bulky threshing machine, a long tiresome journey, partly covered in the dark. Until the eighteenth the days were mostly spent threshing. Then Spencer returned with the machine and Graham followed on the twenty-second with the winnowing machine. Two days later, in return for Spencer's assistance, Graham helped him sow barley. On 2 June he sent two of his horses over to Balgarup with two trusted Aborigines, Billy and Bobbinet.

As has been indicated, Graham and his associates (the diary abounds with mention not only of Joseph Spencer but also E., R. and W. Spencer) seemed to be forever in the saddle, rushing hither and thither, whether for business, sport, pleasure, work, exploring for new leases, hunting or just visiting Billy Cooper's public house 'where they got jolly'.[16] Distance never deterred them. They travelled to all corners of the compass. While he was absent from his property Graham's men would be ramming posts, shepherding sheep, planting cabbages, taking out stumps, finishing the shearing or scabbing sheep. Nor were the young owners afraid of work. The diary tells only too clearly how they drove and sheared sheep, threshed, gardened, ploughed, forged and tended the animals, particularly the horses they loved.

For instance, on Monday 1 October 1860, Graham called at Balgarup in search of his stallion, Slasher. The next day he and Joseph Spencer went out looking for it but heavy rain drove them back. The next day they set out again to scan the Balgarup and Kojonup runs. They inquired at Thomas Chipper's, the mail carter who had established himself just north of the town. While there the solvent Graham paid Chipper for some business they had previously transacted. There being no sign of the stallion among Chipper's horses (Graham contemptuously referred to them as a scurvy lot) the two hunters called into Newstead's to make inquiries, but again were out of luck. On Thursday they rode to Warkelup:

> after a little searching we found him and the two fillies. We could not catch him so were obliged to run him and the mob into Norris's [sic] yard. I then took him, the fillies following, over to Balgarup. Friday, 5th October. Started for Eticup but after having gone a mile the fillies would not follow so I had to take them each to Balgarup and turning Slasher loose with the fillies drove them along the road. But as soon as they got to the Old Swan Road they ran up it and back to Warkelup and I was not able to head them. I turned back to Balgarup as it was late in the afternoon.[17]

On the sixth he set out again for home, arriving about 3 p.m., and made a small yard in the paddock in which to catch the mares at a future date. Soon the place was a hive of industry, in preparation for shearing. Sheep were being washed, lambs picked out, a new piston rod made for the wool press, a garden fence mended and melons planted. All this time there was a constant coming and going of shearers, workers and visitors, including E. and R. Spencer, W. Knight and lastly that jack-of-all-trades, George Maxwell, who was now employed by the botanist Baron von Müller, of Melbourne, to collect specimens of the native flora to the north and east of the settled areas.

In the midst of all this confusion the young proprietor came of age, on 18 October, and as a form of celebration he made a plum pudding. What a bucks party there must have been! There would have been the usual rations washed down with an extra nip of grog and topped off by the great plum pudding made from the suet of the last sheep slaughtered, some sugar and dried fruit from the store, some home-ground wheaten flour moistened with a good measure of spirits and wrapped in a man-sized handkerchief and boiled all day over an open fire. The next day shearing would have continued as usual.

All this time Graham had been brooding over Slasher and the two fillies and on Sunday 21 October he, W. Spencer and W. Knight went to Balgarup for the night. The next morning they visited Warkelup where after a lengthy search they traced the three animals and secured them in Norrish's yard, before returning to spend another night at Balgarup. The following day the horses were successfully driven to Eticup where shearing was nearly finished and preparations were being made for dipping.

During the month of November considerable time was spent in rounding up horses. Hundreds of miles were travelled, from one watering spot to another. Information was gleaned and willingly supplied by all travellers, both black and white. For instance, on 2 November at Poodanup (sic) Graham met Albert Hassell and a worker driving cattle from Jerrymungup (sic) and was told that some of his horses were seen at the Salt River. The worker's name was Jones, a name to be well known soon in Kojonup. Not long after this protracted horse-hunt the soured Graham determined to build stables. Simultaneously, the sheep were being tallied and on 16 November he recorded in his diary that 'the rams came across from Balgarup'.[18]

On 20 November, the Nanamillup establishment ran short of flour and sugar and in pouring rain Graham went to try to borrow some from Balgarup. He found the people there almost as short themselves. Nevertheless, the next day he departed with an emergency supply of twelve pounds of flour and two to three pounds of sugar. On the way he overtook a new settler, one who was soon to become an integral part of the district, Edward Treasure, 'who was taking his things to his run near Malgitup'.[19] They parted at Wadjekanup about sundown.

Graham needed more flour and sugar for his numerous workmen who were now busy mowing and turning the wet hay, as well as for shepherds at their lonely outstations. In desperation he went to see Solomon Drolf and borrowed a half-bushel of wheat and twenty pounds of flour. Treasure was camped nearby and also lent thirty pounds of sugar. Perhaps in compensation, Graham, a competent surveyor, later helped to patch up a difference of opinion between them and chained the distance between their runs, 'Malgitup' (Drolf's) and 'Martinup' (Treasure's).

The summer projects were mounting and everyone was as busy as beavers. When a fire got away a lot of extra work resulted, with stock to be checked and shifted. A trip was made to Balgarup to see if the threshing machine was available but Norrish had already arranged to use it so further inquiries had to be made there before returning home. Towards the end of January Graham and Albert Hassell went first to 'Yeriminup', then to Scott's 'Norlup' property and then to the Tone River. He seems to have been agisting sheep thereabouts. Later, in March, he was absent for four weeks exploring for fresh sheep runs as far south as Nornalup Inlet.

During 1861 his trips to Balgarup became less frequent as the demands of his property increased. His major preoccupation was a quest for more pastures for his larger flocks. With this in mind he visited a place called 'Gnowanyerup' (Gnowangerup) on 29 May, 'Tanbillilup' (Tambellup) on 3 July and later moved further north to Nampup (Nyabing). The expansion of their grazing leases was a constant concern to the pioneer sheep men who had to be prepared for the ever possible bushfire ruining their usual runs, or for their supply of stock water drying up.

On Tuesday 27 August, Graham was expecting some ointment from Balgarup. When the messenger did not appear he set out to fetch it and although he met the man on the road he continued the journey and spent an enjoyable night with his old friend. In the morning he helped Spencer to brand some horses before departing for Kojonup to purchase some pit-saw files from Thomas Chipper. It irked his frugal Scottish nature to have to pay 1s. 6d. each for them. From there he went on to Warkelup, but Norrish was not about so without further delay he made for home where he found yet another established pioneer, Elijah Quartermaine, waiting to see him.

On Sunday 8 September, Graham recorded, 'a heavy snow storm this morning making a home-like winter scene'.[20] No doubt many of the settlers, free and bond, had similar thoughts. But that was all behind them and their new life with all its demanding activities allowed little spare time for contemplation. By the middle of December 1861, Graham knew only too well the monstrous changeability of the seasons of his new country.

> My home and all it contained was destroyed by fire, together with a large stack of hay and a quantity of fencing. The cause of it was a native who set my run on fire, which spread to my house while I was absent.[21]

Within four years he had rebuilt his home, this time a gracious two-storied dwelling, ready to receive his bride, Emma Christina McKail, in August 1865. The new name of 'Fairfield' was bestowed on the property from this year.

THE ALBANY ROAD

Thomas Chipper was one of the first children to be born in the Swan River Colony. His parents had come in the year 1829. In 1853, Thomas was a police constable in Albany where he married Elizabeth Maley on 26 January 1853. He was shrewd and headstrong and objected to the rigid demands of the constabulary. Seeing greater possibilities of advancement in working for himself he resigned and supported by other members of the Chipper family commenced a carting and mail business between Perth and Albany and branched into other ventures whenever they were offered.

In 1857 he obtained the contract for the express mail from Albany to Perth. Previously his contract was Albany to Kojonup. He decided to make a headquarters at Kojonup for changing his horses. At first, he resided in the building erected by George Maxwell, but coveted the site and cottage inhabited by Newstead, claiming that it was the official stopping place of the mail cart. Newstead, however, stuck to his guns, supported by Maxwell,[22] and Chipper had to be content with the area around the Namarillup spring just north of the town on location 7, an original grant to the Leake family.

Here, he built up and housed a fleet of horses, developed grazing interests and when not travelling the road obtained contracts to improve it. The road was in such a bad condition in 1860, with great ruts and poor drainage, that it was even contemplated building a completely new road. In 1861 it was arranged for Chipper to remove a great many fallen trees from the road between the Sound and Kojonup for the sum of £6; and between Kojonup and the Beaufort River for £1 10s. 0d.[23] The bridge at the Beaufort was badly in need of repair and in 1861 the Clerk of Works prepared specifications for it to be improved with sawn timber and 'left it with Mr Smith at the Beaufort to try to obtain tenders from persons near the spot, there being sawyers working for Mr Cornwall'.[24] (Smith was the police constable stationed there.)

Thomas Chipper was soon known personally by all the residents along the entire length of the Albany Road. In being the general carrier, mailman and driver for all those along the rough north-south track, in all kinds of weather, he must have endured many trials. One of his biggest headaches was the keeping up of his supply of horses and seeing that they were at all times in condition for the arduous pulls they were demanded to make through heavy sand and up steep hills. Sleeping and eating in a different place each night, being held responsible for the safety of the mail and the comfort and amusement of his varied passengers and facing the hazardous environment in soaring temperatures or pouring rain were all part of his exacting routine.

Some idea of the conditions on this journey is given by a traveller, the Reverend J. T. Poore, in 1861.

> The distance from King George Sound to Perth, the capital of this Colony is 265 miles, and the journey occupies seven or eight days. The only public conveyance is the monthly mail cart and the intending traveller has need to provide himself with a good skin rug and look well to his commissariat, for he has to camp at night and is dependent for food [on] supplies taken in at the Sound.
>
> Through the kindness of a friend I was well, as I thought superabundantly supplied, but eight days jolting on a cart with constant exposure to the open air, wonderfully quickens the appetite and assists digestion. The road may be described as a good bush track, though some patches of it are very rugged and others deep sand. It was cleared about nine years ago and the miles are numbered on the trees. To Victorian readers it may seem absurd that a journey of less than three hundred miles should occupy eight days, yet to accomplish this, we made early starts, one morning at 2 o'clock and travelled till after sunset, making unequal distances for the sake of water and firewood.[25]

Thomas Chipper was only one of the newcomers of the 1860s whose surname was to have a close association with the district of Kojonup. Another was that of Pensioner Sergeant John Tunney. He was discharged from his original regiment, the 80th, as 'being unfit for further Service'[26] yet he migrated to Australia and carved out an additional career for himself until the ripe old age of eighty-four! He had arrived in the colony on the ship *Dudbrook* in 1853, with his wife and five children. For his supervision of the convicts on the voyage out, Tunney's character was described by the Surgeon-Superintendent as 'extremely good'.[27] This comment, together with his natural intelligence and sobriety combined to mark him as a Pensioner in whom trust could be placed. Soon he was transferred to Albany as sergeant-in-charge and given an office in the Commissariat Quarters. Between 1854 and 1856 two other children were born in Albany.

In connection with his work Tunney made trips to the outstation at Kojonup and became familiar with the farming land there. The first known date connecting him with Kojonup is 1 September 1858, when he was registered as being the godfather of Alice (later Alicia) Catherine, the second daughter of Corporal John Robinson and his wife, Mary.[28]

Shortly after this occasion Robinson became seriously ill and was transferred to the Colonial Hospital, Perth, where he died on 24 February 1859 aged 46, the victim of cancer. The whole of the little hamlet was plunged into grief. For the sorrowing widow, alone in Perth with her two fatherless babies, the secure happy Kojonup days seemed as if they had never been, so wretchedly was she now placed. However, fond thoughts of her were uppermost in the mind of one who had always secretly admired her. After a year he tore himself from his beloved acres to make the trip to Perth to visit her and 'say his piece'. The humble proposal was gratefully accepted by Mary and she married Nathaniel Newstead at the Catholic Church, Perth, on 16 April 1860. Back went Mary and her girls to weave the threads of their lives again with the people and countryside of Kojonup. Over one hundred years later, Charlie Elverd recollected seeing old Mrs Nat Newstead. To his child eyes she was a neat refined old lady, dressed always in a black bonnet and cape. When she took her daily walk down Kojonup's main street she always carried a handbag over her arm and grasped a sturdy walking stick in her hand.

Meanwhile, in May 1863, Sergeant John Tunney purchased Pensioner Caffrey's land, P. 6 and P. 12, for £112 sterling.[29] With five sons Tunney no doubt saw a future for them on the land. However, the only one to settle permanently to farming was the second boy, James, who had been born in Bengal in 1847.

It is said that James began his working life as a clerk in his father's office and later accompanied him to Kojonup to remain and contribute substantially to the district's future.

The distribution of the Enrolled Pensioner Force in 1861 was: Perth (89), Fremantle (13), Rottnest (13), York (6), Toodyay (5), Greenough (6), Bunbury (9), all part time; Albany (5), Kojonup (4), Champion Bay (5), North Fremantle (89).[30]

With the death of John Robinson a new non-commissioned officer was sent to Kojonup. He was Sergeant Robert Loton. The earliest official record connecting him with Kojonup is dated 9 April 1861; he and his wife Ann were godparents for Michael and Ellen Reilly's daughter Ellen.[31] The Lotons, and his brother and sister-in-law, arrived in the colony on 19 August 1853[32] on the *Robert Small* on which Robert Loton was second-in-command of the convicts and Pensioners. Mary Ann, daughter of the Robert Lotons, accompanied her parents to Kojonup. It is believed however that there was also a son. Previous to being stationed at Kojonup, Robert Loton held office at the Mt Eliza station, Perth.

Robert and Ann Loton were devout members of the Roman Catholic Church from which, as children, they no doubt received their basic education. Kojonup was to reap the benefits of this dedicated effort of some Roman Catholic convent.

On 29 April 1862, one of the original Kojonup Pensioners died. William Noonan passed away at the age of 54 leaving his wife Eleanor to battle on in her usual plucky way. Just a few months earlier, in August 1861, the family had been so joyful, celebrating the wedding of the grown-up Bridget to a young police constable, William Grover.

With the coming of 1863 the old identities of Warkelup were also engaged in a frenzy of activities for a wedding, the Norrish family's first. On 17 February, the young (seventeen-year-old) Anna Maria was married to the new Pallinup River settler, Edward Treasure, aged thirty-eight. Probably, the whole Kojonup community was present to witness the ceremony solemnized by Father Coll. Anna Maria chose her young sister, Matilda Mary, and their close friend and neighbour, Elizabeth Walton, to sign the marriage certificate as witnesses, no doubt in the capacity of bridesmaids.[33] After the service the rough stools were most likely pushed aside and singing and dancing, to the tune of someone's fiddle, and interspersed with many a toast, was enjoyed until the sun peeped over the eastern hill. At the end of the festivities the young Anna Maria would have climbed up into her husband's farm cart, said goodbye to her family and left for her new home, Martinup. Mr and Mrs Edward Treasure were to prove themselves discerning and capable pioneers and their property, Martinup, prospered rapidly. The experience Mrs Treasure had received from her family's early farming experiments must have been of immense value at innumerable times, and helped assure that success.

The Norrishes so enjoyed their first wedding that within two months they were celebrating another. This time the eldest son, Richard, was married to an Irish colleen, Ellen Malone, on 15 April, Father Coll once more officiating.[34] Unlike her husband, Ellen had been in the colony only five years, having come from Dublin with her two sisters and a brother, in 1858, on the ship *Emma Eugenia*.[35] Who knows, she could have met her future husband through two of the guests at the previous wedding. Three years earlier her sister, Eliza, had married William Cornwall, who according to the marriage certificate was at that time a farmer at the Beaufort River.

William Cornwall had arrived in the colony on the ship *Sterling* on 14 March 1841, as one of sixteen juvenile emigrants. He was only able to make a mark on his marriage certificate, whereas his wife was able to write her name. Cornwall was never ashamed of his illiteracy; nor should he have been: it did not prevent him from becoming a wealthy businessman.

The two witnesses at the wedding of Richard Norrish, junior, were Eliza Cornwall and William Andrews. The latter had arrived in the colony as a steerage passenger on the same ship as Cornwall, and since then had been closely associated with him, in business. The early years of Cornwall's life in the colony were spent around York, and it was probably through the York merchant, J. Monger, that Cornwall acquired the Beaufort River station.

After their marriage the young Richard Norrishes made their home at 'Marlyup', a few miles past Warkelup. Shortly afterwards, Josiah (the third son) married a Miss Cull of Albany, and established himself further east (in the area where W. H. Graham had earlier set up a temporary shepherd camp) at 'Tambillilup' thereby becoming the respected pioneer of the prosperous Tambellup district. The second of ten children, 'Charlie', was born on 9 September 1869, and was to live to celebrate his one hundredth birthday in the town his parents had helped to found.

By this time there was quite a handful of small children playing around the doors of the Kojonup cottages and the need for a school was discussed by their parents and the visiting Roman Catholic clergy. Increased interest in schools was spreading throughout the colony. In 1856, there were only eleven schools all told, catering for 429 children. By 1860, the number of schools had jumped to sixteen with 874 attending. In 1865, the number had increased to thirty-six and 1586 children were receiving some formal education.[36] One of these new schools was to be found in the little settlement at Kojonup. It was one of a number of 'Colonial Mixed Schools', for boys and girls, opened in country areas by the General Board of Education. Such schools were run along the lines of the Irish National System, the Irish readers being the books used by the children.

Mrs Loton was appointed the first schoolmistress on 3 March 1863, at a salary of £35 per annum.[37] Fees could also be paid (2d. to 6d. a week) and retained by the mistress as a salary supplement but no child was to be denied instruction through inability to pay. The average attendance was fifteen and three children known to have been enrolled were Alicia Robinson, William Elverd and Harry Elverd, but Loton's own daughter most likely helped to make up the numbers. However, by 1867 the fourteen children known to be attending were: Daniel, James and John Shinner; George and Amelia Chipper; William,

Rachel, Bridget and Patrick Reilly; Ellen Forde; Robert Elverd; Mary and Catherine Weir; John Forsythe and William Jones.[38]

In the year 1864 Robert Loton followed his wife in taking on an official Government position. As early as 1855 Commanding Officer Bruce (by then a Lieutenant-Colonel) had complained about the new pre-paid postage stamps and the difficulties he would experience in receiving the military correspondence from Kojonup as no post office where stamps could be purchased existed there. About ten years later Bruce was still complaining and because of his thorough and persistent arguments Kojonup eventually received its first postmaster. How much this was due to the unfortunate consequences of an opium clipper's action in China is problematical!

> The Sergeant at Kojonup is in the habit of sending me Returns and other official papers by the Mail Carrier—whose duty I hold it to be to deliver such letters at the General Post Office with the same regularity as he does the Albany Mails.—Instead of this the letters have, on several occasions been detained in Perth by the Mail Carrier for one or two days before delivery at the Post Office. By the last mail I expected some very important pay vouchers, and not receiving them with my Albany letters I called two or three times at the General Post Office concerning them.—I was so positive that they must have come that I urged a further search for them in the office and a reference to the Mail Carrier.—The result was that yesterday afternoon the missing letters were recovered from the Mail Carrier and delivered to me. I recollect an opium Clipper in China getting into serious trouble by with holding a Mail for a few hours. I think it would be desirable at least to warn the Albany Mail Carrier of the penalty he is liable to,—if such letters can be recognized as comprising a Mail—and should the circumstances of there being no Post Master at Kojonup deprive the said letters of the legal character of a Mail, I recommend that Sergeant Loton be appointed Post Master at that place, without salary so long as his duties consist of the mere forwarding of documents from himself or the other Pensioners.[39]

W. H. Knight, of the general post office, for His Excellency's information, commented at the foot of the letter:

> The inconvenience complained of by Colonel Bruce would be obviated by the establishment of a Post Office and an appointment of a Post Master at Kojonup, and I think that the adoption of this course would result in much benefit to a large number of people who I am informed, live at, or near Kojonup . . . . the letters were not brought into Perth with the first portion of the mail, but with the cart which afterwards brought in the newspapers—and were

not posted until the afternoon—I did not see Chipper when he left them or I would have spoken to him about them as I have before told him that The Colonel was always anxious to get his Kojonup letters as soon as possible.[40]

The upshot was the Colonial Secretary recommended that Loton be appointed as postmaster at Kojonup, without salary. However, someone must have had a change of mind as Loton was officially appointed in October 1864, on a salary of £6 per annum.[41]

Who were these 'large number of people' living near or at Kojonup, as mentioned in the above letter? Some idea can be deduced from a subscription list of those who generously donated to assist the victims of a disastrous summer fire at Greenough, in 1864. Many of the sufferers were probably old campaign comrades of the following subscribing Kojonup Pensioners: Sergeants Loton and Reilly, Privates Forsythe, Newstead, Sullivan, McDonnell, Sweeny, W. Hubble, J. Bates, Rock and Shinner.[42] Among the newcomers there was genuine respect for those like the Norrishes who had been familiar with the district for many years. The year 1865 was a memorable one for Richard and Honora Norrish as on 6 November, Richard and Ellen Norrish had a son, Thomas,[43] the first of another generation of the family to live in the district of Kojonup.

That same year the British Government announced that transportation would cease within three years. This change of policy was due mainly to the high annual cost of the system. It was felt by the British Government, which was still recovering from a series of expensive disturbances (the Crimean War, the Indian Mutiny, the Maori Wars and domestic troubles in Ireland) that as the accommodation in the British gaols was not greatly eased by the system, the expense was unwarranted. Furthermore, the eastern colonies were forever pestering for its cessation, as they claimed that the freed convicts were shipping east and corrupting their society. Following this announcement by the British Government, increased efforts were made in the colony to utilize the remaining numbers of convicts to the best advantage. More thought and activity was centred on improving the roads and making use of existing road gangs to construct police stations at isolated towns.

Constable William Elverd had been on duty in Kojonup in 1862, but had been in the colony as early as June 1846 when a daughter, Elizabeth (later known as Emily), was born to him and his wife, Eliza. In November 1850 his wife Eliza died and he was married again in June 1853 to a widow, Agnes Phillips,[44] who had one son, Thomas Phillips. Prior to coming to Kojonup, Elverd was living in the Vasse. By his second marriage Elverd had six children. The only daughter of this second marriage, Mary Jane, was baptised in the Vasse on 22 June 1856. On the baptismal paper Elverd's occupation was given as 'Police Constable'.[45] On 11 March 1858 a son, John Charles, was born at Busselton, the father being described on the birth certificate as a police officer.

In September 1864, a letter written by the Resident Magistrate of Albany mentions that the constable at Kojonup was instructed that Pensioners at Kojonup were permitted to procure timber for fencing their grants from vacant Government land and that Pensioner Newstead had been fencing a 100 acre tillage lease with timber felled on an adjacent lease 'in the occupancy of Police Constable Elverd'.[46]

The exact site of William Elverd's original home, at this period, is unknown. He acquired locations 52 and 53 (which cover the centre of the present Kojonup town) early in his association with the district and it is assumed that the dwelling was located somewhere on them, possibly north-west of the present 'bottom hotel'. Surviving records that have been found only tend to confuse the issue.

On 27 September 1864, the Superintendent of Police, W. Hogan, wrote to the Colonial Secretary recommending that:

> a reserve of forty acres of land on the town site of Kojonup be declared for police purposes. I am most anxious to see a decent police station and stables erected on Government land and also a fair-sized paddock enclosed to which our police horses can be turned loose at night and thus render their being stolen more difficult than were they to stand in an open stable during the night. The forty acres surrounding the old cemetery would answer admirably.[47]

The letter was duly passed to Surveyor-General Roe who commented at the foot of it: 'the land applied for is vacant and adjoins the south side of lots P. 9 and P. 10'.[48] (A grave is marked on the common boundary of these two lots, on a map drawn up in May 1862).[49]

On 16 November 1864, Hogan recorded:

> I propose . . . to proceed to Eticup to select a reserve for the new police station, authorized by His Excellency, to be established there. Also to mark out a site for new quarters and stables at Kojonup.[50]

(There is reason to believe that previously the horses were kept on Chipper's location which was outside the Kojonup townsite.) Hogan's scheme does not seem to have come to complete fruition, according to statements written by a succeeding Superintendent of Police, N. H. Crampton, in November 1866, when discussing the redistribution of police stations on the Albany road. He wrote:

> At the 125 Mile station the Mounted Constable is at present living in a hired house some distance off the road while his horse is supposed to be stabled and foraged at the Landlord's house fully a mile distant.
> At the Kojonup Station a similar objection exists, the Station being a unfinished Government building not visible to strangers from the road without either stabling or water, both these requisites being a quarter of a mile distant from the Station at a Settler's.[51]

The letter continued by suggesting:

> that a Station be erected on the Government reserve (or arrangements be made with Mr Elverd for the hire of, or otherwise provide a suitable Station) at the 160 Mile for the Constable now stationed there.[52]

From events in 1866 it is obvious that, wherever William Elverd was living, he was comfortably placed. In March 1866, Bishop Hale and party started out from Perth for Albany. Also making the journey south was Sergeant Loton who was of great assistance to the Bishop's party in guiding them over the bad places along the road. On Friday 23 March, they left Williams and made their midday halt at Hogan's (the previous Superintendent of Police). To country folk miles from civilization, time meant little; each day was very much the same as the next. Thus, when the Bishop (who had sent them warning of his coming) arrived, the Hogans were caught completely by surprise, thinking it was only Thursday! However, they hustled about and tried to make amends and 'were entirely attentive and kind'.[53]

It was dark when the travellers reached Gibbs's at the 138 mile. All the male members of the Gibbs family were in the bush but the Bishop 'did very well. Slept in the hut', whilst Kenworthy, his curate, slept in the hayhouse.[54] The Bishop was very impressed with the abundant and excellent water on hand. The place, he wrote, 'belongs to Cornwall. The old place by the Beaufort Bridge is deserted'.[55]

More than likely, during the journey Sergeant Loton had proudly boasted to the Bishop of his wife's little bush school. The Bishop would have been exceedingly interested as he had identified himself closely

with education on his arrival in the colony. While the travellers settled
in at their quarters (this is presumed to be at Chipper's, where the
horses were changed) Loton rushed on to Kojonup to alert his wife
and as many of the school children as possible, it being Saturday. In
his diary the Bishop wrote:

> Went to the school. Nine or ten came on short notice, heard them
> and inspected copy books. Promised to give prizes at 9 a.m. to-
> morrow.[56]

What a terrifying experience for those first little Kojonup school children! To be jolted out of a placid autumn holiday, to be scrubbed and
spruced up, at a minute's notice, and sent off helter-skelter to school
was a nightmare enough, but worse was to follow. Standing stiffly to
attention, with their flushed faces hidden in their readers, their quiver-
ing lips tried to mouth the difficult words for the distinguished visitor
as their teacher hovered nearby, obviously anxious for them to be a
credit to her. The ordeal over they dashed home to tell their parents
of the presentation on the morrow and to spend the remaining hours
of their lost holiday wondering who would be the honoured recipients
of the prizes. In the interim Bishop Hale recorded that he painstakingly
wrote the names of the successful pupils in books he had brought with
him, but failed to record in his diary, for posterity, the names of the
able students.

The next day was Palm Sunday and, as promised, the prizes were
presented at 9 a.m. At 11 a.m. a service was held and 'all who could
come were there'.[57] Two children were baptised: John, son of Mary
and Ambrose Forsythe, and William Thomas, son of Emily and William
Jones, the same Jones who had previously worked for the Hassells.
He had now settled at Kojonup, as a blacksmith, after marrying Emily
Elverd, William Elverd's daughter by his first marriage.

The William Elverds had not been present at the service as Mrs
Elverd was ill so the Bishop later called at their home to baptise two
of their children, Robert and Henry. In recording the baptism the
Bishop described Elverd as the 'Sergeant of Police'.[58] It is possible that
Hale had known Elverd at the Vasse, with which district his wife,
Sabina Hale, was closely associated.

At 3 p.m. the Bishop took his departure and made for Balgarup
where he was the centre of a very unsavoury incident.

> Got to Balgarup, 170 miles. I stopped at the bottom and sent Ken-
> worthy up to the house; he returned, bringing a man, by no means

sober, who said he was in charge. We could have forage and use the house; so we went up. Evident signs of a woman and soon the voice of a female apparently drunk, like the husband. He seemed to be threatening her and she was crying but nothing happened. We had met a cart, three horses and three men conveying the remains of H. L. Cole to Perth. He died at Albany on Sunday last. From this party the caretaker at Balgarup got the drink. They (in the cart) had apparently been drinking also.
26th Mon.
The 'caretaker' seemed pretty much himself this morning. Paid him 6/0 for forage.[59]

This episode was probably discussed by the Bishop with acquaintances on his travels, particularly his friend the Resident Magistrate of Albany, and would have only verified for some their conviction that there was increasing drunkenness along the road. Among the visitors who called to see the Bishop in Albany were Messrs Graham, Edward Spencer and Van Zuilecom.

On his return the Bishop was determined to bypass Balgarup and camped at the 186 mile peg on the night before and made all preparations for a speedy departure in the morning. He arrived at Kojonup at midday on 25 April 1866 and:

Stayed at Elverd's, at their request,—very comfortable. Visited the school. Service in Pensioner Barracks. Attendance very fair.
26th Thursday.
Left 8-30 to reach Gibbs about 2 p.m. Drizzling rain. After very heavy and constant. Mrs Gibbs had asked for service—but no one came. Baptised her child and had prayers.[60]

(The baptised infant was Annie, the daughter of William John and Harriet Gibbs.)

In recording his meeting with Van Zuilecom the Bishop introduces another who was becoming increasingly aware of the potential of the Kojonup district. The Van Zuilecoms were descended from a very old Dutch family which had migrated to England at the time of William of Orange. In 1852, Captain C. L. Van Zuilecom and his family arrived in Victoria and settled in Seymour, where his son, Louis Frederick, remained for thirteen years. The Captain and other members of the family went to India where the Captain was employed by the shipping company, the P. & O. Line, as an agent. In 1866, all the family including Louis, his wife and their three children, came to Albany. The Captain wrote at a later date in explanation: 'I received my prospects of promotion in India, by preferring the more salubrious climate of Australia, even at a sacrifice of emolument'.[61] In referring to his past he wrote: 'I hold satisfactory certificates and testimonials as an officer in Her Majesty's Coast Guard Service, as well as a Commander for several years in the Merchant Service.'[62]

About this time the merchant John McKail had acquired location 3, the property known as Sutherlands, from Joseph Spencer, for the sum of £250. It was arranged for Captain Van Zuilecom to buy it on terms. His sons would live there while the Captain continued to work for the P. & O. Line in Albany. At the same time the Captain 'leased approximately 30,000 acres on various points along the Balgarup River . . . on three sides of the 640 acres held by Spencer and would naturally have had the Mooradup Pool had Spencer not leased it first'.[63] Louis Frederick Van Zuilecom, his wife and three small children and at least one of his brothers were living at location 3, just two miles from Kojonup in 1867 when Bishop Hale made another visit to Kojonup— a very brief, rushed one. He was hurrying to Albany to connect with a ship to take him to England. On this trip he was a passenger on Chipper's cart. At Hogan's, on 27 June, they were considerably delayed, while Chipper negotiated some private business with Hogan. This meant they did not reach the Beaufort halt until well into the evening. Here, there now resided people with the same surname as the Bishop. Time was short so the party was able to sleep only until midnight (in the cart house, between two trusses of hay) and after a quick cup of of tea they were off again.[64] They arrived at Chipper's at Kojonup in good time for breakfast, although not in the best of circumstances. The place was 'occupied by an elderly couple, dirty in the extreme.'[65] Fresh horses were quickly harnessed and with a crack of the whip the impatient travellers were off once more. At midday they were at the 179 mile and by midnight they had reached the Gordon River. Altogether, fifty-five miles had been covered, much of it in the dark. When the travellers finally alighted the heavens opened and the rain fell. One of the party, called Cousins, visited a nearby prison road camp and fetched a firestick to light a fire over which supper was prepared, with great discomfort. A tent was pitched to shelter the weary travelstained passengers as they slept. Such were the conditions one endured on the Albany Road in the 1860s. Whether it was a bishop or a humble conditional-pardon man the hazards were much the same.

Although the rain was certainly not welcomed by Bishop Hale and his companions it would most likely have been received with great rejoicing by the farmers of the southern regions. Drought conditions had existed for some time and this in conjunction with falling wool

14   Above. 'Glen Lossie' in
1927 when owned by
W. H. Penny

15   Below. Side terrace and
gardens of 'Eeniellup' 1970, now
owned by J. Egerton-Warburton
(pp. 112, 134)

16 Foley's wattle and daub
first home on 'Woodenbillup'
with Wayne Marinoni, son of
the property's present owner;
note flattened kerosine tins

17   Mud-bat home built by Hettner, one of Cherry Tree
Pool's early settlers

18   Above left.   G. Hunt of Boscabel uses a steel-wheeled wagon to cart water about 1920

19   Above right.   Hal McKenney, (1970), with Kojonup district's first caterpillar tractor owned by McKenneys of 'Glenoaklands' who used it to excavate many of the district's dams

20   Horse-driven chaffcutter on the Haggerty property, possibly 1906

21   A mould-board, horse-drawn plough on Squatter Jones' property, possibly early 1900s

prices and lower meat values had caused the boom period to gradually wane. Poorer prices did not encourage or induce extensive cultivation, particularly among the smaller agriculturalists. To be offered take-it-or-leave-it prices after driving pigs all the way to Albany or be told that corn could be procured from Adelaide far cheaper than that being offered locally sapped the enthusiasm for farming and other pursuits were seen as more lucrative.

The Norrish family were badly affected. The heavy years of worry and hard work were beginning to tell on Richard Norrish and in 1867 he had a stroke from which he never fully recovered. For a time he lost the power of speech and as he was unable to manage the family's affairs the responsibilities fell to his sons, particularly the second eldest, Thomas, who was still at home.

Although Thomas had no more than a few months schooling all his life, he was a natural student and had developed a liking for books. On inquiring from the various storekeepers he learnt that his parents were deeply in debt. So bad was the situation that more than once the thought of clearing out crossed the minds of the boys. But a family that has surmounted problems as the Norrishes had done for so many years does not willingly turn tail and run. Thomas discussed the matter with the storekeepers who advised him to keep striving and they would not push for a settlement.[66] In desperation to do all possible to aid their beloved father the Roman Catholic members of the family prevailed upon him to be baptised to their religion and this was done at Warkelup on 23 September 1867, his eldest son and daughter acting as godparents.[67] Richard Norrish was then fifty-five.

In accordance with the policy to make full use of all remaining convicts before the British Government removed their officials and finance, a great deal of paper work was passed back and forth about this time between the Colonial Secretary's Office, the Clerk of Works and the police, regarding the working parties on the Albany Road and the police stations needed at different points. Although there had never been any bushranging to the extent known in the eastern colonies a number of convicts had escaped, as evidenced by the remarks of the Governor in November 1866, when commenting on the Albany Road: 'Police Supervision is absolutely necessary throughout the whole line of road, now much resorted to by convicts, illegally at large and other offenders'.[68] In the same month he gave orders for 'a rough bush station to be erected by Convict labour on the reserve',[69] at Kojonup, which reveals that previous plans had not been executed. Warder McMahon and party were detailed to build police stations at the

Gordon and the 131 mile peg. With twelve men working, each station had to be completed in two months. In February 1867 Warder Gray was instructed to move to Kojonup with his party to attend to the road between Kojonup and Balgarup, which was considered to be in a very poor state. Meanwhile, some people in Kojonup did not approve of the idea of a mere bush station for the town and negotiations were under way with officials to reconsider the decision. It was decided to try to exchange the old police reserve in Pensioner Road for a site owned by William Elverd on the Albany Road.

The heightened activity might have permitted an amount of laxity to creep into the handling of the convicts but it was very quickly jolted to a stop when in May 1867 the news spread like wildfire of the escape of three prisoners, reputed to be dangerous, from Fremantle gaol. The three escapees were William Graham, Thomas Scott and George Morris. The latter was shot and captured almost immediately but the other two continued south through York and Beverley. The progress (both real and imaginary) of the outlaws was rumoured everywhere. They were still at large in August and were said to be living off the land and on goods they pilfered from shepherds' huts. Inhabitants in all the southern areas such as Kojonup felt their lives were in jeopardy.

On 10 August four policemen, O'Keefe, Chester, Grover and O'Connell assisted by some Aborigines were detailed to track the convicts. The hunt spread from Moir's station on the Salt River to the hut of William Webb, a shepherd, through the Kyblup Plains to Treasure's station Martinup on to Eticup and hence to Quartermaine's. Word was received that nearby settlers, Haddletons, had seen the men getting away with some provisions from the Haddleton's dwelling. As the search party moved around information was passed to them by Aboriginal groups but innumerable hindrances were encountered. Rain, herds of cattle and flocks of sheep obliterated tracks and sometimes the trail led over gravelly country on which no footprints could be detected.

On 20 August the party's trackers returned from reconnoitring in the Tambolup (*sic*) area with fresh news that the men were nearby. The trackers were apparently influenced by the police to go to the suspected area, under the cloak of darkness, and spy out the land. They returned highly excited to say that they had discovered the absconders in a hut. Graham, the tallest, with gun in his hand, was walking up and down, as if on guard, while the other was resting inside. The police were criticized severely for what was generally thought to have followed. One report said that the police went to the hut and finding both escapees inside, fired into it. The general opinion was that the police sent the Aborigines ahead, with guns, to shoot into the hut. Whatever the case, the two men fled their shelter, only partly dressed and taking nothing but their guns. Graham, however, had been shot in the leg and arm and two days later turned up at a shepherd's camp. He handed in his gun and sent the shepherd with it to Quartermaine, to request that the police be notified. From here he was taken by horse back to Eticup but he found riding painful, so a cart and harness were hired from W. Noonan, junior, and with the police horses in the shafts he was escorted to Albany by Constables O'Keefe and Chester. It was not until 4 September that Scott was finally apprehended in the Blackwood district by Constable McAlinden, and lonely settlers felt they could breathe freely.

Both Constables O'Keefe and Chester proved themselves unequal to their senior office. It was claimed that Grover was quite fearless and exhibited great skill in tracking; also that he had offered to go forward to arrest the absconders in a legal manner with O'Connell, who had offered to accompany him, but they were overruled by their superiors. The official conclusion coincided with the feeling of the populace:

> members of the force should see that even in the capture of men who are reputed to be desperate, neither the laws of the country nor the laws of manliness are to be violated on the impunity. . . . It was right to use the utmost caution but here caution degenerated to cowardice.[70]

Western Australia's penal period could be said to have ended with excitement after seventeen years of moderation. The arrival of the last batch of convicts on 10 January 1868 marked the official close of the convict era. Economically it had been a success, due to the greater activity it engendered in the farming communities. Yet there is little evidence of disappointment at its closure; nor any marked change in the tempo of the life of the colony.

Directly and indirectly Kojonup had benefitted immensely from transportation. In this, the town was typical of other sleepy little hollows of 1850. Along with the increase in population more land had been cultivated and public services had been established in the town for the first time. The north-south arterial road, though still far from perfect, had been improved and had a variety of regular traffic, which kept the inhabitants partly informed on events elsewhere.

Due to its particularly historical birth, based mainly on a group of close-knit families with a common military background, the town of

Kojonup developed its own unique character, which was to be evident to the perceptive for many years to come. Metaphorically, the fabric of the town had been woven and it was decidedly homespun.

REFERENCES

[1] Bishop Hale Diary, p. 12 (309A, held in Battye Library, Perth).

[2] *Perth Gazette*, 26 August 1853, p. 3.

[3] *Ibid.*

[4] *Ibid.*

[5] Bishop Hale Diary.

[6] Thomas Norrish Diary, p. 11 (copy in K.H.S.Recs.).

[7] *Ibid.* p. 12.

[8] W.A.L.Dept.Recs. (copy in possession of author).

[9] Map in O. P. Kost, Field Book, 19 May 1862, p. 54 (held in W.A.L.Dept.; copy in K.H.S.Recs.).

[10] W.A.L.Dept.Recs. (copy in K.H.S.Recs.).

[11] W. H. Graham Diary (in possession of C. L. Hassell).

[12] *Ibid.* 9 March 1860.

[13] *Ibid.* 28 March 1860.

[14] *Ibid.* 21 April 1860.

[15] *Ibid.* 25 April 1860.

[16] *Ibid.* 18 September 1860.

[17] *Ibid.* 4 and 5 October 1860.

[18] *Ibid.* 16 November 1860.

[19] *Ibid.* 22 November 1860.

[20] *Ibid.* 8 September 1861.

[21] R. Stephens, 'Fairfield and its Founder', historical paper (copy in Kat.H.S.Recs.).

[22] C.S.O.Recs., 372, 23 March 1857 and 24 November 1857 (Battye Library).

[23] C.S.O.Recs., 475, 17 April 1861.

[24] C.S.O.Recs., 475, 21 March 1861.

[25] *Inquirer*, 4 September 1861.

[26] Discharge certificate of Sergeant John Tunney (in possession of D. J. Tunney, Kojonup).

[27] *Dudbrook* papers in C.S.O.Recs., 273, 1853.

[28] Baptismal Recs., Roman Catholic Church, Albany.

[29] W.A.L.Dept.Recs. (copy in possession of D. J. Tunney).

[30] G. F. Wieck, Notes on Enrolled Pensioners (Battye Library).

[31] Baptismal Recs., Roman Catholic Church, Albany.

[32] C.S.O.Recs., 268, 19 August 1853.

[33] Marriage Recs., Roman Catholic Church, Albany.

[34] *Ibid.*

[35] *Emma Eugenia* papers in C.S.O.Recs., 412.

[36] David Mossenson, 'A History of State Education in Western Australia', p. 65 (Ph.D. thesis, University of Western Australia, 1961; Battye Library).

[37] Blue Book [Colonial Office] June 1870 (Battye Library).

[38] L. V. MacBride, historical paper, Kat.H.S., 1941 (copy in K.H.S.Recs.).

[39] C.S.O.Recs., 541, 13 October 1864.

[40] *Ibid.*

[41] Information collected from Postmaster-General's Department by K.H.S.

[42] *Perth Gazette*, 29 January 1864.

[43] Baptismal Recs., Roman Catholic Church, Albany.

[44] Facts supplied by Registrar-General's Office.

[45] Baptismal paper (in possession of Alger family, Kojonup).

[46] C.S.O.Recs., 545, 7 September 1864.

[47] C.S.O.Recs., 542, 27 September 1864.

[48] *Ibid.*

[49] Map showing Pensioner allotments, Kojonup townsite, in O. P. Kost, p. 51.

[50] C.S.O.Recs., 542, 16 November 1864.

[51] C.S.O.Recs., 579, 7 November 1866, pp. 2, 3.

[52] *Ibid*, p. 4.

[53] Bishop Hale Diary, p. 97.

[54] *Ibid.*

[55] *Ibid.*

[56] *Ibid.*

[57] *Ibid.*

[58] *Ibid.*

[59] *Ibid.*

[60] *Ibid.* p. 100.

[61] C.S.O.Recs., 602, 30 October 1867.

[62] *Ibid.*

[63] W.A.L.Dept.Recs. (copy in K.H.S.Recs.).

[64] Stephen and Emma Hale arrived in the colony in 1840 aboard the *Simon Taylor*. Stephen was a bricklayer and potter by trade and pursued his work in the district of Guildford for some years. Many of the old buildings in that district were made of bricks fired by him. It is said that in winter he would go to the Abrolhos Islands for a couple of months to catch fish which he dried and salted for lean times.

[65] Bishop Hale Diary, p. 138.

[66] Thomas Norrish Diary, p. 12.

[67] Baptismal Recs., Roman Catholic Church, Albany.

[68] C.S.O.Recs., 579, 14 November 1866, p. 1.

[69] *Ibid.* p. 4.

[70] C.S.O.Recs., 599, 19 October 1867.

7

Acquiring New Ideas

SLY GROG

As early as 1859 there were whispers that excessive drunkenness existed at Kojonup. When sweeping allegations of intemperance among the Pensioners reached the ears of that body's champion, Lieutenant-Colonel Bruce, he rushed to their defence, with his pen. While admitting that two had been struck off duty for such an offence he objected strongly to the contention that they were all guilty, when it was unsupported by one particle of evidence.[1] That liquor was reaching Kojonup was obvious but the source of the supply was a close-kept secret. Bruce suspected the mail contractor and a teamster working for a Perth merchant, but both strongly denied the accusation.

The undercover sale of liquor apparently continued and in time, as was bound to happen, someone saw the possibility of a profitable legal business. This person was S. R. Toovey who applied on 4 January 1861 'for a Road-Side Inn at the Balgarup Brook, on the Road between Albany and Perth, about ninety miles from Albany'.[2] This application was accompanied by a letter from three Justices of the Peace of Albany —H. Camfield, A. Trimmer and E. M. Spencer—in which they strongly recommended the establishment of such a sale of spirits in the Kojonup district.[3] The Governor was not to be persuaded and commented on the corner of the letter: 'Inform the Magistrates that it is considered inexpedient to grant a license at this place'.[4] (Even so, all future owners of 'Balgarup', up to the present day, have referred to the site as 'the pub paddock'.)

To attempt to prohibit the sale of all liquor, on a major road frequented by regular carters all anxious to indulge possible customers, was futile. In June 1861, Webb and Theodore Krakouer both had carts on the road; and Chipper had as many as three carts operating. Police Constable William Elverd was ordered not to report cases of fighting and drunkenness at Kojonup, 'but to confine himself to escorting Pensioners and mails, and such other duties, as they arose',[5] because the centre was too isolated, with no Resident Magistrate to support any charge.

Over the years, with his house built and his acres fenced and cultivated, the settler found time hanging heavily on his hands. The years of yarning and close habitation had revealed all there was to know of his neighbour. The surrounding countryside, once so intriguing, was as familiar as the palm of his hand. Remoteness and a sparsity of money only heightened the tedium, and life became unbearable when tragedy struck: a baby died or a crop failed or livestock realized a pittance. At such times a drop of grog warmed the cockles of the heart. Under its befuddling influence one could laugh again at a neighbour's ancient joke and even recall a few oneself, or dance a jig with the wife.

News of these occasional revellings spread to others who were likewise starved of amusement, and more and more folk were attracted to the centre as it became known that liquor was easily obtainable and that the police were turning a blind eye to the drinking. By 1867 it was officially stated that:

> Kojonup has become notorious as a most drunken and lawless place. The population there and in the neighbourhood is becoming numerous, and a good deal of wrong is submitted to and many offences looked over because of its distance from a magistrate.[6]

The embarrassment inflicted upon Bishop Hale, at Balgarup, would have been considered degrading to him by those in authority. It indicated that drastic action was badly needed: to prevent employees from neglecting their masters' interest, due to intoxication; to ensure that road gangs of prisoners were not exposed to the popular beverage; and to provide suitable lodgings for the travelling public to prevent further degradations to officials. Contempt for the law was so prodigious that in the opinion of the Albany Resident Magistrate:

> spirits were as easily obtained all along the Perth Road as if they were allowed to be sold. I am told that a stream of drunkenness follows the carriers' carts.[7]

In October 1867, two carters of Kojonup were taken to court for 'being notorious grog sellers'.[8] It was divulged, in evidence, that ten shillings was the profit on one gallon of gin.

Six years had passed since Toovey had applied for a roadside inn licence, and with such exorbitant profits being made it was inevitable that others would see the opportunities existing for a legitimate business.

William Elverd had been expanding his activities in the district to the extent where he now owned a big proportion of the centre of the town. This included both sides of the Albany Road as well as the farm block just west of the town known as 'Ongerup', and over 6000 acres of lease-land. Then in 1866 Elverd applied for a publican's licence.[9] He was informed that a permit would only be granted for a wine and beer licence and would necessitate the building of accommodation for travellers, which Elverd, at first, was not inclined to do.

About the same time 'two sons of Sergeant Tunney applied for a gallon license and a Publican's license or a Wine and Beer license'[10] and were told that if they had accommodation for travellers they were likely to be successful in obtaining the required licence.

However, Elverd had a change of mind. It was probably about this period that he was approached regarding the swapping of the old police reserve for some of his land adjacent to the main road. The advantages of owning a public house opposite to the proposed police station appealed to him and he immediately contacted the authorities with his intentions:

> to build a house at Kojonup (opposite the site for the new Police Station) suitable for a Public House and all the necessary accommodation for travellers.[11]

He was willing:

> to enter into a bond not to allow any of the Pensioners at or about Kojonup to have liquors on credit, not to sell or dispose of spirits by the gallon or large quantities to be carried away to Shepherds or others.[12]

As a result of this new application Sergeant Tunney and his family were warned not to erect any building until the outcome of Elverd's proposition was known, as it was very unlikely that Kojonup would be considered capable of supporting two public houses.

By a special licensing meeting held in July 1868, William Elverd was granted, for the sum of £5, a publican's licence for the half-year ending 31 December 1868.[13] Kojonup now possessed its first hotel. It was situated on the north side of the present 'bottom hotel' and was known simply as Elverd's Hotel. In October 1870 the Kojonup Inn owned by the Tunney family was opened for business.[14] The powers-that-be must have decided that if one publican was 'likely to assist the Police to put down illicit selling'[15] two publicans would permit even greater control.

Kojonup was to benefit even further from its unfortunate intemperance. With a public house contemplated in the town the authorities decided that it was vital 'for the comfort and good order of the society and of the road between Perth and Albany, that a Magistrate should be appointed'[16] in the district. Inquiries were made but no one who was willing to 'undertake the office gratuitously'[17] could be found. The Resident Magistrate at Albany asked what salary and duties could be expected, supposing a suitable person was available. Later correspondence revealed that the queries were made on the behalf of Captain Van Zuilecom who in October 1867 was still at Albany but who intended, if he could 'make arrangements for so doing, to join his sons, who were within two miles of Kojonup'.[18] He was 'a person of much respectability and was for some years a member of the Bench of Victoria, residing and acting at Sandridge'.[19]

In applying for the position the Captain showed confidence in Kojonup's future, despite the derogatory opinions prevalent at the time.

> I am quite aware that in a small but increasing Township like Kojonup the Magisterial duties at present would be comparatively light, but as the population increases and the country around about appears favourable for occupation from what I have seen of it, that increased Police supervision will be found desirable.[20]

Nevertheless, he was a business man and was not prepared to be out of pocket.

> I must take this opportunity of stating that although I am not a needy man I should at the same time expect a moderate remuneration for my services, which of course I would engage to give with fidelity and trust impartially.[21]

Van Zuilecom was informed that there was no salary in the estimates for a Justice of the Peace at Kojonup, but that when he had removed there His Excellency would endeavour to allocate some small salary to him for the performance of any magisterial duties that might be entrusted to him.[22] It was not until December 1870 that Van Zuilecom was sworn in as Justice of the Peace (thereby becoming the district's first Resident Magistrate) and a request was made for 'Acts of Council, some printed forms and a supply of Stationery so as to enable him to carry out his duties at his residence in Kojonup'.[23] At some time prior to this date it can be presumed that he had moved to his Kojonup property 'Quanandrup' (which was officially referred to by this name as early as March 1871)[24] and his son Louis, and his family, had gone to live at their homestead block, 'Pardellup', nearer their extensive lease-land.

BASIC BUILDINGS

Towards the end of the 1860s Kojonup was experiencing a miniature building boom with public houses ambitiously going up and the first substantial police station being constructed by convicts. The centre of the town seemed to be shifting from the first durable building, to an area slightly east. The authority of the military which had been for so long the backbone of the little settlement was abrogated bit by bit. No longer did the inhabitants look for protection and command to the gallant little barracks, defensively sited on its hill. The new seat of law, the police station, was located at the bottom of another hill, convenient to the main road. Likewise, it was no flimsy structure, as those who demolished it almost a century later were to discover. In March 1869, Thomas Chipper was successful in obtaining the tender for supplying the timber and shingles for its construction.[25]

If the majority of the adults of the community disregarded the barracks the children were still very much a part of its history. They continued to trudge up the hill for their formal education. However, like its predecessor, the building had been abused over the years and was badly in need of repair. Furthermore, what was acceptable when it was built was frowned upon in 1869. There was a growing awareness by the authorities of elementary standards of hygiene and basic needs.

For some time the General Board of Education had arranged official visits and examinations of the colonial schools, and the Reverend B. Delaney of Albany had been responsible for visiting the Kojonup school. On his last call he had raised a subject which ever since had worried the Sergeant of Pensioners, Robert Loton, and his schoolteacher wife. On hearing of Thomas Chipper's successful tender for the proposed police station, a deferential Loton hit on a solution to his problem and penned the following letter to the Governor, possibly assisted and most assuredly encouraged by his wife.

Honourable Sir,
I have received the men's pay in the mail. They shall be attended to on the last day of this month. I have nothing extra to report. The conduct of the men on Duty under my command has up to the present date been exemplary.
I beg to state I have received a letter from the Revd. B. Delaney from Albany in which he stated that he will have the school broke

up unless there is two proper waterclosets built for the use of the
boys and girls separate. He spoke of it when here which I mentioned to you before.
I have told him the Barracks belong to the Imperial Government
and that it is your goodness to let the children be educated in it
but I will write to you and that it would be no use in me writing
to the Board of Education about improvement in the Barrack
ground. I also beg to call your attention to the state of the Barracks.
It will be unfit to live in next winter. There is a tender accepted
for timber for the police station. The work could be done by the
Party under Mr McMahon. If there should be any extra carting
required I will do it free of charge so as to get the roof secured.

> I am Honourable Sir,
> Your obedient Servt.
> R. Loton.
> Sergt. in Charge.[26]

This letter was forwarded to the Clerk of Works, James Manning,
and he replied waggishly:

The state of the building is quite as bad as anyone can represent it.
The floor is dirt, the roof is so thoroughly ventilated that it neither
keeps out wind or water. A floor and new shingles are absolutely
necessary, but when tenders were circulated there was only one
sent in and that too exorbitant to be entertained. Should it be
approved tenders for the timber and shingles may be invited and
when on the ground tenders for the work obtained separately. In
that case I will prepare details for the levelling etc. As to privies
there are none or if any it is of the most primitive kind. I need not
say these are necessary.
With regard to the party there building the Police Station I consider that work should not be interfered with but that this work
on the Barracks should be done by contract.

> James Manning.[27]

Thomas Chipper was successful in obtaining the contract for the
mahogany and shingles for the renovations to the barracks, as well as
the police station contract.[28] No longer would fidgety pupils be able
to scuff the dirt floor of the front room. It was to be floored with six
inch boards 'cleaned off smooth and uniform'.[29] Apparently, however,
ceilings were not considered essential and the children would still be
able to gaze up into the hip of the little building and contemplate the
underside of the shingles for inspiration. What the children did when
the workmen disturbed their lessons with their incessant hammering
is not known. Perhaps Mrs Loton held lessons among the great boulders
that were strewn around the site. She is almost certain to have been

relieved when the confusion and noise terminated and she was left with a warmer, cleaner, and weatherproof classroom to face the coming winter.

About this time also, Louis Van Zuilecom began building a permanent house on the family holding ten miles south-west of Kojonup. With confidence and inspiration, he and his wife, their eldest daughter, and his brother Albert, set to work to design and execute a home that they considered functional and suited to both the climate and the life they envisaged. It was a brave and successful attempt which reflected the family's individuality and sturdy independent character. To achieve future ease and comfort the women were prepared to carry buckets on yokes across their shoulders, to fetch water from the supply many chains from the house site. The house was of pisé construction, and not the more common mud brick. (Pisé construction was of stiff clay mixed with gravel and rammed between boards which were removed when the clay hardened.) For greater strength around the fireplace, boulders were dropped into the wet clay. Green saplings were pressed into it over doorways and through long walls to act as ties. It has been said that some of these saplings have been found, during alterations over seventy years later, with the sap still in them and the bark quite fresh. The ceilings were of tin, with six inches of soil laid on them for better insulation. This feature still exists in part of the house. Over the years, the parents' resourcefulness overcame the limitations of finance and distance by using available materials for other projects and by establishing an extensive and varied garden. One of the first trees grown was a cedar which still stands. At another time, an avenue of white mulberry trees was planted to feed Louis' silkworms, whose silk he planned to market profitably. Every year the girls of the family lightheartedly set out on their horses to ride two miles down the track to a group of quandong trees, to gather fruit for jam-making.

The building projects were most likely under way in May 1870, when on the twenty-fifth Constable Carmody, native assistant, visited Van Zuilecom's shepherd at 'Manilup' and Elverd's station at 'Ongerup'; and on the twenty-sixth made a lengthy journey taking in Van Zuilecom's property on the Balgarup River, Hassell's shepherd at 'Yaranup' and W. Jeffries of 'Warrenup'.[30]

Elsewhere in the district, failure was being faced and pride swallowed. At Eticup, strong drink had been the downfall of one of its original pioneers, the inscrutable Solomon Drolf. The mortgagee of his holdings, W. D. Moore of Fremantle, foreclosed and Solomon made his last outward journey; he passed the home of his close neighbour,

W. H. Graham, driving his sole possession, a wagon and team, to reside in Kojonup. One cannot help wondering if the successful Graham looked out from one of the upstairs curtained windows of his fine house to witness the passing of his old acquaintance, and if he recalled sombrely the tobacco, sugar and flour they had lent or borrowed, and the multitudinous ways they had assisted each other in those first few years.

However, what was one's misfortune was another's good fortune. In this case no one deserved the chance more than the recipient, Thomas Norrish, now thirty, with behind him a lifetime of striving, deprivation and unselfishness.

The Norrish family were also in debt to Moore. This influential merchant who in a few months was to be one of the successful members of the colony's first representative Legislative Council made a visit to Kojonup and offered to write off Norrish senior's debts of approximately £400 if Thomas would take over 'Ettakup' which carried 824 sheep and a debt of £700.

> The proposition was that the capital debt, plus ten per cent interest, should be repaid over a period of years from the proceeds of wool sales, and Tom accepted it. In August of that year (1869) he went to Fremantle and Moore supplied him with a plough, dray, harness for three horses, all the rations he needed and a bill for £767. The following November he took his first load of wool 196 miles to Fremantle and returned to Ettakup after an absence of sixteen days. This trip he did for four years and found to his joy after the trip in 1872 that the final installment of the debt had been paid by the proceeds, of the clip and the sum of £3/14/0 remained for him. Besides this two bales of wool which he had been unable to get on the load, still remained at the farm.[31]

The district of Eticup was not unknown to the Norrishes. From W. H. Graham's diary it is obvious that they had some interest there as early as 1860, and particularly with Solomon Drolf. With his debts behind him Thomas felt free to ask Christen Ann Wray for her hand in marriage, and she accepted. After the wedding at St John's, Albany, the couple drove the 100 miles to Eticup in a spring cart, camping two nights on the road. Here with high hopes they settled down to become integral parts of the history of that settlement.

Another of the early Kojonup families was finding life consisted of mixed blessings. Tragedy hit the Tunney family when the youngest son, Thomas, twelve years of age, fell into a deep clay hole at Albany and was drowned, on 29 July 1868. Hearing cries for help, a passing

113

teamster called Henri Larsen rushed to the scene and being a powerful swimmer dived into the muddy water a number of times before he located the child's body and was able to bring it to the surface. Under these tragic circumstances, Larsen was introduced to the Tunney family, an introduction which was to result in his marrying one of the Sergeant's daughters, Catherine, five years later.

Henri Larsen, a tall athletic Dane, had gone to sea at an early age. He suffered the rigorous life of the sailing ships until he was twenty-five. In 1857, anchorage was made at Albany and weary of seafaring he cut and ran. When he met the Tunney family he was employed by John Hassell at Kendenup.

The families of the Pensioners were gradually growing up and spreading their wings. Not for them the Blue-coats of their fathers. In 1869 James Tunney married an Irish girl; the couple settled to farming and became known for miles around for their kindness and ready hospitality to travellers. In 1873 they leased a portion of Balgarup from Joseph Spencer; and in 1880 they bought the 'Gracefield' property of Police Trooper E. M. Fahey, which was situated on Slab Hut Gully. Also in 1873, Robert Loton's daughter, Mary Ann, married a widower, Michael Morris, who was one of the mailmen.

Being on the road between Albany and Perth enabled the simple Kojonup residents to rub shoulders with many important colonists. In 1869, Constable Buck arrived driving the police trap carrying His Excellency, the new Governor, from Albany. This was Sir Frederick Weld. On hand to add to the pomp were Police Constables Barron and Jackaman, while Constable Mowan, a native assistant, was appointed temporary orderly to His Excellency.[32]

Another big event which must have helped to break the monotony occurred on 5 April 1870, when John Forrest arrived with his well-equipped party, on the first stage of his trek to Adelaide via the southern coast, to explore and find a practical land route between east and west. The expedition rested four days at Kojonup and was no doubt visited by all the children of the little village as well as many of their curious parents. From Kojonup, John Forrest led his men through Eticup to make their next camp at Treasure's Martinup property. Within five months they reached their destination, in South Australia.

The year 1870 was memorable for another reason: the inauguration of a representative Legislative Council in which twelve of the eighteen members were elected for five years by propertied voters. A handful of Kojonup inhabitants were eligible to vote and on 14 July Constable Carmody left the police station to distribute electoral cards to the farflung settlers Messrs Marchant, Williams, Evans, Kennedy, Magills, R. Spencer, A. Muir, G. Warburton, A. Walton and T. Campbell.[33] Later in the week he distributed cards to those about the town who were to receive them. Apart from such small official acts of duty the dawning of democracy made very little impact on the ordinary colonists, outside the limits of Perth.

The new Legislative Council, with the energetic Governor Weld in the number one seat, was fully aware of the great need to improve the communications throughout the colony and with the world outside. Up-to-date news was rarely received in the colony and the lack was a constant aggravation. More and more prominent citizens were attracted to telegraph, to overcome the situation. It was decided to make telegraphic contact with London, through South Australia, via the route taken by Forrest along the southern coastline.

On 10 June, J. C. Fleming of the Perth telegraph office called for tenders for the supply of sawn telegraph posts for the Williams-Kojonup section and the Kojonup-Albany section.[34] Two years later Thomas Chipper was busy carting the necessary wire from Albany for the contractors.[35] On 26 August 1872, J. Smith arrived at Kojonup to clear the telegraph line with his five workers, James Hurley, M. Guinty, G. Potter, G. Gustlow and T. Lynch.[36] By December 1872, J. C. Fleming, with six ticket-of-leave men, passed through Kojonup connecting the wire.[37]

Undoubtedly, Kojonup's residents would have benefitted in countless ways from the influx of workers for these contracts and the increased traffic through the town. The public houses would have been the first to have a boost in trade but the sale of local products would have brought a little ready cash to settlers along the road. Some of the district men might have been able to procure work from the contractors, Elsegood and Flindell, as the posts were all cut by hand and carted to the road. A member of the Flindell family, Thomas, settled in Kojonup about 1874, as a blacksmith; three children were baptised in the district between 1874 and 1878.

As the contractors reached each station, they were linked up with Perth. On reaching Williams, a young clerk, Frederick Piesse, acquired the necessary instruction and was placed in charge of the telegraph office there. When the contractors reached Kojonup, the terminus was made at Thomas Chipper's which was conveniently on the main road, and his daughter, Mary Jane Elizabeth, was trained to send and receive the vital staccato sounds. In 1872, the telegraph line between Perth and Albany was completed and these two young people, now known to

115

each other at least by morse code, would have assisted in the relaying of the first messages.

Soon the next stage was begun, along the arid coastal country east of Albany, and on 9 December 1877, Perth received its first telegraph message from London along this line. The shell of isolation had cracked.

If the year 1870 was to be remembered by the Kojonup children, it was for a much more near-at-hand phenomenon. The fifth of September began warm and fine:

> but about 11 the sky became overcast and at 12 there was a heavy snow storm which lasted about one hour. The children at the school house enjoyed for once in their lives the recreation of snow-balling; and at Mr Thomas Chipper's house several snow balls were made of the size of a man's fist. The weather was extremely cold and the natives proportionately astonished.[38]

The task of wresting a living solely from their few acres was becoming increasingly hard for the small land-holders. The withdrawal of the convict road gangs (which had been a ready market for any surplus products and a possible source of contracts) as well as the unseasonable conditions, had made it imperative to supplement incomes in other ways. Another generation was establishing itself and once more sandalwood provided a little extra, although the prices paid fluctuated from year to year. William Elverd is said to have assisted some of his clients (sons of early settlers) to assemble the necessities for a trip to the north-east, in search of stands of sandalwood. In September 1870, E. Quartermaine was recorded in the Police Occurrence Book as paying five shillings for a sandalwood licence and Henri Larsen and Michael Morris are said to have been busily employed in carting the sandalwood to Albany. A special sandalwood receipt from the receiving centre of Albany (printed by Evans Brothers of Melbourne) is held by the Tunney family. It is dated 21 March 1877, and is in receipt for 1 ton, 5 hundredweight, 3 quarters, 25 pounds of sandalwood from James Tunney and is signed by R. Tunney (another of the Sergeant's sons) for J. F. T. Hassell (a son of Captain John Hassell).

Before 1870 closed, the Kojonup Pensioners learnt of the passing, in Perth, of the venerable John Bruce, their loyal friend for so many years. He had been staff officer of the colony's Pensioners for two decades. His death could be said to symbolize the end of a cycle in the colony's history: the passing of the military influence.

For Kojonup this change was to be underlined by another death even closer to home, that of Richard Norrish, senior. On 11 January

1871 he died, worn out at just fifty-eight—denied the chance, by a few months, to witness the genesis of local government in the district in which he had seen so many 'firsts'. Like many ex-British soldiers he was buried in the colony without any rolling of the drums or bugle-call, such as was reserved for heroes of a battle field. Instead of one daring courageous act of annihilation Richard Norrish had for years endured harsh conditions and surmounted countless crises when there was no guarantee of assistance or recognition from any soul besides his own eight dependents. Battling against very heavy odds, with his initiative his most trusty weapon, he founded a future for his family. Their numerous descendants, throughout the length and breadth of Western Australia who continue to contribute in their own particular way to the state's progress, are his lasting and most worthy memorial.

As if by some mighty director, the stage was being cleared, the props placed in position and other actors collected for the next big act in the drama of Kojonup.

THE FIRST ROAD BOARD

From the very earliest days of the colony the upkeep of roads and the management of the internal communications had been a headache for the authorities. As the boundaries of settlement were pushed further out and the population increased, the demands for better roads multiplied. Altogether, 'in 1869, the Colony was said to have 110 miles of roads constructed, forty-seven larger bridges and seventy-nine small'.[39]

The Albany Road in particular, because it was so long and passed through remote tracts of heavily-timbered country, had been always troublesome. Being the thoroughfare between the capital and the main port, it was imperative that the road be in excellent condition at all times, yet rarely was this standard achieved. Visitors to the colony, travelling from Albany to the Swan, did not hesitate to complain of the tedious conditions and the shocking state of the road. After a storm it was nothing for the passengers on the mail cart to have to assist in hauling numerous huge trees from the track in order to continue their journey.

Finally, the new Legislative Council decided that the only feasible way to efficiently supervise road maintenance was to decentralize the work more, by establishing local boards responsible for conserving, improving and making roads.

When the District's Road Act, 1871, was first considered it would seem that Kojonup was overlooked as a centre for a Road Board. For some reason not now apparent, in the *Government Gazette* of 24 January 1871, eighteen Road Boards were announced, including the Plantagenet Road Board but not the Kojonup Road Board. On 2 March 1871 the Plantagenet Road Board had its inaugural meeting and W. H. Graham was one of the members elected. As likely as not some Kojonup residents felt slighted by this omission and the subject could well have been a bone of contention in the local bar-rooms. The settlers of the Blackwood and Williams districts had been similarly overlooked.

Obviously, some behind-the-scenes overtures ensued because on 12 December 1871, a new list of Road Boards was published and this time there were twenty-one, the new ones being Kojonup, Williams and the Blackwood.

Prior to this, on 20 May 1871, the following notice had been posted in Kojonup by the recently-appointed Justice of the Peace, C. L. Van Zuilecom, and a copy forwarded to the Colonial Secretary.

> A public Meeting will be held at 'Elverd's Hotel', Kojonup on Wednesday . . . , 31st day of May at 7.00 in the evening for the purpose of electing a 'Road Board' for the Kojonup District. All persons interested in the state of the roads are requested to attend the meeting. Mr James Manning will be present and give such information as may be required as to the object of the meeting.[40]

When the appointed day came, twenty-two of Kojonup's inhabitants assembled in a spirit of co-operation at the hotel, to inaugurate the district's first local government body. The meeting was chaired by the district's Justice of the Peace, C. L. Van Zuilecom, and when nominations were called the most vocal were Robert Loton, James Tunney, John Tunney, Michael Reilly and S. Shinner, all connected in some way with the Enrolled Pensioner Force. On the other hand, of the seven members elected (Thomas Chipper, W. H. Graham, William Elverd, Robert Loton, Louis Van Zuilecom, Thomas Norrish and James Tunney) only one was a Pensioner and one a descendant of a Pensioner.

The members selected Louis Van Zuilecom to be their chairman and Albert Van Zuilecom and John Cronin were appointed as auditors. (Cronin was the son of a Pensioner who had come to the colony in 1855. Members of the family had been known in the area as early as 1866. He had been proposed by George Norrish.) John Tunney, junior, was employed as secretary, his salary being £20 per year.

The area designated as the Kojonup Road Board was announced as:

Bounded on the Northward by the South boundary of the Williams District; on the Westward by the West bank of the Arthur River and by a line southward from the junction of the Arthur and Balgarup Rivers to the North shore of Lake Matilda; on the South-ward by a line from Lake Matilda to Point Hood.[41]

However from time to time some confusion arose over the boundaries with adjacent Road Boards, particularly with the Plantagenet Road Board, both Boards claiming some identical locations. It was not until 1887 that the boundaries were substantially redesignated.

The Government proposed to distribute almost £9000 among the Boards.[42] Of this sum Kojonup received, as its first quarterly install-ment, £66 8s. 11d. A similar amount was received in October and by the last day of the year there was a balance of £17 1s. 6d.[43]

During the six months, £6 6s. 10d. was spent on books and station-ery; 1s. 6d. on postage stamps; 13s. 6d. to W. Jones for notice boards and the remainder was paid to various people for work done on the Albany Road. J. Carrots was the main beneficiary, receiving altogether £42 6s. 0d. for three contracts. These were to repair twenty-seven chains between the 165 and 170 mile trees; to make a culvert and clear away trees between the 194 and 195 mile trees; and to drain between the 160 and 195 mile trees. Newstead was quick to obtain extra work and combined with a Mr Johnston to repair the main road between the 159 and 161 mile trees, for the sum of £22, plus £7 2s. 6d. for clearing out drains between the 160 and 161 mile trees. Others to benefit were S. Pouton, M. Boddington, T. Parker and W. Harris. (The latter received £5 to keep an eye on the road north of the town, between the 136 and 160 miles during the whole six months.) R. Tunney received £11 3s. 0d. for clearing a tree off the main road, making a dish drain between the 154 and 155 mile trees instead of a culvert, and repairing a culvert between the 158 and 159 mile trees.

The method of assessing payment is perplexing. R. Tunney received only 3s. for clearing a tree off the main road; L. Toovey received 5s. for clearing away a tree between the 204 and 205 mile trees; and S. Pouton received 15s. for clearing two trees from the main line.

In the second year Henri Larsen received £139 10s. 0d. for a contract but very little until 1883 when he once more completed a large contract and received £152 15s. 0d. (The fact that he obtained the licence at the Kojonup Inn in 1874 probably accounts for his disinterest.) When

Loton was the secretary-chairman, in 1881 to 1882, his son-in-law, Michael Morris, was by far the most successful tenderer. Other names to appear in the accounts ledger as the years passed were Reilly, Balmer, Forsythe, Dearle, Delaney, Horley, Treasure, Masters and Watts.

Despite the careful provision made at the inaugural meeting to elect two auditors, when the time came the accounts were examined and found correct by someone else—J. E. C. Hare (Resident Magistrate of Albany) and Robert Tunney. (As a comparison to these modest figures, in the year ending 30 June 1969, the Kojonup Shire Council spent $43,991.37 on road maintenance and $109,928 on road construction.) Unfortunately, the records of these first five years of the Road Board are sparse and fragmentary. Louis Van Zuilecom continued with the Board until 1903. In 1874 and 1875 he performed the duties of both chairman and secretary, receiving the fee of £20 for the latter position. This salary was the same as that paid to Thomas Phillips in 1884 when he became secretary, which he remained for twelve years. (Phillips was a son of Mrs William Elverd, by her first marriage.)

The first indication that Board members regarded themselves as having any responsibility other than the main road was in 1882 when one of the Krakouers received £14 to repair the Spring, the town's official water supply.

The Board was loathe to commence rating, and it is doubtful whether the land-holders would have been in a position to pay them, no matter how trifling. Instead it relied solely on the Government grant to keep its section of the Albany Road in repair. Later, cart licences were collected to augment the income and in 1881 an indefatigable Loton collected £84 5s. 0d. in this way, and charged the Board £6 7s. 6d. for the service.

The first chequebook was bought in December 1882 and was not replaced until 1884. The accounts for 1887 reveal that the chairman, Joseph Spencer, was reimbursed £7 16s. 6d. for personally paying for sundry trees being cleared from the road. In the same year he also received £15 for travelling expenses incurred when inspecting the roads.

After the inaugural meeting the Board continued to meet at Elverd's Hotel. Subsequent meetings held there were on 16 September 1872, and on 6 February, 18 April and 24 April in 1873. By 1 March 1875, meetings were being conducted at the Kojonup Inn where Henri Larsen was the current licensee. The venue of the meetings seems to have changed as frequently as the licences of the local public houses. For instance, in 1885 and 1886 Mrs H. Larsen was paid £2 for the rent of a room for a year. The following year a room was hired from Jas. Flanagan for the same amount. (This was at the 'bottom hotel'.) In 1890 a similar amount was paid to W. House (Mrs E. Treasure's second husband) for a room, and in 1891 a room was rented at the Royal Hotel from Palmer, William Cornwall's son-in-law.

The Kojonup residents were initially enthusiastic to form their own Road Board but there is no substantial evidence that there existed any ardent desire for the democratic way of life. The majority of the inhabitants simply did not have sufficient means or time for such idealism. The vital consideration was how to make a few extra pounds for basic needs. This was the prime reason that only established (not necessarily prosperous) farmers were elected to the first Road Board. No wage-earner could afford to tarry for a meeting when opportunities existed to earn some extra money. Mainly, the Government and locals alike considered that the Road Board was formed to keep the Albany Road in repair, for the convenience of the travelling public and, especially, the mail cart. For instance, in June 1872, the colonial mail was delayed for some time because a culvert was carried away by a heavy flow of water at the 184 mile peg. The mailman reported this to the police constable who recorded that he passed the information on to John Tunney, who was then one of the members of the Road Board.[44] The chief attraction of the Board to most of the locals was the chance it gave of earning a little money close to home.

Ultimately, those men who did give of their time and intellect to the first Road Boards tested and amended the foundations, with the commonsense of the average man, until it assumed the comprehensive form that functions so efficiently today. The present institution, successor of the humble little Kojonup Road Board of 1871, has now, besides 1072 miles of roads to supervise, a programme which extends to the provision of sewerage, health services, traffic control, library, civil defence, bush fire control and sporting and social amenities for a population of 2700 people.[45]

REFERENCES

[1] C.S.O.Recs., 431, 1859 (held in Battye Library, Perth).
[2] C.S.O.Recs., 483, 4 January 1861.
[3] C.S.O.Recs., 483, 7 January 1861.
[4] *Ibid.*
[5] C.S.O.Recs., 602, 8 October 1867.

[6] *Ibid.*
[7] *Ibid.*
[8] *Ibid.*
[9] *Ibid.*
[10] *Ibid.*
[11] *Ibid.* memo.
[12] *Ibid.*
[13] C.S.O.Recs., 621, 8 July 1868.
[14] Main C.S.O. Index, R.M., Albany, October 1870.
[15] C.S.O.Recs., 602, 8 October 1867.
[16] C.S.O.Recs., 602, 14 October 1867.
[17] C.S.O.Recs., 602, 8 October 1867.
[18] *Ibid.* 24 October 1867.
[19] *Ibid.* (Sandridge is old name for Port Melbourne).
[20] *Ibid.* 30 October 1867.
[21] *Ibid.*
[22] *Ibid.* 15 November 1867.
[23] *Ibid.* 663, 14 December 1870.
[24] Police Occurrence Book, 418, 2 March 1871 (Battye Library).
[25] *Government Gazette*, 2 March 1869.
[26] C.S.O.Recs., 643, 10 March 1869.
[27] *Ibid.*
[28] *Ibid.* 1869, Specifications, no. 49.
[29] *Ibid.*
[30] Police Occurrence Book, 418, 25 May 1870.
[31] J. F. Hillman, 'The Life of Thomas Norrish', W.A.H.S. journal *Early Days*, vol. 1, October 1938, p. 23.
[32] Police Occurrence Book, 24 September 1869.
[33] Ibid. 14 July 1870.
[34] *Government Gazette*, 10 June 1870.
[35] Police Occurrence Book, 10 June 1872.
[36] *Ibid.* 26 August 1872.
[37] *Ibid.* 16 December 1872.
[38] *Inquirer*, 14 September 1870, p. 3.
[39] Noel Pavitt Clapham, 'The Development of Local Government in Western Australia 1838-1906', p. 69 (B.A. thesis, University of Western Australia, 1949; Battye Library).
[40] Identical information held by the Kojonup Shire Council and K.H.S., no reference given.
[41] *Government Gazette*, 19 December 1871.
[42] Clapham, p. 83.
[43] Kojonup District Road Board Ledger, 202 (Battye Library).
[44] Police Occurrence Book, 23 and 29 June 1872.
[45] Facts compiled for the Annual General Meeting of Electors of Kojonup Shire, 30 June 1969.

8

||||||||||||||||||||||||||||||||||||||||||||||||||||||||||||||||||||||||||||||||||||||||||||||||||||||||||||||||||||||||||||||||||||||||||

The Seventies

Until the late eighties, when gold was discovered, the colony of
Western Australia made little spectacular progress. The generally
declining progress curve was reflected in Kojonup. On the whole, the
agricultural centres were affected by falling prices for most farm
products, poor seasons and fewer markets. The market for wool was
not so severely affected and those who had the foundations of a flock
were able to make a modest profit. The small land-holders of the
district survived by living frugally, relying on their own resources to
provide their daily diet, and obtaining small contract work whenever
possible. A type of mixed farming was to exist in Kojonup for almost
seventy years. At times it was no more than subsistence farming of
a very low level.

The beginning of the seventies was still favourable for the grain-
grower and J. R. Quigley was encouraged to build a flour mill in
Williams to grind the bumper crops being experienced in the southern
areas. In July 1872, it was reported that the mill had been constantly
at work, due to the good crops from the Arthur, Kojonup and Williams
districts: 10,000 bushels had been ground to that date.[1]

Captain John Hassell would have been one of the big graziers who
was still active and prospering in the district. In 1873 he had the
contract to supply forage to the police in Kojonup. The following year
M. Cronin and L. and A. Van Zuilecom also supplied corn and hay to
the police. According to family records,[2] in 1873 John Hassell held
leases in Kojonup amounting to 75,684 acres including:

Paula Valley (*sic*)	10000	acres
Yarranup	20000	,,
Carlcatup	10000	,,
Warkelup	10000	,,
Unnamed	2250	,,
Jackaneerup (*sic*)	10000	,,
Position uncertain,	6000	,,
possibly adjoining	5534	,,
Yarranup.	1900	,,

It is thought that Frank Hassell was running the Kojonup lands as a separate entity, and this may have continued until the properties were divided among the sons in 1894.

In April 1872, Bishop Hale, on a return trip from Albany, held an evening service on a Tuesday at Elverd's Hotel. Thirty-eight people, including children, were present, among them W. H. Graham and family and Manning, the Clerk of Works. The next morning the Bishop went to Chipper's for breakfast before continuing his journey to the 124 mile peg, where he held another service. He conducted his next service in Kojonup in December the same year, but by then William Elverd had died and the police station was used for worship.

During his first visit it is possible that the Bishop discussed with some of his congregation the passing of the Elementary Education Act, in 1871, by the new Legislative Council. Under this law, district Boards of Education were formed and controlled by a Central Board of Education. Not long after, on 28 May 1872, the district's returning officer, C. L. Van Zuilecom, issued the following notice:

> To the Inhabitants of Kojonup and vicinity.
> By virtue of a writ issued to me by His Excellency the Governor.
> It is hereby notified that on Saturday the eighth day of June that at the hour of Noon, an Election will take place at the Police Station of five persons to form a district Board for Kojonup under the provisions of the Public Elementary Education Act.
> A full attendance is particularly requested.[3]

This meeting was protracted until 4 p.m. and the five members elected were the Reverend B. Delaney, Mesdames Chipper and Elverd and Messrs J. Tunney and W. Weir.[4] A further meeting was held on 2 July to elect a chairman but the constable omitted to record the successful candidate. Later Tunney resigned and his place was taken, appropriately, by Miss Lizzie Robinson, the first white child known to have been born in Kojonup.[5]

Under the new system the antiquated Irish readers were dispensed with and new methods were introduced. Gradually, compulsory schooling was to be enforced for all children between six and fourteen years if they lived less than three miles from a school. The teacher's salary was to be calculated partly on attendance and partly on the results of the regular inspections. By this 'result' system a teacher would be entitled to fifteen shillings for a pass in reading, writing and arithmetic and ten shillings for a pass in geography and grammar. On 13 May 1876 the police constable recorded the arrival from Albany of Adkinson, the school inspector. He was to hold the public school examinations in Kojonup that day, so it is to be presumed that Mrs Loton had to face this ordeal every year until 1885, when her teaching career came to an end with her death. In 1881 she is reported to have received £59 1s. 0d. for teaching fifteen children.

Children were no different in those days: some were good, others not so good. In January 1871 the police caught a settler's son and an Aboriginal boy and brought them before the Resident Magistrate, Van Zuilecom, for removing from William Reilly's hut one single barrel gun, one powder flask, one shot belt, one horse rug, one flannel shirt and a quantity of other articles. Justice was done by the European boy being handed over to his father with instructions for him to be flogged, and the Aboriginal boy being taken in charge by the Magistrate, with a view to retraining him.

C. L. Van Zuilecom seems to have had a very real compassion for the Aborigines and wrote in 1872 that there were:

> several old and indigent natives in this district to whom during winter months a blanket and a little flour would be a most desirable gift. In the season 1871 Mr Hare sent me up ten blankets for distribution. Last winter I received flour which was thankfully accepted. I also gave away during the last two winters about a half ton of flour and a bag of sugar from my own stock but I fear from anticipated short yields of wheat this season I shall not be in a position to repeat the donation, under these circumstances if the Government deems it desirable I shall be very glad to distribute carefully either blankets or flour next winter, to the much infirm and aged natives who may require a little reasonable help.[6]

Probably as a result of this appeal a supply of blankets was sent to Kojonup in August 1873. Many of the needy old Aborigines who received them would have been in the prime of life when the white man had first come to the district. In their lifetime they had been part of two completely different cultures. As they accepted the white man's offerings they must have sometimes reflected and compared the last days of their fathers with the changing scenes of their own.

The new generation of Aborigines was becoming increasingly disenchanted with the white man and his life. They were not interested in working for him, nor in sharing their women with him. As their natural mode of life became more difficult to follow they resorted to stealing to satisfy their craving for the introduced foodstuffs. In April 1871, John Wilmott reported to the constable at Kojonup that a shepherd, Joseph Cherull, at Yarranup, had been robbed of a quantity of flour, tea and sugar by three natives, Balgarup Tommy, Jordie and Mary.

But lawlessness was not confined only to the Aborigines. Constable Armstrong was called to investigate a wide variety of complaints committed by the white population, including drunkenness, disorderliness, stealing a fowl, being out after hours and neglecting a master's business, threatening language, violent assault and even speeding (when a ticket-of-leave man was drunk and furiously rode through Kojonup at night). A 'reversal' of justice was executed when a former convict summonsed an employee under the Master and Servant Act!

A much more serious crime was reported to Constable Armstrong on 8 July 1872 when he was hurrying to Albany on official duty. A settler, William Balmer, had found the decomposed body of ticket-of-leave man 'Yorky' Marriott. Until April, Marriott, 'a quiet, thrifty, hard-working man',[7] had been employed by Thomas Norrish of Eticup, from whom he had received £47 5s. 2d. in wages. He had left to take up a tillage lease that he was purchasing from James Lambe, a tanner and currier. It was situated at Slab Hut Gully, about twenty miles south of Kojonup.

In June another ticket-of-leave man, William McDonald, came to work for Marriott and there was some talk of them going into partnership, if McDonald could obtain some wages owing to him by Thomas Chipper, for sandalwood cutting. The unfortunate outcome of this association exemplified how one ex-convict could make good, given a chance, and another, through a series of set-backs, which undoubtedly bred a feeling of hopelessness, resorted to the vilest of action to gain his own selfish ends.

It was Marriott's custom, each Sunday, to visit his neighbour William Balmer who lived four miles away. According to the Balmers he was always clean and respectably dressed. When he did not turn up for two Sundays, Balmer and 'Yankee' Taylor, who lived at the Balmer's, called to see him on their way out horse-hunting. They discovered the body outside the hut, by a wrecked cart, and all cash missing. It was subsequently proved that McDonald was guilty of murder and he was hanged at Albany on 12 October 1872.

The district had barely recovered from the shock of this crime when Constable Armstrong was called to Balgarup to investigate the killing of Nobby, an Aborigine. Thomas Mustow, who was one of John Elverd's labourers was working with Nobby, log-rolling; he saw another Aborigine, Tommy, attempt to spear Nobby in the leg but Nobby moved and the spear found a more serious spot. The disagreement concerned an Aboriginal woman. In fairness to Tommy, Constable Armstrong explained that it was 'common custom with natives to spear each other in the leg when aggrieved, without at the same time harbouring any intention of inflicting any serious injury'.[8] Nevertheless, Tommy was committed to five years penal servitude at Rottnest, for manslaughter.

In June of the same year Constable Armstrong arrested another Aborigine, Jimmy, suspected of killing a female Aborigine, Polly, employed as a shepherd by Joseph Spencer. In the afternoon, the accused and Polly had been seen at Balgarup by an intelligent half-cast, Bill Warren, and some of the Tunney children. As there were no real witnesses to this killing the accused was found not guilty.

In August 1873 two Aboriginal prisoners had escaped from Constable Fahey and taken his revolver, and it was claimed that the native assistant had done nothing to aid the constable, even when called upon to do so. Elsewhere, similar situations had arisen and the practice of employing Aboriginal constables was gradually dropped.

Meanwhile, life continued more peaceably for others. Sunday, 18 February 1872, was a great day for the Roman Catholics as Bishop M. Griver visited them and confirmed James Shinner, William Reilly, John Tunney, George Norrish, John Annice, Edward McKenna, John Forde, Robert Grover, James Forde, Thomas Forde, Michael Joseph Morris, Alice Haddleton, Joanna Barron, Mary Ann Shinner, Margaret Elizabeth Harris and Rachael (sic) Reilly.[9]

On 9 February 1873, Constable Armstrong and his wife Elizabeth had their small daughter Harriet Agnes baptised by the Church of England clergyman Mr Gegg; then in October, W. Wardell-Johnson baptised W. H. Graham's son, William Montrose.

The admirable way in which Magistrate Van Zuilecom attended his official duties found favour with the authorities and he was asked to consider going to Williams once a month, as a visiting magistrate. In reply to this request Van Zuilecom wrote to the Colonial Secretary:

> I heard you were expected at Kojonup, Saturday evening and hoped to see you before you left on the following morning but am sorry to say the only horse I kept at home managed to get out of the stable, Saturday night and could not be found until after nine o'clock on Sunday morning when I immediately drove over to Kojonup vexed enough, to find you had started on your homeward journey only a few minutes previous. The note I left for you at Mr Tunney's Inn I presume you received.[10]

In this note Van Zuilecom had explained that he could not afford the time to visit Williams every month but offered to go every quarter. This proposition was not acceptable to the authorities and a new magistrate, G. G. Growse, was appointed to Williams. In June 1874 the whole situation was reversed and Magistrate Growse was asked to hold court once a month in Kojonup, owing to the sudden death of C. L. Van Zuilecom on 18 February 1874 at the age of sixty-four. When Van Zuilecom was first taken ill Dr Brown, who was farming at the Arthur River, was brought to Kojonup to attend him but to no avail.

In June 1874 Bishop Hale travelled south to St Werburgh's where he consecrated the little church which had been planned for so long by Lieutenant Warburton. On the Bishop's return journey he recorded that he consecrated the cemetery at Kojonup.[11] He is almost certain to have visited C. L. Van Zuilecom's grave near the huge granite boulders two miles south-east of Kojonup.

The new magistrate was not satisfied with the arrangements at Kojonup and wrote:

> I have the honour to request that the room at the Police Station, used as Court House, be furnished with cupboards and I enclose a tender for the work which I consider reasonable.[12]

In this tender William Jones, senior, agreed to erect a cupboard with two doors, for two pounds.

About this time the social centre of the town was undoubtedly Elverd's Hotel, or as it was more commonly known by then, the Semblance of Old England. Trade was very brisk, mainly due to the popular young barman, Stephen Hale, who in 1875 married Mary Jane Elverd. The 'Semblance' became the headquarters of a very active cricket club; the first known organized match was played against Eticup on 30 July 1874. In a two day match arranged on 5 and 6 November 1874, against the '135 mile' eleven, Kojonup won by three runs the first day and lost by twelve runs on the second day. On 1 December 1874 another match was played against Eticup and the next day the local boys' appetite still not being satiated, a game was arranged between 'the boys of Kojonup upper' and 'the boys of Kojonup lower',[13] the latter being the victors.

Another attraction at the 'Semblance' was the opening of a store in one of the rooms by Abraham Krakouer, in September 1874. How long this arrangement lasted is not known.

On New Year's Day, 1875, Constable Armstrong, and probably most of Kojonup, journeyed to the 125 mile for a race meeting. This was practically the last time many of the people of the district were to see Armstrong. On 10 January, when hunting for the Aborigine Bobbinet who was accused of killing another Aborigine, he was fatally shot by the frightened Bobbinet. This was the same Bobbinet who in 1860 had worked faithfully and contentedly at W. H. Graham's property. A lot of water had flowed under the bridge since those days. When the news reached Kojonup the little community was stunned.

On 19 January Bobbinet was still at large and Louis Van Zuilecom sent one of his Aboriginal workers into town with the message that the killer was thought to be hiding out two miles from Van Zuilecom's. There were no constables at the station so the townsfolk made up a search party of Sergeant Loton, Thomas Chipper, William Reilly, W. Prosser and Stephen Hale, and went to the aid of the Van Zuilecoms, but no trace of the fugitive was found. Bobbinet was eventually captured and before his execution he is said to have written a letter of appeal, with the assistance of a clergyman, to his brother Paddy, entreating him to remain with the worthy Graham and not to fall into lawless ways. A haunting sequel to this story occurred on 31 August when Bobbinet's three children were ordered to Perth in charge of Thomas Chipper.

Before this tragedy had struck Mrs Elverd had been worked into a great fluster on being informed by Constable Hogan that His Excellency Governor Robinson and party would arrive the next month to spend a night and that she was to make arrangements for their accommodation. It requires no stretch of the imagination to picture the scenes that ensued; the scrubbing, dusting, washing and cooking that a one night stay by Governor Robinson at the old 'Semblance' involved for Mrs Elverd and her helpers.

Many times in the past Kojonup had been maligned by the authorities for its intemperance but the boot was on the other foot in 1876. On 10 June of that year Sub-Inspector Finlay sent the following lengthy telegram to the Superintendent of Police:

Lance Corporal Carmody reports 'The Resident Magistrate Mr Growse came to the station and opened court morning of 31st ultimo, he was drunk, at noon adjourned, came again at 1 p.m. to resume business, he was much more intoxicated and had to be laid on a sofa for considerable time before he could stagger back to Hotel, next morning, came again Drunk, tried to do business and acted in a most extraordinary manner. Both days the confusion and scene in court may be easily imagined but hard to describe.[14]

In the meantime, there had been considerable pairing off of the younger generation. John Norrish had been courting Margaret Noonan; and Henry Quartermaine had been a frequent visitor to Warkelup where the little Matilda Mary had grown into a fine young woman. As no clergyman of their faith was due at Kojonup in the near future the young couples decided to go to Albany and have the Reverend B. Delaney perform a double wedding. It is said that on the appointed day Margaret Noonan, who obviously inherited her mother's inexhaustible spirit, walked the four miles to Warkelup and from there she and John travelled to Martinup where they met up with the other young bridal couple. With various members of their respective families they boarded a wagon and gaily set off for Albany. The ceremony was conducted on 4 February 1875, and for her witnesses Margaret Noonan chose her sister and brother-in-law, Eleanor and Michael Cronin, whilst Matilda Mary chose her sister Anna Maria Treasure and her brother Joseph Norrish.

The last of the Norrishes, George, was married two years later, on 6 August 1877. He married Margaret Sheehan, a young girl who had come from Perth to be governess to the Treasure children. George and Margaret set up home at a property half-way between Warkelup and Eticup called 'Oakfarm'. Margaret was to live to the remarkable age of 102.

Another notable wedding was that of the two young telegraphists at Kojonup and Williams. It is said that they had pursued their courtship by morse code. Their wedding was held at the humble little barracks by the Reverend W. Wardell-Johnson. Many years later this capable young couple, Mary Jane Elizabeth Chipper and Frederick Henry Piesse, were to dwell in a much more splendid building, the magnificent 'Kobeelya', in the new centre of Katanning which Piesse was to be instrumental in founding.

But that was a long way in the future. For the present, the newlyweds went to live at Williams and when Piesse was busily engaged as clerk of court his wife attended to his telegraph duties. Piesse, who was earning £20 for his job as clerk, applied for a raise and in supporting his claim the magistrate described him as 'a very painstaking officer who gives me great satisfaction'.[15]

As all these young people made their great plans for the future, for others of Kojonup their hour had come.

Solomon Drolf had been eking out an existence in a hut at Thomas Chipper's. One cold Sunday in June 1877, Mrs Chipper thoughtfully sent some food by her son George and a farmhand, Robert Donovan, to the old man who was confined to his bed. The invalid was feeling the cold so his visitors made a fire in the fireplace. One of the big logs used must have been hollow and after the men had departed it flared up and soon the whole hut was ablaze. The old man somehow struggled outside and was still alive when Mrs Chipper and others came racing to the scene, but he died not long afterwards. What unfulfilled dreams of the youthful Drolf were buried with his aged body will never be known.

On the other hand Eleanor Noonan, at the age of seventy-four, was fit as a fiddle and had accomplished much of what she had planned. Her children were all happily married and settled on their own properties. Being still very active the capable old Eleanor enjoyed visiting her various children. In February 1877 she was staying with her daughter, Mrs Grover, of 'Indinup' and it was arranged for her son-in-law's brother Robert to drive her to visit her other daughter, Mrs Michael Cronin, who with her husband had taken up land eighteen miles to the east. Not far from Indinup the horse bolted and the gallant old lady was thrown from the cart and killed instantly. The stunned young driver rushed back to Indinup with the tragic news and soon all Kojonup was mourning with the grieving family.

In September 1876, the widowed Mrs Elverd died. The hotel and the Elverd assets were left to the eldest son, John. Thomas Phillips took over the licence of the 'Semblance' and that year he was one of the auditors of the Road Board's accounts. The other auditor was Magistrate Growse's successor, Dr Rosselloty. A likeable, one-time inhabiter of the East Indies, the new Resident Magistrate for Williams and Kojonup was described, years later, by Mrs Thomas Norrish as 'of ruddy countenance with a bushy beard and a mop of white hair; and in summer dressed for the tropics'.[16] Being a qualified doctor his regular visits to Kojonup were very convenient for the residents, although it is doubtful if some of his remedies would be approved today. In April 1881, Constable McGlade sent a telegram to him: 'very bad with dysentry, cannot keep anything on stomach, what can I do.'[17] Dr Rosselloty replied:

> Take 20 drops of chlorodyn every two hours; after three doses one teaspoonful castor oil in brandy and water, then continue chlorodyn if necessary.[18]

Henri Larsen's great strength and fearlessness made him well suited to the bar trade. More than once the police were called to settle trouble at the different hotels. One night, not long after Henri had taken charge of the Kojonup Inn a customer is said to have become raving drunk and threatened all in sight with an axe. It was left to the bold Henri to disarm him and take him to the lock-up. During the night the man is said to have hanged himself from the cell door, with a silk handkerchief.

Another change which took place before the seventies ended was in postal arrangements. In 1878 Robert Loton relinquished his position as postmaster and Alicia Robinson, one of his wife's first pupils, was appointed as postmistress. It is possible that at this time the post office was established in a little house opposite the police station. Besides a postmistress, there were also two telegraph assistants in 1879, H. C. Chipper and William Thomas Jones.

William was one of Mrs Loton's brightest pupils, and it is very likely that he obtained the job, at thirteen, on the recommendation of both his teacher and the ex-postmaster, her husband. As well as possessing a keen intelligence, William was an only child, the apple of his mother's eye. As most of the children of the district came from large needy families, his upbringing was very different from theirs. He developed a restless, ambitious confidence which was to stay with him to the very end. For his job of telegraph messenger and post boy for the town he received £12 per year.[19] Perhaps his mother had visions of her son working his way up to a position of official prominence but such a process was too slow for the alert William and after two years he left the Postal Department and obtained work around the district with established graziers like his father's old friend, Hassell, or worked with his father learning the blacksmith trade. Whatever it was he was always inquiring and observing.

At the age of fifteen his mother gave him sixteen hoggets, possibly to help augment his income. In his spare time he would graze them on the surrounding hillsides. It is said that one day as he drove them down the Albany Road to some pasture, a group of men standing on the corner spied him and a wag said, with an exaggerated gesture, 'There goes the Squatter'. The name caught the fancy of the locals and was to stick to him for ever, and it is by this name that he is commonly known today.

In a few years Squatter had built his flock up to 180 and when he was otherwise occupied he employed a boy to shepherd them for him. Unfortunately this proved more expensive than expected. The lad

22 'Balgarup' with owner A. Egerton-Warburton near horse. From left: a visitor (name unknown), Jessie, Mrs Egerton-Warburton, Reginald (Rex). Door at left led to kitchen next to fruit shed. House is at left, not shown. Trolley made by A. Egerton-Warburton for carting water in two wooden beer casks was also used to bring carcases to the killing tree where they would be hung from the gambol swinging from the tree

23 Photograph probably taken at opening of first official schoolroom, 1894. At back: Miss Cullinane. Back row: Lilly Bagg, Jane Cullinane, Charlie Elverd, Teddy Flanagan, Les Treasure, Billy Flanagan, Jimmy Jones, Freddy Norrish, Hubert Bagg, Albert Elverd, Arthur Watts, Annie Larsen. Front row: Adeline Elverd (in front of Jane Cullinane), Emily Jones, Sissy Krakouer, Willy Elverd, Dolly Flanagan, Billy Bignell, Henry Jones, Frankie Larsen, Cecil Larsen, Edith Bignell, Harry Bignell, one of the Newhills and his sister

24 Picnic race-meeting group, including the Watts (Mary at left in frilled apron), Happs and Bailye
at Kojonup racecourse behind 'Glen Lossie', 1908; note saucepan boiling on campfire

25 Kojonup's first tennis club, taken beside the state school, 1903. Back row: Mr Peach (schoolmaster)
Edmund Bagg, Herbert Jones (police constable), Bessie Little (postmistress), Herbert Van Zuilecom
Louis Van Zuilecom, Mrs Peach, Mrs Herbert Jones, Mrs Grundy, Lilly Bagg. Second row: Emily Jones
(with H. Jones' baby), May Watts, Sissy Norrish, Gertrude Grover, Mary Watts, Blanche Van Zuilecom
little Jones (son of H. Jones), Ethel Bagg, Clara Dearle. Sitting: Fred Van Zuilecom, Emily Norrish

was heedless and allowed the sheep to wander into poison country so that 110 were lost in ten days. It was a severe lesson for Squatter, and one which he was never to forget. He learnt by sad experience the lethal qualities of the poison plant and became increasingly aware of its presence.

As he sat on a rock watching his depleted flock fattening and their wool growing longer he probably dreamed great things for Kojonup, should the poison plant ever be completely eradicated. His active mind no doubt turned the problem over time and time again, as he strolled the green hills round the town. Meanwhile he persevered in increasing his flock, once more, and by the time he was eighteen it had grown to 200. At twenty he rented a small pastoral lease on which to settle the flock and bided his time.

Another marriage of significance in the seventies was that of Elizabeth Robinson, the first known white baby to be born in Kojonup. She married Samuel Bagg, the son of a Pensioner, in 1878. They were to rear five children of their own and Elizabeth was to become sought after throughout the district as a capable midwife. To young and old she was to become known affectionately as Granny Bagg.

At the end of the seventies the Government announced the establishment of a mail service to be conducted by the Police Department between Perth and Albany, twice each way a month. The van drawn by four horses would be able to carry three adult passengers as well. The distance was to be divided into eight stages corresponding as far as possible with the police stations on the Albany Road. The mail horses were to be under the control of the constable in charge at the different stations, where the horses would be changed. The through fare was to be £4 with the children under ten years at half price and intermediate journeys at a minimum of ten shillings. In readiness for the new mail service tenders were called for the erection in Kojonup of a four-stall police stable, in October 1878.

But what of private contractors like the lively Thomas Chipper? These official plans were to terminate his carting business, although members of his family were to become well known as drivers of the Government mail coaches. In 1879 he married for a second time but simultaneously sundry creditors began pestering Thomas for settlement of their accounts. In response to their demands the property which he had fostered since the 1850s had to be placed in the hands of a receiver.

Yet another of Kojonup's original Road Board members was preparing to leave the district. W. H. Graham and family were to lease their property 'Fairfield' to Louis Van Zuilecom and go to live in Tasmania for approximately ten years. The Van Zuilecoms now had eight children (another had died three days after birth). The youngest, Blanche, had been baptised by W. Wardell-Johnson on 18 October 1877. Throughout the lease years the family divided its time between the two places. Sometime during these years 'Pardellup' was named 'Eeniellup', the spelling many years later being changed to 'Yeenyellup'. The property 'Quanandrup', bequeathed to Louis by his father, seems to have remained with the family for a time, although its exact history is hazy. Altogether, the family must have been kept extremely busy and constantly on the track. Perhaps this is why Louis relinquished the position of chairman and secretary of the Kojonup Road Board to Robert Loton in 1881.

REFERENCES

[1] A. H. Chate, 'The Williams', W.A.H.S. *Journal and Proceedings*, vol. 4, pt 5, 1953, p. 25.

[2] Personal correspondence from C. L. Hassell, 2 October 1969.

[3] C.S.O.Recs., 721, 30 April 1872 (held in Battye Library, Perth).

[4] Police Occurrence Book, 418, 8 June 1872 (Battye Library).

[5] *Perth Gazette*, 12 June 1874, p. 2.

[6] C.S.O.Recs., 721, 14 December 1872.

[7] Dora Bulbeck, 'Westraliana', *Countryman*, 12 June 1969, p. 34.

[8] *Western Australian Times*, 9 October 1874, p. 2.

[9] Recs., Roman Catholic Church, Albany, supplied by D. Bulbeck.

[10] C.S.O.Recs., 721, 10 October 1872.

[11] Bishop Hale Diary, p. 199 (309A, Battye Library).

[12] C.S.O.Recs., 781, 8 June 1874.

[13] Police Occurrence Book, 418, 1 December 1874.

[14] *Ibid.* 10 June 1876.

[15] C.S.O.Recs., 781, 11 January 1877.

[16] A. Burton. comp., 'Memories of Mrs Thomas Norrish', W.A.H.S. journal *Early Days*, vol. 1, October 1938, p. 29.

[17] Police Occurrence Book, 418, 19 April 1881.

[18] *Ibid.*

[19] J. S. Battye, *The Cyclopedia of Western Australia* (Adelaide, 1913), vol. 2, p. 768.

9

The Eighties

With the coming of the eighties more and more of the descendants of the early pioneers were reaching the conclusion that all work and no play makes Jack a dull boy. No longer were they satisfied to congregate and meet distant relations and friends at the occasional wedding, spasmodic church services or funerals. The highly successful sports meetings of the seventies had whetted their appetites for something more. The mention of organized entertainment becomes more common in the surviving Kojonup records of the eighties. An urge to organize to raise money for a particular purpose was tentatively being tested and being found both popular and financially successful.

Without a doubt, at 11 o'clock on Monday 13 September 1880 everyone for miles around would have collected at Thomas Chipper's to witness one of the district's earliest clearing sales and a fair-like atmosphere probably prevailed while nearly thirty years of effort by the Chipper family went under the hammer of auctioneers G. F. Wilkinson & Co.

The property to be sold consisted of:

LOT 1—All that allotment of Land known as Kojonup location No. 7, containing 1500 acres, more or less, in fee simple, with all buildings thereon; this being the well-known HOMESTEAD and FARM now occupied by Mr Thomas Chipper.

LOT 2—The valuable runs abutting on or used in connection with the same.
Full particulars of these runs will be furnished on the day of Sale, by the auctioneers.

LOT 3—A block of fee simple land containing 40 acres, more or less, called 'Kojonup Location 84'. This lot abuts on Lot 1, on its western side.

Also at the same time will be offered in Lots—
A number of Horses, Woolscrew, thrashing Machine, Chaffcutter and other Property and Effects.[1]

The buildings on the property at this time were the small original part of the present homestead, with a stable, shed and small thatched cottage slightly north-east of it. (The latter is thought to have been the original hut built by George Maxwell when he was mailman in 1852.) The shed was said to measure forty feet by twenty with large doors at either end through which the mail cart could enter and leave. The stable contained stalls for twelve horses and a harness room on the south end. It was of pisé construction.

The successful bidder was Albany merchant, Alexander Moir, who obtained possession of it for £570, but Thomas Chipper remained living there until 1888 although under what arrangement is not known.

Another change of land tenure in 1880 was the resumption of Muradup Pool from the leaseholder, Joseph Spencer, and the proclaiming of it as a reserve while Spencer was leased the adjoining 3000 acres.

Perhaps one of those interested in Thomas Chipper's forthcoming sale was the traveller who left the following pen sketch of Kojonup as he saw it, in the early eighties.

> At 60 miles from Williams and 35 miles from Spratt's you come to Kojonup—one of the first permanent settlements formed on this line. It has a very compact appearance. There are several well-formed streets, the land is good. Albeit there is a good deal of poison growing on the rocky rises running here and there, and many head of stock are occasionally lost in consequence of its presence. This is amongst the chief drawbacks of this locality. The district has seen its vicissitudes, but one thing is to be said, greatly in its favour I think—a very large proportion of its 'Old Settlers' have stuck to it, and I don't know that they have done the worse for acting upon this decision. Many of the farmers are military pensioners. Among them I found Sergt. Loton, although well advanced in years, has a good deal of activity in him yet, is Chairman of the Road Board, and is very generally respected . . . I found two hotels, both well conducted apparently, and managed by Mr Larsen and Mr Hale. The town proper possesses only a few houses. There are the Post and Telegraph Offices, a store or two and the Police Station, the Resident (Dr. Rosselloty) holds court at the police office, but generally there is not much for him to do. One of the principal farms I saw near Kojonup was that of Mr Thomas Chipper; but the land is all well adapted for agricultural purposes, and yields good crops where care is taken. The rainfall in this part of the Colony, unfortunately, notwithstanding the high elevation, is scarcely ever sufficient even in a moderately wet season; and the result is obvious—the country cannot carry stock without the expense of water lifting . . . . The remedy for the shortness of the

supply of water on this fine strip of country is . . . the construction of tanks and dams. Social matters are not altogether disregarded, but very much more might be done, and with the great advantage, towards the moral and social improvement of the inhabitants.[2]

Not so long before it would have been inconceivable for a traveller to pass through Kojonup without even noticing or mentioning the barracks. The little building still had a purpose as the schoolhouse for a handful of children but the police were contemplating using it for police quarters. In reply to queries about his residence Robert Loton wrote in 1881 that 'the verandah will soon fall if not repaired, windows and doors broken'.[3] Times had certainly changed when a Superintendent of Police could receive a letter from the Sergeant of Pensioners at Kojonup and comment on the bottom: 'What are the Kojonup Springs?'[4] Inspector Howard after examining the little old building estimated £12 would put it in very good order, and replied for the enlightenment of his superior that:

> The Kojonup spring is on the Barrack reserve close to the house. The water is unfit for human use but stock use it. There is a constant supply and about 70 head of cattle and horses use it daily. The spring is unenclosed.[5]

The Surveyor-General realized the situation and added a compassionate rejoinder, 'I would first like to know whether we would displace any old pensioner'.[6] It would appear that as a result of his hesitation nothing came of the proposal and the aging Mrs Loton continued to live and teach the 'three Rs' within its walls.

Apparently, Abraham Krakouer's first venture into the retail history of Kojonup, at Mrs Elverd's hotel in 1874, had been worthwhile so that in 1880 he launched out and established a business in a building on the Albany Highway, just south of the junction of Pensioner Road and was complimented in the press 'for the improvements he has made to our little town since commencing business here'.[7]

Once more the management of the Kojonup Inn changed hands. Henri Larsen and his wife went to live in a white stone house in Pensioner Road, south of Spring Street. It was always referred to as 'the old white house', and was eventually demolished when the road was widened. A loose stone wall surrounded it, built by the energetic Henri to keep out the wandering stock that frequented the Spring area. At the back of the house was a large stone stable, as the careful housing of the horses was equally as important as that of the riders.

Hotel life was too inactive for the strong Henri. He preferred the outdoor life of the road worker and he became extremely skilful in this type of work. His place behind the bar, at the Kojonup Inn, was taken by the turbulent John Dearle, who is immortalized in an amusing account of a court sitting in Kojonup in April 1882.[8]

Dearle v Delaney

. . . Messrs. Parker and Parker appeared for the plaintiff, and Mr Burt for the defendant . . . .

John Dearle, the plaintiff, a publican, storekeeper, and farmer, residing at Kojonup, said that in May, 1873, he lived on the Blackwood, and that in that month he got married to the defendant's sister. A few weeks afterwards the defendant, who was then a mere lad, came to live with them, of his own accord. He remained with them until the end of 1879, when witness sold his farm and removed to Kojonup, the defendant accompanying them, as one of the family. He used at first to do a little shepherding, but he got tired of that, and then took charge of a team. He was always treated like a son, rather than a servant, being supplied with clothing, food, and pocket money. He was never promised any wages, but at the end of 1880 witness offered to provide him with a team on condition that he would cart sandalwood from Kojonup to Albany for witness receiving in return for his services a share of the profits. In pursuance of this agreement he carted some 15 tons of wood, the property of the witness, to Albany, and this was the wood which the plaintiff now sought to recover, the defendant having disposed of it in his own name, and had the proceeds placed to his own credit. During this time he was being treated as a member of the family, and no question of wages was ever gone into between them. The wood was never given to him in part payment of wages, nor had he any authority to sell it on his own account. The wood in reality, belonged to Messrs. McKail & Co., they having advanced the plaintiff the money to purchase it from his predecessor, when he took over the public house from him. It was not until about fifteen loads had been delivered that the plaintiff discovered that the defendant had disposed of the wood on his own account. When witness made the discovery, he proceeded against him criminally, but the case was dismissed, and hence the present claim.

Cross-examined by Mr Burt: Within twelve months after the defendant came to live with us, he took charge of a flock of 700 or 800 sheep. He had charge of them for about two years, and was afterwards employed as teamster. When we took the public house at Kojonup, he assisted at the bar. We used to have balls occasionally—'cushion dances' as they used to be called, and, after one of these gay and festive occasions, he and I had a quarrel, and I said to him we had better part. He then left my service, and claimed wages in respect of the time he had been in my employ, but I refused to pay him. Some time afterwards we made it up again, and he made himself generally useful, on the farm and at the public house. I took him back for the sake of his sister—my wife. I did not offer to pay him what was owing to him, with sandalwood, instead of money. During a great deal of his time he did nothing, but walked about 'like a gentleman', and had a servant to wait upon him. He used to get as much money as he liked, but I never charged him with it. He even had a race horse, which he fed and trained at my expense. I did not object to his doing so for he served me well, and we lived on good terms until after the eventful occasion of the 'cushion dance' and the subsequent occasion when he disposed of the sandalwood in his own name . . . . I always supplied him with cash, and he had always plenty of money in his pocket.

Mr Burt: I thought there was not much money knocking about Kojonup.

Witness: We generally manage to have a 'bob' or two.

His Honor: As between man and man, don't you think you owe him something for his eight years' services?

Witness: I don't consider I owe him anything.

His Honor: It was hard lines indeed to cause this young man to be arrested for felony, when there was not a tittle of evidence to support such a charge.

Mrs Dearle, wife of the plaintiff and sister of the defendant, was the next witness called. Her evidence was in the main, simply confirmatory of the story told by the previous witness . . . .

To His Honor: It is a nice comfortable business that we have at Kojonup. I have no idea what profit it brings in a year,—perhaps £200 or £300, or more. We were quite a happy family until the row about the 'cushion dance' took place. We did not get anybody in the defendant's place, after he left, but did his work amongst ourselves.

John Watkins, a wheelwright, living at Kojonup, said he knew the plaintiff and the defendant and was acquainted with the relations that existed between them. . . .

To Mr Burt: I am a neighbour of Dearle's and keep his books.

His Honor: Did it appear to you they were doing a profitable business?

Witness: Yes they were doing pretty well.

His Honor: What do you mean by doing pretty well?

Witness: They were taking about £50 or £60 a fortnight, or at the rate of about £1400 a year.

His Honor: A wonderful country! . . .

Mr Burt then called the defendant, who said he was employed in various capacities for several years in the plaintiff's service. Occasionally he drew money from him, and on one occasion got a number of sheep in part payment of what he regarded as wages due to him from the plaintiff. The day following the 'cushion dance' already referred to, they had a row, and plaintiff told witness they had better part. Witness said he was agreeable, if he would pay him what he owed him for his services, but this he refused to do. Witness met him sometime afterwards and told him he had obtained legal advice with regard to his claim against him for wages and that he was told he could recover, but that he did not like to go to law with him, if he would settle with him. Plaintiff said he would give him sandalwood as payment instead of money, if witness would accept it, and witness agreed to do so, at the rate of £3-5s. a ton. He estimated that he got about fifteen tons of wood, altogether, which he conveyed to Albany, in his own team, and there disposed of it to Messrs. McKail & Co. He was engaged about six months in carting it to the Sound. At a later period of his service, the plaintiff offered to take him into partnership, giving him a share of the profits, but witness refused the offer, as he had another project in view, intending to take a farm of his own. When he finally quitted his service, witness asked him to settle up, but he could get no satisfaction, and shortly afterwards the plaintiff charged him with the larceny of the sandalwood, but the case, as already said was dismissed.

At this stage of the proceedings a heavy shower of rain drove all the witnesses into Court, and among them a matron with a baby in arms, which baby became somewhat demonstrative and noisy on being admitted into the building. His Honor asked if the baby was connected with the case? Mr Burt said it did not appear on the record. His Honor ordered the mother and child into the custody of the Sheriff, who provided accommodation for them in the juror's room, where the infant pleader resumed his address to the court, with renewed vigour. The rain having meanwhile abated, mother and baby were directed to withdraw; so they went, without further interruption . . . .

His Honor . . . gave judgment for the defendant for £72-16s, and on the application of Mr Burt, certified for costs on the higher scale. His Honor added that he was glad the evidence in this case had enabled him to find a verdict for the defendant, who he said, had been most improperly treated by the plaintiff, in respect of the criminal proceedings instituted against him.

The Court then rose and adjourned until next day.

Dearle v. Krakouer.

This was an action to recover the value of goods alleged to have been sold and delivered by the plaintiff to the defendant, at various times. The plaintiff is the gentleman who figured in the same capacity in the case heard the day before, and reported above, and the defendant is a storekeeper and auctioner, carrying on business at Kojonup.

Messrs. Parker and Parker appeared for the plaintiff, and Mr Burt for the defendant.

Mr. S. H. Parker in opening the plaintiff's case, said the whole question in dispute resolved itself into a matter of accounts, and the degree of reliance to be placed upon the evidence. The plaintiff on one hand disputed almost every item in the defendant's set off, and the defendant on the other hand disputed nearly every charge in the plaintiff's claim.

. . . .

John Dearle, the plaintiff, an amusing old gentleman, gave evidence as to the items for which he claimed. The first item was a claim of £50-3s. in respect of goods and liquors sold and delivered, which included, among other heterogeneous articles, pork, and pepper, sugar, and ale; a carriage lamp and salt butter; a lump of plum pudding alleged to have been snatched from the plaintiff's kitchen table by the defendant; and a quantity of spirits, chiefly rum, supplied to a gentleman rejoicing in the musical nickname of 'Singing Billy'. (The plaintiff produced a book, containing an account of these items and upon the book being handed to the Chief Justice for his inspection His Honor, commenting upon its dirty appearance, said he was afraid it afforded a very clear insight into the inner life of Kojonup.) There was also a claim in respect of articles of furniture alleged to have been broken by the plaintiff —the combined result of infirmity of temper and the potency of the Kojonup beer.

His Honor said in respect to the value of some tumblers broken that he would allow so much for them.

Witness said that was too little.

His Honor: You had better hold your tongue, sir, or else you'll get nothing at all.

Witness also claimed in respect of board and lodging furnished to the defendant's sister, for which he charged at the rate of 15s. a week. An animated discussion took place with reference to this charge, Mr Burt saying he was prepared with evidence to show that even at the 'Semblance of Old England' hotel—the most fashionable hotel at Kojonup—the same female had only been charged at the rate of 10s. a week for board and lodging. With reference to this observation, witness said he was prepared to prove that he kept a better table than the 'Semblance'; that he had never had a female by the week,—and that he told the defendant he would not charge his sister any more than anybody else.

His Honor: That was very kind of you.

After hearing the plaintiff's evidence with regard to the other items constituting the claim of £50-3s., His Honor said—subject to any evidence which might be adduced to the contrary for the defence —he would allow the plaintiff £37-11-4d. in respect of that claim.

Cross-examined by Mr Burt, the plaintiff said he was not on good terms with the defendant; that they had a row.

Mr Burt: What about?

Witness declined to answer.

His Honor said the question was a proper one, and that the witness would have to answer it.

Witness: Well it was about my wife.

His Honor: Oh, I see, a case of jealousy.

Witness: No your Honor, a case of a man's 'better half' being ill-treated.

Mr Burt: Did you not have another dispute with the defendant?

Witness: Not that I know of.

Mr Burt: What about the 'beef case'?

Witness: That 'beef case' seems to be a great annoyance to you Mr Burt. I paid for the beef and eat it. What more do you want?

Mr Burt: Then you are a beef eater, Dearle?

Witness: Oh, yes I like a bit of beef, like most Englishmen.

The witness was then cross-examined with regard to each item, in respect of which he claimed, and also with reference to the defendant's set off, consisting chiefly of articles said to have been supplied to the plaintiff or his wife out of the defendant's store, amounting in the aggregate to £34-16-8d. The principal items appeared to be chaff, provisions and clothing; lollies for the little ones, cigars for himself, and hose for his 'better half'; peas and gunpowder, packs of cards and a cribbage board; also two pairs of inexpressibles, with reference to which there was a considerable conflict of evidence.

Mrs Dearle the plaintiff's 'better half', was next examined. She did not carry the case much further than the old gentleman himself, except with regard to a loaf of bread for which the plaintiff was charged a shilling (His Honor said he felt inclined to allow that item, after hearing Mrs Dearle's evidence but Mr Burt said it would never do for the Court to let it go forth that a shilling was a fair charge for a loaf of bread. His Honor said he did not think the Court would be compromising itself by doing so in this instance, —the loaves at Kojonup were no doubt of larger dimensions than city loaves.) The witness was even more emphatic than her husband in disputing the various items constituting the defendant's set off, and was so assertive with reference to a certain frying pan that His Honor said he was almost persuaded to strike it out of the account.

A man named Watkins, who kept the plaintiff's books, gave evidence in support of the claim, but he proved nothing very material to the issue.

Miss Krakouer, a sister of the defendant, and who has the misfortune of being blind, was the next witness called. She gave evidence of having boarded at the plaintiff's house, and of having been treated with the utmost kindness and consideration by him. Her brother was responsible for her board at the plaintiff's.

His Honor: And I hope he may be induced to do still more for you.

The Defendant informed His Honor that since he was a lad he had done all within his power to support his afflicted sister, and not long ago had disposed of his business in order to take her to Melbourne, to see if anything could be done to restore her sight— that, if His Honor had been in the colony in the 'olden times' he would have known this and refrained from making any remark upon the subject.

His Honor said he was very glad to hear the defendant's statement. For the defence.

Mr Krakouer gave evidence with regard to his set off, and also the plaintiff's claim. He disputed the greater part of the claim, and gave a somewhat different complexion to the remainder of the items, to that put upon them by the Dearles.

The Court at this stage adjourned, during the usual interval, for refreshments. On resuming,

Mr Parker said the parties had been in consultation during the adjournment, and he thought the simplest plan to settle the case would be to adopt the course usually followed when a juror is withdrawn, but as His Honor was the only juror in the present case, it would be obviously impossible for His Honor to withdraw from himself.

His Honor: Cry quits.

Mr Burt said he would agree to cry quits, if His Honor would give judgment for one side or the other, for a shilling.

His Honor: I am inclined to give a shilling to the defendant, but without costs. I think the plaintiff is animated by a great deal of litigious feeling, and if he takes my advice he will take back that brother-in-law of his (the defendant in the previous action,) who seems to me a very fine fellow.

Mr Dearle: Never!

Judgment, by consent, was then entered for the defendant, for one shilling, without costs.

John Delaney later was to become well-known in the district. At the age of two years he, with his parents and sister Winifred, had come to the colony on the *Escort* in 1860. However their father died within six months and their mother went to work for a time for Lady Richardson-Bunbury, near Picton. In 1882 Delaney married into the Hale family which lived north of Kojonup, close to the Albany Road. About this time he was also employed by Thomas Chipper, driving the mail coach. Delaney came to enjoy this type of work and in the 1900s built up an extensive mail service throughout the Kojonup district.

In 1874 William Noonan had been established in the sandalwood industry for some time and on 22 January he passed through Kojonup with his teamster and 'two teams loaded with sandalwood'.[9] Noonan's brother-in-law, William Grover, also found it a lucrative sideline to enable him to develop his farm 'Indinup', and when he was sometimes away his wife, the courageous Bridget Grover, was doubly pleased when any Kojonup residents who were journeying east in search of the valuable wood dropped in to see her. She was always anxious to hear the latest news of her old home town, and her diary of 1882 mentions visits from Robert Forsythe, John Elverd, Sam Bagg, William Reilly and T. Bettridge. In this way an immense 'grapevine' was served; notes passed, families kept in touch, seasons and crops compared. Sometimes the news was not very happy, such as the time when Bridget learnt of her little niece, Amy Harris, being lost in the bush. Despite extensive searching the little girl's remains were not found until months later.

John Elverd was well respected in Kojonup. In December 1875 he was appointed temporary constable, to take charge while the police were absent at a court case east of Eticup. On his father's death he had become a man of property in the town. According to the clamorous John Dearle 'it was simply a farce calling it a Town. The present owner will not dispose of any of the land unless he gets treble its value'.[10] This was not quite true. On 30 May 1882, John Elverd transferred to 'the Standing Committee of the West Australian Branch of the Church of England',[11] for five shillings, the land on which the Church's buildings now stand. The witness to the deed was 'Robert Forsythe, farmer of Kojonup'.[12]

Another remunerative occupation for the local men, and one far more adventurous and exciting, was horse-hunting. For years horses had escaped from their owners and bred in the bush. Most owners spared nothing to retrieve a reputable horse but to do so could take weeks so that among the bush ponies was running the progeny of many a thoroughbred. The wild ponies seemed to develop a sixth sense towards the poison plant and thrived in hidden grassy hollows of the Kojonup district to become a particularly hardy type of animal suited to the strenuous demands of a settler. While attempting to catch these valuable animals the young men of the day not only became expert in the saddle but also developed a passion for horse racing. On 15 February 1882 a public meeting was held at the Kojonup Inn to arrange a race meeting on 22 March. The stewards appointed were F. R. Hassell, G. Norrish, H. Larsen, J. Elverd, S. Hale, J. Dearle, starter, and T. Norrish, clerk of the course. A six event programme was advertised by the honorary secretary H. J. Cooke, the races being the Maiden Plate, the Ladies' Purse (consisting of sovereigns presented by the ladies of Kojonup and Eticup), Kojonup and Ettikup (sic) Stakes, Hack Race and the Hurry Scurry, for untrained horses, (once around the course).[13] The entrance fee was to be 2s. 6d. but the advertisement failed to mention the location of the race course. It is very probable that earlier meetings were held but this is the first known to be conducted in the town. (In later years Race Day, to coincide with St Patrick's Day, was to be one of the town's most popular occasions and the thorn in the side of the local schoolteacher. A practicable and pretty race course off the Collie Road was constructed by the enthusiastic supporters. It was sold after the 1914-18 war and the money raised assisted in establishing the present showgrounds.)

The early pioneers' dependence on the horse for transport gave rise to the practice of holding more than one function, whenever there was a likelihood of people gathering. For example, when an important court case was to be held and it was obvious that there would be an influx of jurymen, witnesses and spectators (and the surviving records of Kojonup court cases indicate they were well worth travelling to hear and see) a cricket match and dance were often arranged for one of the days.

Long journeys were of necessity leisurely, with careful provision being made well in advance for the watering and feeding of the horses, quite apart from the personal requirements of the travellers. The few facilities and many hardships—open fires, earthen floors and no indoor plumbing to name just a few—make the numerous tales of selfless hospitality, in the records of the past, even more creditable.

It had long been the custom in Kojonup to observe the passing of the old year and the coming of the new with a series of functions. Knowing this it occurred to some of the Roman Catholic adherents that it might be a profitable venture if they held a 'bazaar' during the holiday festivities to raise funds to enable the town to finance its own resident priest. There were substantial reasons for such optimism. For some the season had been good with excellent closing rains and a bumper hay crop—which was a most essential commodity to the horse-reliant community.

One of those in the district who most keenly saw the need for a resident priest was Bridget Grover. Consequently, on 30 December 1882 she accompanied some of the Roman Catholic Sisters and a Miss Gibbons from Albany to Kojonup. On 1 January they reached 'Balgarup' and visited Mrs Morris, Loton's daughter, who was settled with her husband on land on the opposite side of the road from the celebrated Balgarup. The party was able to send a telegram from there to the Sisters back in Albany, announcing their safe arrival. From there they journeyed on to the barracks. 'Poor old Mrs Loton was invisible',[14] so Bridget 'had to go to Mrs Larsen to find a place for the sisters'.[15]

After they had enjoyed a meal she took the horses up to her parents' old house which she found almost a ruin, and then returned to the barracks to assist the Sisters in setting up the bazaar. It opened for business on 2 January and was 'not very largely attended but did pretty well considering'.[16] The next day they were up early but found no buyers so closed till after the cricket match that was played between Kojonup and the 125 mile team. The latter won, which meant that both sides were now quits and it was arranged to have the final match played during the next month.[17]

On the fifth the party started early for their return to Albany by way of Warkelup where they were served morning tea. They continued on to have dinner with Mr and Mrs Richard Norrish, junior, and from there they went to spend the night at 'Gracefield' with the hospitable James Tunneys.

Two photographers set up temporary businesses in the town during February 1883. H. Sibyer's efforts were generally voted as the best and most of the time there was a group of interested people congregated around his tent.

Nearby, John Dearle was living in clover. Stephen Hale had lost his publican's licence because his agent neglected to apply for a renewal. John Dearle was, therefore, the only publican in the town and was doing a roaring trade, so much so that he was intending to add six rooms to the old 'Kojonup Inn'.[18]

Meanwhile on the other side of the world, in Moravia, Father Joseph Chmelicek, a man of fifty years of age, felt compelled to volunteer for missionary work. His application was received in Rome at the same time as Bishop Griver of Western Australia was there, anxious to recruit priests to assist him in his diocese. The application was passed on to him for consideration and duly accepted.

In 1883 Father Mateau of Albany wrote to his Bishop of the very great need for a Roman Catholic priest in Kojonup. At the same time Father Chmelicek arrived in the colony, spent a few months in Guildford and short stays elsewhere and eventually was sent to Kojonup, saying mass for the first time on 3 February 1884.

Father Chmelicek was an extremely gifted man, an accomplished linguist, learned in medicine, a herbalist and a competent horticulturist. He was tall and powerful and like many European men of that period tended to have a stiff military gait.

146

At first he stayed with the Henri Larsens but later shifted to a hut near the old Noonan dwelling. Here he kept a few fowls, some cows, planted a variety of fruit trees and grew vegetables to sell in the town to supplement the small income that he received from his church members. In 1891 he purchased part of location 45 and sub-lot P. 4 from William Noonan and extended his farming projects, all the time taking a keen, intelligent interest in the growing of herbs and observing the indigenous plants. Two small boys, Albert and Charlie Elverd, would sometimes weed his garden and receive in payment a pint of sweet rich milk. As he became known about the district he was loved for his kind understanding nature and respected for his wide knowledge, particularly his vast appreciation of herbs and their healing properties. It is said that Mrs John Elverd was forever grateful to him for curing her of a goitre, by means of a herbal mixture.

His clerical duties spread from the Williams to Tenterden and east to Eticup and he travelled around his area in a cart in which he would sit reading while the horse wandered from side to side, cropping at tit-bits at the side of the track. It is said that once, when his horse was unable to pull his single furrow plough through the heavy ground he coupled a young bull to the plough as well and so completed his job.

One of his rambling journeys would have been in the direction of Bridget Grover's homestead at Indinup. Visitors continued to call at the property and on 22 December she recorded nostalgically: 'Old Mr Newstead came for his last turn', as mailman.[19] After thirty-one years the old soldier had to step down for a younger man—the irrepressible Dearle.

Often when Bridget's callers arrived dusty, weary and thirsty, they must have wished for some easier way of travel. The problem of distance, the getting from one spot to another with a minimum of trouble and the maximum of ease and speed still had to be solved in the colony. The new Governor Broome and his Lady had found it necessary to go by sea from Albany to Fremantle, when they first arrived in Western Australia. Their small son and companion were sent overland and Lady Broome recorded, from Perth:

> As we were sitting down to dinner a telegram arrived from Louis and Catherine to say they had reached a place called Kojonup and were going to sleep there that night, having got so far quite safely and with beautiful weather.[20]

In charge of the post office at this time would have been Miss M. J. Ryan, Alicia Robinson having married Abraham Krakouer. Between

1885 and 1889 Miss Louisa Roe was postmistress. It was demanding work. Her time book shows she worked every day of the week for two shifts, finishing at 9.30 p.m. except when the mail from Albany arrived when she could be busy until well into the morning. Somehow she found time to become acquainted with a dashing young kangaroo-hunter from South Australia who was in the district with his two brothers and a friend called Riddaway. In a specially arranged shooting match against the locals, the visitors proved their superior skill with the rifle. Louisa Roe eventually married her young man, Frank White, and Miss Ryan returned to take over the office for another ten years, the last eighteen months as Mrs John Larsen.

Another new face in the town was that of Miss M. Cullinane who had taken over the schoolroom after Mrs Loton's death on 24 May 1885. After his wife's death Robert Loton seemed to fade from the local scene. He is said to have suffered severe financial loss from bush-fires. His property in the town was acquired by Joseph Spencer. The old Sergeant of Pensioners eventually died in Fremantle in 1897 at the age of 90.

In a period when immorality was condemned maliciously and hypo-critically, Miss Cullinane reared her fatherless child Jane, and in so doing won the respect of those among whom she discreetly lived. Her courageous stand was not common in bigoted small-town communities and there is evidence that more than one young Kojonup girl committed suicide rather than face the hostile censorious standards of the day, as an unwed mother.

In 1884 whispers were floating down as far south as Kojonup that railways were the answer to the transport problem. The Government mail coach system was not as efficient as had been hoped, but the lack of money prevented the Government from drastic alterations.

It was only natural that as the rumours increased residents along the Albany Road presumed that any change in the north-south transport system would follow the same track as the road, thus utilizing the existing towns such as Kojonup.

However, the outspoken and influential York settlers opposed any move that would not directly involve them. Their outcry was heeded when the Government began talking to private companies about the construction of such a railway in return for land. In 1884, it was announced that Anthony Hordern had formed, in London, the Western Australian Land Company to construct and maintain a railway from

26   Miss Mary Watts, sidesaddle, with Henry Milton of Katanning, 1905, the year she was judged
best lady rider in the Great Southern District

27   Champion horsemen: the Kojonup team which won the state polo championships, 1966. From
left: Ivan Haggerty on Lucky, Mark McGuire on Tanya, Stan Haggerty on Chief and Des Reid
on Lilly

28 Land guides Joe and Jack Norrish with interested selectors, early 1900s

29 An outcamp; note meat bag, camp oven, grinder for sharpening axes

Beverley to Albany, on the land-grant principle. The following year the line between Chidlows Well and York was completed and the year after the line had snaked its way as far as Beverley.

For the railway to pass twenty to thirty miles east of the Albany Road was a bitter pill for Kojonup. The inhabitants listened covetously to all the fresh news brought from the east by the travelling sandalwooders. Slowly the Great Southern Railway line progressed simultaneously from Albany and Beverley. Sometimes the truth seemed stranger than fiction. The company was to receive 12,000 acres of Crown land for every mile of completed railway!

One of the first to rethink their future plans were the Piesse brothers of Williams. Frederick Henry Piesse had given away the poorly-paid Government job to go into partnership with his brother, C. A. Piesse, as merchants. They now organized portable stores and followed the progress of the construction railway gangs, profitably supplying their needs.

After the official opening of the line in June 1889 the old Kojonup inhabitants incredulously watched the meteoric rise of their new neighbours, Katanning and Broomehill. Not only did a train run through daily but buildings appeared like mushrooms after the first rain; and behind the stores, hotel and houses were usually the astute Piesse brothers.

The full realization of what the recent momentous changes taking place twenty-odd miles east of Kojonup would do to that town and its district hit the inhabitants forcibly in 1888 when the mail coach ceased to run down the Albany Road, to Kojonup.

> The coach has ceased running to Kojonup having struck off at the Arthur River to catch the railway. This being so the question is asked how is Kojonup to get on without mail communications? Will Kojonup, as a certain Government official remarked on a recent visit, when the railway is finished become a thing of the past? Surely the Government will not allow the only recognised township between Perth and Albany to fall into oblivion. It behoves them now the alteration has taken place in the mail service to make arrangements whereby Kojonup will have a weekly service between Albany and Perth. This could be done by arranging with Mr Baggs, mail contractor, to run direct to Moojegen [sic] from Kojonup, and vice versa instead of via Eticup as at present. He could thus meet the train from Perth and deliver the mails for Albany. . . . I hope and trust the Postmaster General will look into the matter and not leave Kojonup out in the cold when the coach is taken off this end of the road.[21]

As Kojonup licked its wounds some conception of future railway requirements and the need to utilize the individual's rights of expression in the democratic system was being fathomed.

> I have heard that a memorial is to be forwarded to the Government (with a view of it being brought before the Legislative Council) by the Roads Board on the Perth and Albany road, asking for an increase in the vote for next year. The Government and the Legislature should, when the matter is brought before them, take into consideration, the large amount of work to be done, owing to the completion of the Albany-Beverley railway at the beginning of the year. New roads will have to be constructed to bring Wandering, Williams, Arthur and Kojonup into communications, they being shut out by the railway. Surely if this railway is for the public good the Legislature should vote sufficient money to the different Roads Boards to make roads so that the settlers may derive some benefit from it. It is impossible for the Roads Board on the Perth-Albany road to do anything extra with the small amount allotted to them as it takes all they have to keep the main line in repair, in fact they can hardly do this to satisfaction. As the members of the Roads Board give their time gratuitously, attending meetings very often at great inconvenience, they should certainly be encouraged in their work and not disheartened as they are at the present.[22]

Although Kojonup was being cold-shouldered by the Government, private individuals were confident that business could be profitably negotiated there. Up to the eighties William Cornwall had tended to have more of a business interest in Williams than Kojonup. He had opened the Bridge Hotel at Williams in 1871 and had advertised 'good beds; wines, spirits, ale and porter'.[23] His wife was naturally drawn to the Kojonup district since Mrs Richard Norrish, junior, was her sister. In 1883 Cornwall bought Abraham Krakouer's premises and all his stock for £2000 and R. Hoops was made the manager.[24] The Road Board was a customer in 1884 with the purchase of a measuring tape and stationery for fourteen shillings. In 1887 the Cornwalls opened Kojonup's third hotel for business. The first press correspondence was not altogether favourable:

> Our new hotel, 'The Royal' is now open for the convenience of the public but, judging from appearances the 'Old English Hotel' seems to carry the sway.[25]

It is not to be thought that such comment would trouble Cornwall for long. He was a hard-headed business man and had proved more than once that most ventures he dabbled in ended up showing a profit.

Typical of the man was his comment when someone laughed at seeing him pretending to read the daily paper—upside down. 'Anyone can read it the right way up' he replied.

Sometime before he opened the hotel Cornwall had obtained an interest in 'Quanandrup', the property of the Van Zuilecoms. His farming interests then stretched from Kojonup to Williams but he made his headquarters at the Royal once it was built, and interested himself in all manner of businesses on the side. He was frequently the contractor to the police for forage and in 1887 he had the additional contract to reroof the police station, for £85 13s. 6d. with the unsightly but useful galvanized iron which was soon to replace the wooden shingles of buildings in every part of the colony.

By 1887 the Treasures were also establishing themselves in Kojonup. The industrious Edward had died the year before and the property 'Martinup' was left to his son, Levi. Mrs Treasure returned to live in the Kojonup district she knew so well. Her movements were wide and varied. She bought the Semblance of Old England; the original Noonan holdings (and lived there for a time); 'Norlup', the property of the Scotts, on the Blackwood; and the old Elverd property known as 'Ongerup'. The purchase of the latter was to prove tragic when in October 1887 her eighteen-year-old son, Elworthy, was accidentally killed. The custom was still to wash the sheep before shearing and young Treasure had been busily engaged all morning in doing this. He returned to the shearing shed and before climbing over a hurdle handed his Winchester rifle to one of the Elverds. The trigger touched the fence and the rifle went off, the ball penetrating the young man's spine.

Towards the end of the eighties a new name appears in the district records. In 1889, Frederick Watts of Albany rented from Moir the 1489 acre Chipper property, for £30 a year. On taking over the place the Watts family found the buildings in a state of great disrepair and had to spend some time renovating them to their liking. One room was added to the homestead and later a stone barn was built by stonemason Thomas Riley. The foundation stone on its north-west corner was ceremoniously laid by Mrs Watts after her husband had first carefully placed in position a bottle containing full particulars of the occasion.

Watts was a devoted horticulturist and soon an extensive orchard, vegetable plots and beautiful flower garden were thriving, watered by a dam constructed north-east of the house. The first crop grown by the Watts in 1889 weighed about three tons and the sheaves (which

151

were reaped by hand) were stored in the original old house. Two brothers, Jack and Joe Foote, were employed to thresh it by hand with a flail. The first wool clip was sent to Albany by train, from Broomehill, which was then the principal station in the vicinity. The second year Watts took his wool to Albany himself and returned with a five-foot damp-weather Martin stripper with which he stripped not only his own crop but many in the district, going as far as the Williams to strip eighty acres.

The Watts family were great entertainers and during the summer when the watermelons and stone fruit were plentiful many happy garden parties were held. The young people of the family were expert riders and when district shows became common the name Miss Mary Watts headed the lists of prize winners in the equestrian events for many years. At the end of their ten year lease the Watts family had grown very proud of and attached to their property and bought it for £1000, naming it 'Spring Villa' after the 'Namarillup' spring located on it.

Although poor seasons were being experienced by settlers in other parts of the colony in the late 1880s, Kojonup was enjoying a measure of prosperity. Crops were heavy, particularly that of James Tunney of 'Gracefield'; and good clips were being shorn. In addition, rumours were becoming more persistent of great prospects, backed by the same wealthy, smart Sydneysider, Anthony Hordern, who was behind the Great Southern Railway. It looked as if Kojonup was going to benefit more directly from the railway, after all. The Western Australian Land Company applied for several poison leases in the district and it was whispered that great plans were underway for land development. As early as 1880 leases covering thousands of acres were finalized, the rents being calculated at £1 for every thousand acres. Lease 8/266 of 27,726 acres covered that area south of the Balgarup River. Of all the new poison leases the development of this one was to make the earliest impact on Kojonup.

The prevailing buoyant conditions were sufficient to attract business men such as Neary, agent for the four-year-old A.M.P. (insurance) Society, to visit the town and to spend a week there. 'As a result of his visit proposals on the lives of Kojonup residents . . . Wood, Kelly and Larsen were accepted by the Society'[26] and would have been among the earliest policies issued in the district.

Social events of an organized nature continued to increase during these more palmy days. They varied from a picnic at which 'Mrs Wall and Miss Cornwall were ready in passing the sweetmeats and sandwiches around to all comers',[27] to a shooting match 'at which there were no less than forty-five entries'.[28] Those to receive a prize were H. W. Scott, £11; J. Nelson, £6; W. Norrish, £4, and a J. Holland, £1 1s. 0d. In just a few years this same J. Holland was to make even a greater name for himself in the colony, and the skills and bush lore he had amassed during these peaceful times were to prove of untold value in the changing days ahead. At the moment, the people of the south were too absorbed in their own day to day events to get over-excited about stories they might hear of gold finds in the very north of the colony. Such apathy was soon to change.

REFERENCES

[1] *Inquirer*, 18 August 1880, p. 3.
[2] *Ibid.* 4 August 1880, p. 3.
[3] C.S.O.Recs., 1437/92, 26 September 1881 (held in Battye Library, Perth).
[4] *Ibid.* 28 September 1881.
[5] *Ibid.* 25 November 1881.
[6] *Ibid.*
[7] *Inquirer*, 18 January 1882, p. 5.
[8] *West Australian Times*, 21 April 1882, p. 3.
[9] Police Occurrence Book 418, 22 January 1874 (Battye Library).
[10] C.S.O.Recs., 1357/8, 17 July 1881.
[11] Personal correspondence from Diocesan Secretary, Church of England, Bunbury, 1 May 1969.
[12] *Ibid.*
[13] *Inquirer*, 1 March 1882, p. 3.
[14] Bridget Grover Diary, extracts (in possession of Mrs A. Wilson, 'Indinup', Katanning).
[15] *Ibid.*
[16] *Ibid.*
[17] *Albany Mail*, 31 January 1883, p. 3.
[18] *Ibid.* 28 February 1883.
[19] Grover Diary.
[20] Letters from Lady Broome, in Alexandra Hasluck, *Remembered with Affection* (Melbourne, 1963), p. 45.
[21] *West Australian*, 10 October 1888, p. 3.
[22] *Ibid.*
[23] *Herald*, 5 August 1871, p. 1.
[24] *Albany Mail*, 31 January 1883, p. 3.
[25] *Inquirer*, 9 November 1887, p. 5.
[26] Personal correspondence from J. G. Sawyer, A.M.P. Society, 9 June 1970.
[27] *Inquirer*, 9 November 1887, p. 5.
[28] *West Australian*, 10 October 1888, p. 3.

10

Growing Responsibilities

In 1890 responsible government was granted to the colony of Western Australia. Three years later the Legislative Assembly of thirty-three members was to be elected by all men in the colony aged twenty-one and over, and it was no longer required for a member to be a man of property.

But, at the beginning of the 1890s the position of the Kojonup Road Board remained very much the same as it had been when it was first inaugurated in 1871. It was still the only official Road Board centre for all that country between Plantagenet and Williams, east of the Blackwood district. Naturally, the fast-growing parvenues to the east were not going to tolerate this situation for much longer. On the other hand, if the Kojonup settlers were to get any benefit at all from the railway easier access to the closest railway station was essential. Gradually the Kojonup Road Board found itself forced to extend its jurisdiction to roads other than the initial Albany Road. Nor was Kojonup the only little settlement having to face change. If Kojonup residents felt they were being eclipsed by Katanning, Eticup was doomed to fare even worse. It was faced with extinction; its place being taken, heartlessly by the fast-growing railway centre of Broomehill, just a few miles to the east.

In 1889, W. H. Angove was paid £5 9s. 2d. by the Kojonup Road Board to survey the Broomehill Road. In the same year G. Norrish, T. Norrish and F. Watts were paid sundry small amounts to do several clearing contracts along the track, and J. J. Garritty was paid for work on the Carlecatup crossing.

The first mention of the Kojonup-Katanning road in the Kojonup Road Board accounts ledger was in 1891 when W. Elverd was advanced £60 to clear the track. The following year the Board received, in addition to its usual grant, extra amounts for special works: £25 for the Kojonup-Katanning road, £17 10s. 0d. for the Broomehill-Kojonup road and £35 for the Blackwood road.

This last grant was no doubt to improve communications between Kojonup and the development work being pushed ahead on lease 8/266 by the Western Australian Pastoral and Colonization Company Ltd, to which it had been transferred under the agency of Alexander Forrest. About this time, Robert John Irving came to Kojonup as the company's local manager.

> He was a tall man, over six feet in height, a regular dictator and a dyed in the wool Englishman.[1]

To Kojonup residents, for some unfathomable reason he was to become known as Dr Irving.

Irving's instructions were to clear the land of poison plants and to survey and fence it into thousand-acre blocks. This was easier said than done. However it provided welcomed work close at hand for many of the men of the district, such as William Elverd, John Larsen, Harry Priest, Jack Lambe, Jack Ford, Harry Thomas, Ted Mews, Bill Reilly, Watty O'Keefe, Joe Coulbern, Dick Burton and two dozen Chinese who had previously worked on Hassell's Palinup estate.

'A tin hut' was erected by Martin Costello as a storehouse for provisions, fencing equipment and other implements, and a homestead was built for 'the Doctor' close to the site of the present Jingalup town. The company's first well was excavated in 1891 by John Larsen, Jack Ford and Harry Priest for £1 per foot. It was sunk forty feet and lined with split posts. Two days before they had finished, the men ran out of rations. Rather than delay the finish they lived on damper and billy tea for that period, and then had to walk the twelve miles into Kojonup before they could partake of a good square meal.

John Larsen also excavated the first dam on the property, this time assisted by Watty O'Keefe and Harry Thomas. It was near the tin hut and was always referred to as 'the tin hut dam'. It was laboriously sunk with only mattocks, shovels and wheelbarrows as equipment. Two years later the 'old Government dam' situated on the Jingalup Reserve was excavated by the Chinese workers.

So that the Chinese would not lose precious time getting lost in the bush between their camp and their working site Irving had single furrows run from the tin hut to the work points, as a guide line and the Asians would tramp along it in single file. Some faint traces of these plough marks are still visible in the area.

On the whole, the life of the Chinese could not have been very pleasant. Irving was most particular that his European employees did not mix with the Chinese. In 1894 the latter were employed in constructing the 'Quailiup Dam', supervised by overseer McLeod. Three of the Chinese were provoked to attack the overseer with hoes. Badly lacerated he found his way back to the tin hut and sent young Tom Larsen, with all haste, to fetch Constable Nicholson from Kojonup. Tom Larsen years later recalled:

> It was dark when we arrived at the Chinamen's camp where the three Chinamen were arrested. The constable gave me his revolver to guard the prisoners while he handcuffed them to a tree. This I remember was on a bitterly cold night and the Chinese who were dressed in their national clothes must have been very cold. On the next morning, still handcuffed together, the Chinese were made to trot the fourteen miles to Kojonup. They were later tried in Albany where one was sentenced to nine months imprisonment and the other two to three months each.[2]

All this activity must have been of great interest to the Van Zuile-coms, nearby. Blanche, the youngest, was away at school in Albany, and greatly prized the letters written to her by various members of the family from 'Fairfield' or 'Eeniellup'; letters full of the day to day farm activities so missed by the homesick country schoolchild. In July 1891 her brother Charles wrote from Fairfield: 'We have been out tammar shooting today and we had very good luck. We got thirteen tammars and one eagle-hawk.'[3] In August of the same year her father wrote from Fairfield: 'There is going to be a shooting match at Kojonup on tomorrow, Monday, when Hebby [Herbert] is going to try his skill. . . . Tomorrow, the Grahams arrive and are to take charge, so we shall all be very busy packing up.'[4] In November 1891 her sister Caroline wrote from Eeniellup with details of the forthcoming Broome-hill Show. Her father was sending some wool, some bacon and a couple of hams. The girls were intending to exhibit some eggs, scones and some wildflowers. 'Your little boronia is just coming into flower and I water it every night and I am trying to revive your little pitcher-plant.'[5] A few days later her father wrote to her from Eeniellup:

> The garden is looking lovely. . . . We had some strawberries. . . . There are lots of apples, grapes and peaches coming on, fair crop of plums, not many pears, the cherries will not bear this year—too young, also the chestnuts and walnuts. There are a nice lot of gooseberries. . . . English lilacs, Spanish broom and laburnums are lovely. We are getting a fearfully dry season, I am afraid we shall be short of water.[6]

The letters told of continual stock losses from the poison plants and the nuisance of the ever-prevalent common cold.

Perhaps others of the letters would have mentioned Henry Ranford, the Government surveyor, who was well-liked in the district, particularly by the children.

Mrs Thomas Norrish said of him:

> How the children loved his coming. It always meant new puzzles and conundrums and games and he emulated the (mail) coach's arrival with a great flourish of whip and lusty hoorays.[7]

Ranford had been in the district as early as 1872. At his temporary camps he would welcome parties of his friends and in return be a popular guest at their homesteads. He was a well-read, broadminded personality who had a wide circle of friends in all walks of society. In 1899 Ranford, a widower, married Emily, the daughter of Louis Van Zuilecom.

Two other old families of the district were faced with adjustment to new circumstances as the nineties began. Honora Norrish, the first woman settler of Kojonup, died in 1890. She is said to have left seventy-five descendants. In 1891 the Elverds were again to lose the head of their family at an early age. John, who had shown so much promise, died of pneumonia in 1891 at the age of thirty-four, leaving a young wife and five small children in straitened means. As a result the influence that this family had seemed destined to have in the town gradually waned.

Progress continued to be made on a large scale in neighbouring Katanning. Every few weeks fresh news and rumours sifted through to the older settlement of new achievements and future plans of an unbelievable magnitude. By 1891 a flour mill was actually located there. It was only a matter of time before this prosperous railway town and its neighbour to the south would assert their independence of the sleepy little hollow of Kojonup, twenty miles to the west, and be granted their own local government facilities.

In 1892, the returned W. H. Graham was made chairman of the Road Board. T. Phillips was still secretary but among the members were some new names: J. F. H. Hassell, R. C. Climie, J. J. Garritty, R. F. Krakouer, J. J. Treasure and Richard Burridge who replaced L. F. Van Zuilecom. On 30 September 1892, the whole Board resigned and the Katanning and Broomehill Boards were excised from the Kojonup Road Board. Those elected to the new Board were J. J. Treasure (chairman), John Tunney, R. J. Irving, W. H. Jones, John

Delaney, John Dearle, Chas. Bell, with T. Phillips still acting as secretary. Kojonup Road Board was on its own again.

The three new Road Boards were just beginning to find their feet when a tremendous piece of colonial news rocketed around the world, altering the lives of thousands of people and substantially changing the history of the colony of Western Australia.

In September 1892 Arthur Bayley and John Ford discovered gold 110 miles east of Southern Cross. When Bayley arrived in the Cross with his saddlebag bulging with gold there was almost a complete exodus of men from the town within a couple of days. A little over a year later an even more spectacular field of gold was discovered by Patrick Hannan, Flannigan and O'Shea, twenty miles further east. At the end of the year the Dundas field was discovered to the south, at Norseman; and other important finds were made or claimed almost every few months.

Immigrants flocked into the colony from the other states, through Esperance, Fremantle and Albany. Some who arrived at the latter port made their way to the goldfields through Kojonup, barely giving the little town a backward glance. Those who were more financial travelled north from Albany on the Great Southern Railway line. Naturally, the feverish enthusiasm of the newcomers for the goldfields rubbed off on some of the rustic lads, but on the whole they reacted cautiously.

One of the first to consider pulling up roots was the able rifleman, John Holland. He foresaw the need for a more direct route from Albany to the goldfields and determined to blaze the trail himself. While waiting for the worst of summer to pass he laid his plans with three other experienced bushmen, David and Rudolph Krakouer and John Carmody. (Mrs William Noonan, junior, was a Carmody.) 'We were all natives of Western Australia and our equipment consisted of five Western Australian ponies, a light dray, a 100 gallon tank and provisions for five or six months.'[8] They determined to set out from Broomehill and travel as directly as possible to the goldfields. Their weeks of careful planning, together with their thorough knowledge of the Western Australian bush, paid off. They covered the 320 miles in two months and four days, cutting the travelling time by two weeks. They arrived at Coolgardie just one day after Paddy Hannan reported the discovery of his find. This track was to become a regular route for the diggers arriving at Albany. As well, it was of inestimable value to those who hoped to make their fortunes, not from the yellow metal itself but from the supplying of provisions to the dependent gold seekers. Holland claimed the expedition cut the longest cart track ever made in one stretch in Western Australia.

John Delaney and his brother-in-law, T. Blackmore, were quick to see the worth of the Holland track. They shifted their households to Broomehill in 1895 and at a suitable time set out along the track with a team each and were soon carting all manner of things between Southern Cross, Kalgoorlie, Coolgardie and Menzies.

J. J. Treasure decided to try his luck in 1894 and resigned from the Road Board and was off to the Dundas goldfields, where he was engaged in mining as well as the hotel trade and carting. During the four years he spent there he drove the first wagon team through from Esperance to the Dundas field, his passengers on this occasion being the members of the first Warden's Court which officiated there.

Another to go to the same fields was J. J. Treasure's brother-in-law, J. M. Flanagan, who worked at the St Agnes and Princess Royal mines. He became actively engaged in the fast-growing town of Norseman, being a founder of the Progress Association and instrumental in establishing the first newspaper and hospital. Such experiences were to benefit Kojonup in the future.

Henri Larsen also went in the same direction, finishing up forsaking the gold fever for the job with which he was more familiar: superintending the opening of the road to Norseman from Esperance.

The lure of the goldfields was being felt elsewhere in the town. When John Larsen first began work for Robert ('Dr') Irving he was paid 25s. a week. By 1893 it was necessary to raise the pay to 30s. a week. Soon this was no incentive to those who had the wanderlust for the goldfields. John Larsen, along with others of the company's employees, packed his swag and travelled east.

The flamboyant Irving was finding that the cursed poison plants were not so easily eradicated; they had the persistent habit of suckering if not completely grubbed. The result was disastrous to the livestock. Such setbacks along with inefficient management were making the company's project far from profitable, especially when there were now more lucrative fields of investment in the colony. In 1897 on '29th September, Kojonup location 325 was excised from the Lease 8/266 and granted freehold to the Land Corporation of Western Australia Company Limited for the sum of £210 sterling'.[9]

As the news spread of the company's failure many of the local battlers smiled secretly to themselves as they recalled how their warnings of the poison plant had been boastfully brushed aside by outsiders. From this failure was born the conviction of many old identities that the poison plant in many ways was a blessing in disguise, as it discouraged large-scale development by speculators. There are however many farmers who would not support such an opinion—those who have spent many back-breaking hours grubbing the curse just to lose scores of sheep from one overlooked plant.

One of those who still had more faith in familiar fields was Squatter Jones. In 1885 he had married Tilly, one of the capable daughters of Edward Treasure. In 1893, while other young men were saying good-bye to their young wives and marching off to make their fortunes digging on the Golden Mile, Squatter Jones purchased 1000 acres of poison country and began the tedious task of grubbing. Many were inclined to ridicule his ambition and condemn his optimism as mere foolhardy stubbornness, but five years later he acquired an additional 3000 acres adjoining it. By the turn of the century he had proved the truth of his conviction. He was the owner of 10,000 acres including 5000 acres freehold, which was part of the Leake family's original grant and the 230 acres known as 'Ongerup', which had been owned by his maternal grandfather, William Elverd.

The picture of the goldfields which has endured is one of great camaraderie when, in the face of the adversities of makeshift, grime, heat, flies, unquenchable thirst and disease, the men of all ages held out a hand to those who were in need, and far from loved ones. The glint of the nuggets had not extinguished all the finer qualities intrinsic in man. Yet it is sometimes overlooked that these very traits which were so evident must have been nurtured previous to the romantic vital days of the gold rush, in placid little agricultural villages among struggling pioneer families and in happy co-operative colonial school-rooms.

This spirit of mutual help and comradeship is typified in the letter written to Will and Tilly Jones to wish them a Merry Christmas by an enterprising old friend, Raphael Krakouer, who had gone to the Dundas fields with Charlie Elverd, senior, and another mate, Tom, whose surname is not known.

Dundas Dec 9
1894
(my address is Dundas via Coolgardie
cyclist)

Dear Will,

Just a few lines to let you know I have not forgotten you altogether. Hoping you are all in the best of health has it leaves me and Tom at present but poor Charlie has had a very hard time of it with inflammation of the lung. I had him here for twelve days, next door to death and I have only got three rooms yet and there is only me and Tom to do every thing. But we done the best we could for him has he would do the same for us, has if we were a brother.

And I can tell you I was getting played out myself has trade is pretty brisk so I have not got much time to spare and Manager of the Mabel mine and his wife came down and they made me shift him up to their place and if it was the Governor's son he could not be better cared for and I think he is out of all danger. The managers wife is a regular lady and if Charlie was her son she could not do more for him. It is two miles from here. Tommy has been up to see him today and he is a lot better so I think he will soon be about again.

Will I suppose you have heard before this I am a publican. It is a grand billet here where trade is brisk but we have to do all our own house work which comes pretty rough on us has I cannot get my wife to come up here yet. I don't know why but I think it is the fresh rum she gets on while I am away.

I suppose Kojonup is has dull has ever. When you answer this tell me all about it and how old Dearle is getting on. Is he still in the pub? Tell Till to have plenty of sucking pig when I come down. I will be their some time in February if I don't get none of the sickness that is about here. Their are a lot of people laid up here now but me and Tom has escaped so far and I hope we will continue so.

Dear Will I think I must draw this to a close has it is getting late. Wishing you and Till and the children a merry Christmas and happy new year.

I remain your forever friend

Raphael

Tell Till I would like to have a shot at the fowls they will have for Christmas dinner.[10]

How the hard-living Joseph Spencer and his contemporaries would have thrilled to the adventure of the goldfields in their day! But that was a thing of the past. In January 1891, Joseph Spencer died leaving his property heavily encumbered. His land holdings consisted of Kojonup locations 23, 28, 29, 39, 42, 46 and sub-lots P.8 and P.9. The total area of his leases amounted to 39,760 acres. Everything was taken over by the Bank of Australasia and in 1894 the legendary Balgarup was handed over to Augustus Egerton-Warburton, a son of Lieutenant George Egerton-Warburton and a nephew of the former owner. For £400 he purchased 700 acres. Previous to this Augustus (or Gus, as he was known) had been living in the Lake Muir area and he continued to farm this property for some time but he and his large family made Balgarup their home.

No time was lost in turning to profit the rich acres of their new property. The orchard was vastly improved and soon it was supplying the goldfields with apples. To assist his industrious family Warburton employed many locals for varying periods. In 1893 some of those engaged were Fred Mutton at £2 per month; Richard Kennedy, £1 per month; H. Toovey, £1 5s. 0d. per week; A. Moore, £3 per month; Snowden, £1 per week.

There was seemingly no end to the transactions carried out, simultaneously, by this energetic family. In 1894 beef was sold at 4½d. per pound to John Dearle (120 lbs.), Mrs Richard Norrish (120 lbs), James Tunney (52 lbs.). Later the price went up to 5d. and John Dearle was sold 22 lbs. and Miss Cullinane, 9 lbs. In July 1894 forty head of cattle were sold to A. Muir for £150 and six pigs were bought from Mrs Norrish for £3 12s. 0d.

Patrick Miniter was employed in a variety of ways. He charged 2s. 6d. an acre to ringbark 50 acres; 1s. 9d. an acre for another 100 acres; 1s. an acre for another 100 acres and 8d. for a further 50 acres. He also received 3s. 6d. per chain to split posts, erect and complete nineteen chains of seven wire fencing. Later he completed some more fencing at £13 10s. 0d. per mile.

On 12 January 1894 the family's flock was listed as 1320 ewes, 1680 lambs and wethers and 80 culls. In the same year the family was running six mares with fillies, a stallion, five miscellaneous horses plus their draughthorses. In September 1897, the following sheep were sold:

40 lambs at 8/0	L. Weise
100 lambs at 8/0	Hugh Climie
43 sheep at 9/0	Hugh Climie
700 mixed sheep at 5/0	William Cornwall
9 rams at 10/0	William Cornwall
40 culls at 3/0	James Tunney
20 culls at 8/0	George Dunn[11]

Another who was making great strides in the district was Mrs John Norrish. In 1892 her husband died leaving her with six young children. Like her mother before her such a predicament was a challenge. With boundless energy she extended her interests, tackling every job that arose, from mustering to droving cattle, and carrying her family and friends along with her by determination and a ready sharp wit. Keenly observant and with a background of half a century in the southern areas, she became recognized for her extensive knowledge of the countryside, historical landmarks and tales of the past.

But the precincts of Kojonup could not hold her. Sometime between 1885 and 1899 she leased 5000 acres adjoining the Muradup Reserve, previously held by C. L. Van Zuilecom. (Between 1890 and 1899 Squatter Jones leased 5000 acres on the opposite side of the river.) At different times she bought property at Kulikup, farmed at Dinninup as well as Kojonup, bought and ran hotels in Albany and Kojonup and bred and raced horses profitably due in no small part to her intuitive knowledge of animal husbandry.

When recalling the past it is very easy to view all our pioneers through rose-coloured spectacles and see no faults. Ever since the world began man has been a complexity of gentleness and cruelty, trust and suspicion and those in Kojonup were no different. In the nineties the ingenious Father Chmelicek was the target of some relentless malicious gossip which terminated in his being accused of immoral practices. Rumours of the scandal reached Bishop Gibney and as was the custom in such circumstances he wrote to the priest requesting to see him. It was incomprehensible to this Moravian celibate that anyone would consider him capable of repudiating his ordination vows. Life in the insular Kojonup environment must have been many times irksome for the scholarly priest and the thought that his Bishop would question his integrity cut him to the heart and was the final straw. The whole subject was abhorrent to him and he objected to having to explain himself. In silent retaliation, at the age of sixty-two, he removed himself, crushed in spirit, from the Kojonup town and its people to a little mud-brick hut on the Jackaneedup creek about six miles from Kojonup, just off the Katanning road.

The biggest proportion of Kojonup inhabitants, both of his own church and others, did not believe the vicious tales and those like the elderly Mrs M. Reilly and Margaret Norrish would visit him with small gifts of food, or young newly-weds would call for his blessing. One person, not of his church, who came to know him well and to whom he could converse at an intellectual level was the popular Government surveyor, Henry Ranford. It distressed him deeply to see the old man fading away among the squalor of his hermit's retreat. More than once he wrote to Bishop Gibney, whom he knew personally, in the old man's defence. In one letter he described Father Chmelicek as 'this highly educated simple minded and kind (trusted) aged priest'.[12] In February 1907 he wrote: 'As God is my judge I believe Father Chmelicek to be the soul of honour.'[13] Two years later the old man was found dead by his bed with his rosary grasped in his hands. He was buried in a little cemetery on Noonan's land by Father Michael

Reidy of Katanning. (In 1885 this land had been leased for 999 years as a burial ground by William Noonan, then an Albany innkeeper, to William Grover, Michael Cronin, John Norrish and his wife, and Jane Noonan.)

Contrary to popular belief, Father Chmelicek had not been rejected by the Roman Catholic Church and evidence exists that he periodically had received an allowance from the Church. He was regarded as a retired priest and his wish to be left to himself respected. There is reason to believe that others did not respect the old man's privacy to the same extent and in 1906 he applied to the Road Board for the road through his land to be closed. The matter was left in the hands of the secretary for settlement.

In 1892 when Albert Elverd first attended school it was still held at the barracks. Two years later the first official schoolroom was built, on the corner of Pensioner Road and Spring Street, in sight of the barracks where Miss Cullinane and her daughter lived. Some of his school pals were his cousins, Charlie and Maurice Elverd, and Jimmy Jones, Harry Larsen, Hubert Bagg, Gordon Nicholson, Sonny Ford and other Elverd boys. Among the girls were the Watts children, Octavia Spencer, Cecilia and Emily Norrish, the Palmers and Adeline and Grace Elverd. Sometimes Miss Cullinane had the Newhill children to stay with her (no doubt to keep up the numbers of her class). They were related to her, and attended with her own daughter, Jane.

> We children were no angels. The noise could be heard fifty yards away sometimes. Miss Cullinane could not keep control. When the inspector was coming she would appeal to us and say: 'Oh! my dears, do be good and try your hardest.' She would be trembling all the time. We used to work on slates, some had lines on them and we liked them the best. We would hide them the night before and when school opened the next morning we would charge in to get them. Miss Cullinane was a Roman Catholic and always had prayers and a hymn for the children of her faith after school. She never gave the cane although she had a stick which when the noise was at its loudest she would slap hard on the table. However, she often wore a thimble and would flick us in the ear with it if annoyed with us. She led a rather secluded life. In those days the uprights of the first Barracks were still standing and we children used them as bases for the game of rounders which was very popular then, even the adults played it on a Sunday, where the hospital is now. The rule was one out, all out. One of the favourite games with girls as well as boys was sliding down the big flat rock on the seat of our pants; but our Mothers did not like it.[14]

It is claimed that when the new schoolroom was opened by Mr F. Watts a dance was held to mark the occasion. During the evening twelve hat pegs, the only dish and the key were removed. Later it was discovered that the policeman who was eccentric had taken the articles.

The housing of the Royal Mail seems to have had a very precarious existence in Kojonup. As well as the previously mentioned location, the post office was for a time situated in the south portion of the building erected as a store by the Krakouers. Then in the mid-nineties a post office was built next door to the school in Spring Street—a strange location, considering all the town was then on the Albany Road. The reason might have been that the Government did not possess any land in that vicinity.

Another building that stood in Spring Street, by 1897, was the Agricultural Hall. It was located on the north side of the barracks. It took over the barracks' role as the centre for social gatherings, a change that must have been much appreciated by the tenants of the barracks.

In the second half of the nineties the days of the prospector were finishing, and reef and deep-shaft mining, organized by large companies financed with overseas capital, were fast taking over. There was less likelihood of striking it rich and the idea of spending one's days digging deep in the bowels of the earth did not appeal to those who loved the freedom of the great outdoors. Gradually, many of Kojonup's sons who had left for the distant fields of the gold towns realized that they were not suited to the dry, dusty hubbub and rush of a mining life.

One of those who came wandering back to the old familiar haunts of Kojonup and to the folk with whom he felt an affinity was Henri Larsen. In 1895 he took up virgin land at Muradup and named it 'Muradup Farm'. On it he built a wattle and daub house with a Danish influence: an enormous fireplace that took huge logs to fill it and had seats provided in its construction.

Another to return was J. J. Treasure who settled on land just west of Kojonup, known by the old identities as 'Little Ongerup' but called 'Glenburn' by Treasure. With his usual enthusiasm he set out to build up an impressive line of stud stock in both horses and cattle. By 1898 he was once more a member of the Road Board and chairman by 1900.

165

Yet another to come back was J. M. Flanagan who took up land a
few miles beyond Warkelup and in 1897 replaced T. Phillips as secretary of the Road Board, holding the position until 1907. John Delaney
also returned to Kojonup. He took up farming land in 1899 and renewed his interest in Road Board affairs immediately, being elected
to the Board in 1898. (He had previously been a Road Board member
in 1892 and had resigned in 1895.)

Besides these returned prodigals, complete strangers from the goldfields were wandering through the Kojonup district, liking what they
saw and deciding that it was the spot where they would like to farm.
One of these visitors was James Jeffery. He too had been at the Dundas
field, with a team of horses and wagons. About 1897, he had started
from Esperance and travelled west with his team until he came upon
the Yarranup country so well-known to the early sheep men. At once
this South Australian knew it was the land he had set out to find. He
was joined by his brother, W. Jeffery, who in 1904 became a member
of the Road Board.

The two brothers conducted a systematic ringbarking and clearing
programme in the area as under new land regulations (designed primarily to encourage more settlers into agriculture and to place farming
on a sounder footing) such activities enabled the farmer to obtain
financial assistance to expand further. Another incentive that was to
be a tremendous boost to small rural communities was the Homestead
Act of 1893. Under this act a settler could obtain a free block of 160
acres if he lived on it for seven years improving it by degrees. Obid
Bignell and his family took advantage of this in the second half of
1890. Weary of the goldfields where he had been engaged in a carting
business he came south looking for farming country. He bought land
four miles from Kojonup on the Katanning Road and by 1901 he too
was a member of the Road Board.

Yet another family was disillusioned with the goldfields and chose
to settle in Kojonup, about 1900. The C. H. Bailyes selected a homestead block about six miles north of the town. They built a galvanized
iron house and divided it with hessian to make four rooms. Like many
of the house-proud women of the day who were deprived of a raised
wooden floor Mrs Bailye would boil red gum from the eucalyptus trees
in a big tin and pour it over the carefully swept earthen floor. It would
set with a shiny hard surface which lasted about a week. Soon the
seven Bailye children were enrolled at the Kojonup school and would
travel there in the family's old spring cart, drawn by an equally old
draughthorse named Rory.

The life of these new settlers was very similar for the first few years. Once a house was up and a reliable water supply obtained, from a spring if lucky enough to have one nearby, or by the strenuous and dangerous method of sinking wells, everyone in the family concentrated their efforts on clearing completely a small yard of the dreaded poison plant so that stock such as a milking cow could be safely grazed. Another great fear was the possibility of bushfires. On 11 January 1899 John Watts rushed to the police station at 7 a.m. to report that a large bushfire was raging in the vicinity of the Albany Road and the race course and his house was in danger. About twenty Kojonup inhabitants turned out to help fight the fire and were able to save all his wheat crop.

Cricket was still being played with anyone who could field an eleven. With so much new land being opened up a surveyor's team thought they would be able to show the locals a point or two but had to concede victory in the end. On a number of occasions in the nineties, race meetings were held, and other forms of gambling were in existence too. For instance, in April 1899 the police raided one of the public houses and disturbed most of the town's most worthy citizens thoroughly enjoying a game of dice.

By 1897 Kojonup had an Agricultural and Horticultural Society and still existing are several well-preserved, attractive first prize certificates which were awarded to the Watts family to testify to this. In February 1898, the Society held an autumn show. The occasion was planned around a series of other events.

The twenty-third of February began with a court sitting attended by W. R. Adam, Resident Magistrate, and two cases were heard. At 3 p.m. the show was opened by the Resident Magistrate, and was to stay open until 9.30 p.m. During the same afternoon a cricket match was held against Katanning, Kojonup being the victor. Some of the Katanning supporters took the opportunity to inspect the show.

The following day a race meeting was held between 11.30 a.m. and 5.30 p.m. The acting-clerk of the course, Richard Kennedy, was thrown from his horse and was unconscious for twenty minutes, at some time during the day. That night the Race Ball was held in the Agricultural Hall from 9 p.m. until 3 a.m. The next day a scratch cricket match was held and it is not surprising that it was 'only moderately attended'.[15]

A sequel to this cumulative entertainment was a complaint from James Fowles of the Weld Hotel, Albany, that he had been robbed of a variety of articles whilst visiting Kojonup for the sports. When staying at the Royal some of his clothes were taken and the description given of the articles not only indicates what the well-dressed dandy of the day wore, but also introduces a new concept of travel which was becoming increasingly popular among those of the new generation who were weary of the constant demands of the horse. James Fowles was missing one soft cream shirt with small flowers, one white necktie with red flowers, a gold scarf pin, white handkerchief, brown socks and a pair of bicycle socks, dark brown with flowered tops.

These earlier shows were apparently only displays of produce, mainly fruit and vegetables, and it was not until 4 November 1898 that the Kojonup Agricultural and Horticultural Society held its first *annual* show. It is generally known that the first shows were held where the hospital now stands. According to the press report of this first annual show 'the grounds had only been in the hands of the Society a few weeks',[16] but great improvements had been made to them and this together with the delightful weather contributed in making the occasion most successful. The day concluded with a dinner at Norrish's hotel for the official guests which included L. L. Cowan, (Secretary of the Agricultural Department), Crawford (a dairy expert) and Craig (Chief Inspector of Stock) and the committee, L. F. Van Zuilecom (president) and J. M. Flanagan (secretary). After this everyone went on to the Show Ball at the Agricultural Hall.

The prize list of this first annual show reads like a muster roll of all Kojonup's old families. The best dairy cow was owned by Mrs James Tunney, the morning milk weighing 28½lbs. The prize for the best cow for breeding beef was awarded to Mrs Margaret Norrish. J. J. Treasure's Clydesdale stallion, Hero's Lad, won a first prize; so too did his black mare, Violet. The best mare for breeding for export was considered J. B. Tunney's Actress; and the best draught mare, Western Australian bred, was A. Egerton-Warburton's Dobbie. In the sheep section, J. J. Treasure took first and second prizes for the best merino ram and Mrs Margaret Norrish took first and second for the best ram (any breed), while W. T. Jones took the prizes for the best pen of five fat lambs and five fat wethers. The first prize for the best two fleeces went to T. Norrish and the second prize to W. T. Jones. The best three bundles of green fodder were exhibited by A. Egerton-Warburton and W. Norrish. Other sections covered produce, poultry, flowers and vegetables and the names of Bagg, Watts, Van Zuilecom, Dearle, Delaney, Larsen and Elverd are sprinkled throughout.

Life must have seemed very civilized to those like Thomas Norrish who could remember the same site when the little barracks had stood alone. But not sufficient progress had reached Kojonup to eliminate many heartaches such as that when six months later a sorrowing Squatter Jones and his wife returned mentally exhausted from seeing their two-year-old daughter buried to find their four-year-old little girl was dead with the same dread disease—diphtheria.

REFERENCES

[1] Information on pages 208, 209, 210 from Anthony Barker, 'The History of Jingalup', p. 21 (Teachers Higher Certificate thesis, 1959; held in Rooney Library, Education Dept., Perth).

[2] *Ibid.* p. 25.

[3] Extracts from Van Zuilecom letters (in possession of John Warburton, Kojonup).

[4] *Ibid.*

[5] *Ibid.*

[6] *Ibid.*

[7] A. Burton, comp. 'Memories of Mrs Thomas Norrish', W.A.H.S. journal *Early Days*, vol. 1, October 1938, p. 30.

[8] *Great Southern Herald*, 15 November 1963, p. 11. Condensed from a paper read by the late John Holland at Bulong in 1906.

[9] Barker, p. 32.

[10] Letter from R. Krakouer to W. T. Jones, 9 December 1894 (held in K.H.S. Recs.).

[11] Extracts from Balgarup Diaries (in possession of D. Crabbe, Kojonup).

[12] Letter from H. Ranford to Bishop Gibney, 5 May 1904, in notes on Father F. J. Chmelicek collected by Rev. Martin Newbold (in possession of Rev. Martin Newbold, Kojonup).

[13] Letter from H. Ranford to Bishop Gibney, 14 February 1907, in *ibid.*

[14] Personal conversation with A. and J. C. Elverd, 8 August 1969.

[15] Police Occurrence Book, 418, 25 February 1898 (held in Battye Library, Perth).

[16] *Albany Advertiser,* 10 November 1898, p. 1.

11

Metamorphosis

Ushered in with the twentieth century were many new problems, concepts and schemes for the colony of Western Australia and, likewise, for Kojonup. The first major decision to be faced for the whole colony must surely have been the question of federation. The realization that there were topics other than regional to concern them was brought home to the Kojonup Road Board when they received a telegram from the Hon. F. H. Piesse announcing that he would address a meeting in Kojonup on 23 July 1900 at 8 p.m. on the subject of federation. The Road Board decided to make the most of the visit and ask for £150 grant for the Road Board, £100 for the Agricultural Society and £50 for a recreation ground.

The family of A. Egerton-Warburton considered federation of sufficient importance to squeeze the announcement 'Mama and Papa went to Kojonup to vote for Federation'[1] on 31 July 1900 in between more mundane diary jottings of sales and purchases of wheat and eggs, the movement of hawkers, the planting of cabbages and the employment of men. For Mrs Egerton-Warburton, as for all the women of Kojonup and Western Australia, it was a unique experience, being the first time women of the state had been given a vote. Altogether, seventy persons cast their vote between 9 a.m. and 7 p.m. at the little post office in Spring Street, after which the policeman, on his horse, delivered the ballot box to Broomehill where it was conveyed by the modern railways to be counted with every other vote in Australia. A new era was on its way!

Symbolically, perhaps, only ten days before a labourer James Casey had reported to the same policeman that a two-room cottage at Warkelup was burned down and his swag had gone with it. Offhandedly, the policeman recorded that 'it was a very old thatched cottage'.[2] It was in fact the same which Richard Norrish and his family had inhabited so gratefully half a century earlier.

Another momentous event at the turn of the century on which Australia was to focus considerable attention was the war in South

Africa. The Kojonup settlers were to reap some financial benefits from the war. In February 1901 military officials arrived in the town to buy eight horses for the sixth contingent. A year later the police were notified to inform the residents that the second Commonwealth contingent wanted to buy another forty or fifty horses and a large muster was to be held in Katanning on 21 February, but only the best horses would be purchased.

The district was also called upon to support the war. The mayor of Perth wrote to the Road Board requesting subscriptions to his patriotic fund for the Transvaal war. Over £5 was raised on the spot and it was decided to leave the appeal at both hotels for further donations.

In March 1901 a different appeal was made. After a race meeting and before the Race Ball a Mr Kreiger, returned soldier from South Africa who had been recommended for the Victoria Cross, gave a short lecture on the war. Although the lists of Western Australian volunteers include the name of W. Norrish no record survives of great enthusiasm for enlisting among the young men of the countryside. It could be that the gruesome tales of their military forefathers were still too vividly in their minds for them to be willing to forsake the quiet security of Kojonup for doubtful adventure and almost certain bloodshed.

A more conclusive break with the past was felt by the residents when the police constable announced he had received a telegram revealing that Queen Victoria had died and the day of her funeral, 2 February 1901, would be observed as a bank and general holiday, and a day of mourning. If there still existed any deep-seated sentiment of loyalty for the grand old lady who had been on the throne for sixty-four years, it was not sufficient in the one-time outpost of her military command to interfere with the locals' thorough enjoyment of a cricket match against the Arthur River team and the dance that followed at the 'Semblance', just the night preceding the official day of mourning. (This, in fact, was the last time the police constable referred to the 'Semblance'; henceforth, it became known as the 'Commonwealth'.)

In July 1901, the Duke and Duchess of Cornwall and York visited Western Australia and Constable Jones with his police horse Feather left on the Katanning train for two weeks duty in Perth during the celebrations. His experiences must have enthralled many locals when he returned.

This succession of grand displays in the state gave rise to pompous expressions of patriotism and gaudy parades everywhere, such as one of the items at a Kojonup school concert on Easter Monday, 5 April 1902, in aid of the school's prize fund. The children, with the girls all

171

dressed in white with blue sashes, performed a flag display of choruses and marching, explaining the history of the Union Jack. Perhaps such sensations impressed some of the children more deeply than was imagined and partly accounted for the emotional response that some young adults were to make twelve years later, in support of the 'mother country' and the red, white and blue.

At the moment, however, although such events helped to make rural people such as those in Kojonup realize that they were not completely shut off from the rest of the world, it was still the parochial problems that made the greatest impact in their lives.

It is generally acknowledged that the factor which most of all helped to vitalize the colony's static society was the rapid growth in the population initiated by the goldrushes. Kojonup continued to benefit from the side effects of this inflow of families. When the men grew disappointed in their search for the elusive gold they reflected further on the agricultural land they had passed on their way to the fields. Many of these men had come originally from farming communities and the incentives held out to would-be farmers by the Western Australian Government's liberal land laws, particularly the Homestead Act, and the new Agricultural Bank with its declared policy of cheap and ready rural credit, were very attractive to many. Their views that farming in the west looked most promising was relayed to friends in the east and almost every week newcomers were known to be settling somewhere nearabouts or making inquiries concerning land.

Many were attracted to properties nearer the railways, and some were prepared to go even further east, but there were still others who had come from a small rainfall area and were reluctant to once more face similar conditions, and were attracted by Kojonup's heavier annual rainfall. As the twentieth century progressed the Government promoted immigration from the United Kingdom, by the offer of free or assisted passages. Gradually, new homesteads appeared in the most unlikely places and old maps are marked with innumerable 160 acre blocks where some enterprising settler of this period tried for some years to make good, only to eventually walk off or sell to faster growing neighbours.

In the month ending 14 February 1903, it was claimed that twenty people had applied for conditional land purchase in Kojonup amounting to 2425 acres and twelve had applied for Homestead farms covering 1884 acres. These 't'othersiders' as they were mostly called by the locals were regarded with suspicion at first and one Kojonup store-keeper was heard to mutter after having made up a big grocery order for a newcomer: 'Those blooming t'othersiders, they'll eat us out.'

Nevertheless, the common interest of sport was to help to break down the initial strangeness, although some local champions did not appreciate having their nose put out of joint by more adept new-comers. Cricket continued to be the most effective means of bringing people together and the spread of settlement could almost be followed by the matches arranged. In the early 1900s cricket was played against the Blackwood, 'Oakfarm', 'The Glen', Arthur River, Katanning, Broomehill, Carrolup and later with Muradup.

Other sports were also claiming supporters. In April 1903 the Kojonup Tennis Club felt so confident that it was considering throw-ing out a challenge to the Katanning Club. During the winter months of the same year some exciting football had been played against Carrolup. By September both sides had won a match and in the finals Kojonup was the victor with 4 goals, 4 points against Carrolup's 3 goals. However, the losers had the excuse that they had been short of players and had been forced to take substitutes from their oppo-nents. The best players for Kojonup had been Egan, Norrish, Ranford, Walker and Petersen, while for Carrolup they were Longmire, Norrish, Lynes and Ranford. Later in the month the cocky Kojonup side had to eat humble pie when they were beaten by Marracoonda.

It is interesting to note that the local Aborigines also had a liking for sport and as early as 20 March 1901, the police constable recorded that they were congregating for a big hockey match. More than one Kojonup octogenarian claims that this was a game of their own de-vising and by no means copied from the white settlers. It was played with such intensity, belligerence and noise that when word spread of a forthcoming match many keen sportsmen made a point of being in the vicinity that day.

The Longmires who were prospering at 'The Glen' had some close relatives in South Australia who were experiencing very bad times due to a succession of droughts since 1896. In 1903 their relative W. H. Haggerty accompanied by his son Ern and a neighbour's boy William Yates came to visit the Longmires and to consider the pros-pects of the western state. Haggerty selected land near the Muradup Pool and then returned to South Australia to organize the removal of the families.

On 4 March 1904 the Yates and Haggerty families with all their cattle, horses, poultry and household effects landed at Albany, having made the trip across the Bight in a freighter, the *New Guinea*. From Albany the cavalcade set out for Kojonup. Mr and Mrs Haggerty went first in their buggy to arrange the next camp and to have the billy boiling for the others at the end of each tiring day. Mrs Yates followed in their buggy and pair with three of the children and Mr Yates, with one of his sons, drove the wagon while another boy Cecil, riding Haggerty's old school pony Toss, kept the cows moving.

The journey took nearly a week and when they reached Kojonup their arrival caused quite a stir. They camped just north of the town, where the Roman Catholic school is built. They located Jack Bilston who had been farming before the turn of the century with his brother Reuben on the Blackwood (Reuben had first come to the state to work on the Albany to Esperance telegraph line) and he agreed to pilot them to the Haggerty's land 1½ miles south of the present town of Muradup, on the Balgarup River. The next day they all had a pleasant surprise when Walter and Ern Haggerty arrived from the goldfields, where they had been working. These two young men had caught the train to Katanning and had come the rest of the way on bicycles, following the road to 'Eeniellup' and turning off when they noticed signs of wagons leaving the track.

After a few weeks the Yates had found their homestead blocks, just north of the Muradup Pool, and went to camp at the Pool in order to be closer to their holdings. Probably in relation to these newcomers the press reported in June 1904:

> Judging by the large numbers of strangers who have come here lately with the idea of selecting, it appears that this long forsaken district is going to advance at last.[3]

In October of the next year it was written:

> A good deal of settlement is going on west of Kojonup; indeed, there is a greater population in that portion of the district than around Kojonup itself.[4]

Soon the Haggerty and Yates families were busily engaged in building their first house—all bush timber, galvanized iron and hessian. The older Haggerty boys did share cropping for the Holly brothers whom they had met through the Longmires. The first year the wheat averaged sixteen bushels and the next year twelve. They also engaged in mallet bark carting and any other lucrative contract work available, and the money obtained was handed to their father.

Further west from the Haggerty's on the outskirts of the Kojonup district another farmer, a former Queenslander, was having great success with some rich black soil he had carefully selected. In the middle of heavy bush, miles from any neighbours, a Mr Foley had built up a splendid farm which was bringing him profitable returns despite the fact he had to transport his produce fifty miles to the railway. In 1905 this skilled agriculturalist had a thriving orchard of three-year-old Cleopatra apple trees and regularly supplied 'the metropolitan and Kalgoorlie markets with large quantities of the most perfect fruit'.[5] Besides apples this resourceful farmer cultivated English fruits such as gooseberries, raspberries and currants as well as a wide range of vegetables, stone fruit and melons, on the fertile isolated country he had the courage to choose.

In April 1903 rumour had it that the Western Australian Land Company intended spending £50,000 in improving its enormous leases in the Kojonup district, but residents with long memories were very sceptical. Soon after it was reported:

> T. H. Kappler has accepted the contract to clear, fence and grub 15000 acres of the Western Australian Land Co's immense Poison Lease. Six men have been put on to commence the work. The contractor remarked yesterday that 'the Company were just going to see what the result of this job is like before going on with the rest of their lease'.[6]

As the Kojonup folk suspected, it was to be left to individuals to finally bring much of this land into production, people like M. L. Ashe and his boys. They had arrived from Tasmania in 1902 and had selected four homestead blocks on part of location 325, termed the 'Jingalup Estate'. When they first arrived their only possessions were a spring cart, a pick and axe, some stores and five shillings in cash. Once a shack was built for Mrs Ashe the men set to work with a will to clear, poison grub and fence the land, but it was three years before they were able to put sheep on the country. The Agricultural Bank only advanced money for ewes and the ruling price was 7s. 6d. each. The first wool clip consisted of one bale and a few bags and was sold for 10d. lb.

All this time many old identities were making changes in their lives. In March 1900 there were 43 males and 34 females in the town and 60 males and 31 females living within the Road Board district.

Young Albert Elverd was soon considered of an age to earn a living and at ten had done some shepherding for £1 a month. He would usually be given about fifty to one hundred weaners to shepherd. Sometimes the chief shepherd, George Reilly, would give him a few extra shillings to mind the whole flock (anything up to 1500 sheep) while he went to play Sunday cricket.

But Albert's first main job was in 1901 when he was fifteen, as a house boy to L. F. Van Zuilecom. He received 30s. a month and for this he had to rise first, light the fire, call Mr Herbert and Mr Fred and serve them breakfast. (Miss Van Zuilecom and her father would breakfast later.) He then hurried to milk the four cows and to return to do all the washing-up. Later he would get in all the wood for the day and attend the pigs. Another dreaded job was working in the smoke house, keeping wet straw on the fire so that the smoke would not diminish. However, when the ham was fully smoked it was delicious and well worth the smarting eyes, running nose and general discomfort.

Miss Van Zuilecom was a wonderful housekeeper. When she went visiting to Perth she gave Albert detailed instructions on how to cook the meals, particularly the bread. The family entertained a great deal and one visitor that Albert particularly remembers was the Church of England minister, Rev. J. A. Howes of Katanning. There was to be a service in the Agricultural Hall and everyone was rushing around preparing to leave. The kind clergyman saw the young lad standing bashfully nearby and said: 'You can come with me.' His heart leaping for joy the boy climbed aboard the minister's sulky and they set off jauntily for Kojonup, leaving the rest of the household to follow in the buggy and pair. He felt very grand as they drove through the streets of Kojonup.

Despite all the work Albert enjoyed his sixteen months at 'Eeniellup' but in 1903 his father became an agent for Henry Wills and Co., skin buyers of Albany and wished the lad to go out possuming to increase business, so Albert had to leave the Van Zuilecoms.

Another service which Rev. J. A. Howes conducted at Kojonup was the wedding of Reuben Bilston and Florence Mary Watts on 23 September 1901. This social occasion had the honour of being reported in the first issue of the Katanning newspaper the *Great Southern Herald* and the account gives an excellent indication of the local etiquette of the day and the style of ladies' fashions. The bride 'was elegantly attired in white silk with tucked yoke and chiffon trimming and orange blossom'[7] while her handsome and accomplished sister, Miss Mary Watts, wore cream cashmere with blue trimmings and a picture hat and the two other bridesmaids, Misses Cissie Krakouer and Florence

Bailye had similar frocks in blue. The best man was E. Bilston of Burrocoppin.

A reception was held at Spring Villa and 'a large number of wedding presents, including both the useful and ornamental were tastefully displayed on a side table'.[8] Later the guests returned to the Agricultural Hall and dancing was enjoyed until daylight. Among those present were Miss Van Zuilecom, white muslin de clime, with pale blue sash and valenciennes lace; Miss Warburton (Balgarup) black skirt, pink nun's veiling bodice with guipure lace and pearl necklet; Miss Climie (Ballochmyle) black silk; Miss O'Callaghan (Kojonup) canary silk trimmed with black velvet; Miss E. Jones, cream muslin, blue trimming; Miss Norah Norrish, white silk skirt, old gold blouse; Mrs Lambe, blue cashmere; Miss Clara Dearle, pink satin and Miss Rose Tree, pink muslin with white lace.

In August 1902 the young bridegroom was to be elected secretary of an Anglican committee formed to organize the building of a church in the town. £20 was donated at the meeting and a subscription list was sent around the district.

Earlier in the year a concert had been held in the same hall in aid of the building of a Roman Catholic church, although the programme indicates that an ecumenical attitude prevailed at such times. The evening was presided over by Anglican L. F. Van Zuilecom and his family figured largely in it. H. Van Zuilecom sang 'They all love Jan' and F. Van Zuilecom sang 'Gathering Shells'. Other items were performed by Miss C. Krakouer, a recitation 'Boka'; Mrs Bailye, 'Kate O'Shane'; J. M. Flanagan, 'Blow the Candle Out' (encored); H. G. Jones, 'Thy Voice is Near' and the overture was played by Mrs J. W. Norrish.

Before 1902 ended Mrs Ambrose Forsythe, the mother of Kojonup's first Anglican family, died at the age of eighty. 'The coffin was carried from her late residence to the cemetery and was followed by all the residents of Kojonup, walking.'[9] After the first few years of their arrival in Kojonup this Pensioner family grew more and more retiring, humble and frugal. Of all the children—Margaret, Ambrose, Johnny and Robert—only Robert married and then late in life to the widowed Mrs John Elverd. Whereas other Pensioner families like the Noonans flourished in their new environment the Forsythes withdrew into themselves, hardly noticed by the more active residents. Little remains to show that they ever contributed to the settlement of the original town.

Miss Cullinane left the Kojonup school in 1900 and there followed a succession of teachers. In April 1901, a Mr Young took over and soon fitted in well with the little community. He learnt from the men how to set snares and each evening would do his rounds of nearby possum haunts. He was the first teacher to stay for any length of time who was not a Roman Catholic and the Anglican families were delighted when Mrs Young held Sunday school for the children. Once when an Anglican clergyman remained for a meal with the Youngs he was served possum as poultry. There was great merriment among the neighbours when Mrs Young related how the august gentleman had praised her delicious poultry meal and had asked for a second helping!

Young was a great lover of trees and it is said that he planted the pepper trees that grow in front of the barracks which was then the schoolteacher's residence. In July 1902, he received forty-two trees from the Department of Woods and Forest and the following children were chosen to plant some of them: Thomas Oliver (Mrs Young's son from a previous marriage), F. Bailye, A. Watts, A. Dearle, Henry Jones, Agnes Dearle, Emily Jones, Doris Oliver, Grace Adams, Adeline Elverd and Maud Elverd. On 4 August a big occasion was made of Arbor Day. Another twenty trees were planted in the morning by the twenty-five children who were present, followed by a lesson entitled 'Trees and their uses'. Later, Mr Flanagan addressed the pupils and presented certificates to those who had been successful in their last exam. In the afternoon sports were conducted and £2 7s. 6d. was distributed as prizes, after which the parents and visitors handed out refreshments.

A week later the children enjoyed another day of sports, to celebrate the coronation of King George V. Like his predecessors, Young was forever complaining of the absentees when the adults held sporting functions, shows and race meetings. Poor attendance affected his salary and in September 1902, after two days with only six children present one morning and none the next, he determined that in future he would have the days omitted from the quarterly average.

That year the children were successful in gaining quite a few prizes at the Katanning Show, as well as the local show. Yet the next year a new teacher arrived and his opinion of the children's work was far from complimentary. After the monthly examination in February he wrote:

Drawing: Freearm Instruction,; the children had very little idea of this subject and were sitting in the wrong position.
Drill: The children hardly know their left from their right and *new* nothing of the physical drill.

Reading: Read too much of a sing-song style and do not pronounce the h's and read ink for ing, etc.

Arithmetic, mental: Not satisfactory in any standard for the tables are very badly known.[10]

By July this teacher had been transferred and it would appear the children were not sorry. His place was taken by a Mr Archibald. That year the average enrolment was 19.9, but the following year for a time it dropped to 8.9, mainly because the Lambe family left the district.

One of the seasonal problems was the scarcity of water. In those days when the excellence of one's starching and ironing was an item of great importance, the lack of water for the weekly wash was keenly felt by the ladies. In summer, some would take their clothes to the Spring to do the washing. In March 1900 Mrs Margaret Norrish complained that a tub and boiler she had left there had been damaged.

Another well just west of the Spring was called 'Charity Well' as local Aborigines and destitute ageing men would camp there. Some ladies did their washing there and sometimes these visiting ladies would report to the police if they saw any particularly needy cases. In July 1898 Mrs Larsen had told the constable of Ben Gaylor who was very ill and it was arranged for the old man to go to the Katanning hospital for treatment. In the days when there were no social service benefits, 'charity' was a word frequently used.

The year 1902 was very dry and the Road Board was granted an additional £50 to improve the water situation at the Spring, the recognized town supply. It was decided to use the money to supply additional troughs and to improve the approach to the Spring. T. E. Larsen was given the contract to do the work.

As in the past, associated with the dry conditions were devastating bushfires. In 1901, 5000 acres of summer feed owned by Squatter Jones went up in smoke. Samuel Bagg was lucky to have his standing crop saved. That year it was thought expedient to extend to 1 March the date for opening the burning season. No one knew when the fire menace would strike. In April 1904 it struck, with a vengeance, the Van Zuilecom's property. The threshing and winnowing machines and a large hay shed were destroyed as well as 13 tons of hay, 4 tons of hay straw and 2 tons of barley. The family considered themselves fortunate that the stables and adjoining barn were saved.

By the early 1900s some of the more progressive of Kojonup's farmers were becoming aware of the state's new Department of Agriculture and the technical advice it could give. When Squatter Jones lost two cows and looked like losing a third, he called in the Government vet who after inspecting the sick animal diagnosed the complaint as being due to eating greedily of rough dry grass. In April 1902 R. Warburton, inspector of stock, addressed a meeting on the diseases of animals. Farmers were becoming more aware of the need to improve their blood stock and for a time in the early 1900s a Government shorthorn bull was stationed in the district and its progeny were soon winning prizes at the local shows.

In September 1903, Dalgety and Co. imported some very fine merino rams for W. T. Jones, W. Cornwall and the Treasure brothers from the stud of Murray Bros.; and three shorthorn bulls were on order for J. J. Treasure, R. and E. Treasure and W. T. Jones. Mrs Margaret Norrish had also ordered some merino rams through her agent, H. Wills and Co.

Not all the farmers were as careful with their animals and at the end of 1901, although it was considered the best season ever with abundant grass, a stock inspector called G. A. Glen had to quarantine many sheep in the district, owing to the prevalence of tick, and as a result the numbers in the sheep section at the 1902 show were down.

To clean up the flocks, dipping was enforced. One of the first dips was constructed near two wells in the main street opposite the police station. It was made of galvanized iron and was filled by bucket from the wells. Shepherds would bring the sheep in from the bush and yard them in a small adjacent paddock that was enclosed with a slab fence.

These same wells were a favourite camping site for teams of mallet bark carters. Some nights there would be as many as five or six teams camped there. Any team that arrived after all the others had turned in for the night was far from popular in the morning. By 1904 the mallet bark industry was booming and in July of that year seven parties of eight or nine had left the town and were out in different directions, seeking the bark. Abraham ('Chubb') Krakouer had negotiated a large contract and employed teams of men to collect the bark. At fifteen Charlie Elverd was in one of the teams and for ten weeks work he received ten gold sovereigns. When he walked down the street with them clinking in his pocket he felt like a king.

Poison plants continued to be a grave problem and nobody was more aware of it than the local Road Board. Consequently it was considered money well spent when, in January 1903, Charlie Elverd was paid 8s. a day to clear the poison off the roads, a chain wide. In 1905 there was an increasing tendency to specialize in sheep wherever it was

30　Clearing the country

31　Business centre at Kojonup about 1906, now demolished. The formal attire of the National Bank
　　manager at left on the verandah contrasts with that of the storekeeper at right

32   Kojonup *c.* 1904, looking from barracks up Spring Street, with the post office at right, later the head-master's residence, now privately owned. Left background, the Royal Hotel. Cart occupants may be J. J. Treasure and son

33   Kojonup *c.* 1904; Albany Road looking north from Broomehill Road corner at right and Blackwood Road turnoff at left

financially possible. Arguments were put forward that they were less trouble or that the weather was more suitable to grazing than farming. A certain optimism was being felt in relation to the poison plants.

Some people claimed:

> In recent years great progress has been made in clearing the land of poison and settlers have found out how to minimize the scourge by dividing the land into a number of paddocks, by grubbing and by heavy stocking with sheep etc. Consequently, the poison plant has not its former possibilities of disaster to stock.[11]

To make such bald statements in Kojonup was tempting fate and in the same month J. J. Treasure had the misfortune to have his valuable imported shorthorn bull die from eating poison.

It is difficult to conceive today the hundreds of hours of tedious backbreaking work that went into clearing some of the best farms around the Kojonup district. Whole families, from the mother to the toddler, would be put to the task of 'specking' for the plants. At one property a visitor found all the family moving over a paddock in a line, each child taking a turn to walk beside the mother and read a page of his reading book.

It is not possible to say for certain who was the first person to develop the most successful method of poison grubbing. There is some reason to believe that the system of knocking out the York Road poison with a mattock, packing the hole tightly with fresh soil and patting it down firmly with the blade of the mattock was brought to the district by a South Australian, Ted Forbes, who developed the method on a property at Moodiarrup owned by a Mr Towns. He passed on his ideas to the Elverds when he joined their team. It was this method that was used extensively by the teams working for Squatter Jones. When others saw the success achieved, with little regrowth, it was soon copied. The only criticism oldtimers made of the method was the difficulty sometimes in finding sufficient clean soil in a badly infested paddock, to pack into the holes.

Another plant that was suspected of being poisonous about this time was the stinkwort. In 1903, the local press interviewed Kojonup's two publicans on the subject. John Dearle was convinced it should be eradicated:

> The Government should put a lot of men on in every district to set to work and grub the crimson coloured weed up, instead of messing about appointing inspectors to travel around and inspect the stuff. A nice picnic the inspector is having at seventeen bob a

day. I've heard as how that's the screw he's getting. Good luck to him if it is so, I say, but by the same rule why not put a lot of men to kill the weed?[12]

W. Cornwall had different views. It was written:

Rare indeed are the occasions on which Mr C. drops his voice to a whisper and imparts an opinion confidentially. His practice is generally to express himself in a resounding voice calculated to awake the heaviest sleeper . . . what a lot of nonsense they are talking about stinkwort. Why it's fodder, as good as clover, and my stock are all eating it. And so long as they do no Government in the world will make me destroy my fodder. No siree. Why our local policeman will tell you that his horse and cow eat the stuff too. It's a pity the inspectors hadn't something better to do; some of 'em are big enough and ugly enough to take to real hard work instead of inspecting stuff which is good fodder.[13]

The Government eventually gave a grant one year so that men could be employed in grubbing it out along the roads but in the end more people came to accept Cornwall's views and just lived with the pest.

In a home where poison grubbing and the tools employed were as common to the children as the cutlery on the table, a father relaxing by the fire one night put down the book he was reading and said, 'Ah! the nomadic life, that's the life for me.' The littlest of the family looked up and agreed, 'Yes Daddy, I think a no-mattock life would be best, too.'

The prevalence of the noxious weeds certainly did not frighten off all would-be settlers. In January 1906, the acting land agent at Katanning, R. Cobham, visited the district to obtain some statistics concerning settlement. Within a radius of fifteen miles north, south and west and of ten miles east of the town he estimated there were 142 families. Other figures compiled were:

Freehold land, first class:	130,981 acres
Second and third class:	61,524 acres
Ringbarked country:	7050 acres
Wheat grown:	2858 acres
Oats grown:	703 acres
Barley grown:	200 acres
Total area cleared:	8792 acres
Orchards:	121 acres
Horses:	1130
Cattle:	514
Sheep:	10,495
Pigs:	200[14]

One of the new settlers would have been Arthur Liddell and his family who had come from the eastern states and settled just east of Kojonup town in the Warkelup area. About the same time the Watts family found themselves in financial trouble and were forced to give up their much-loved Spring Villa and shift to a small block on the Collie Road. Their former home was bought by a benevolent Fremantle gentleman, J. McHenry Clark, who renamed it 'Glen Lossie'. He paid £2000 for it and was soon renovating the house to suit the needs of himself and his daughter and son-in-law, Mr and Mrs Tom Fitch. (Two rooms were built onto the north end of the homestead and later another owner, C. H. Neumann, added another on the south end.)

In 1905 McHenry Clark was elected to the Road Board and was chosen chairman for two years, when he was replaced by J. J. Treasure but still remained on the Board. In October 1907 he proposed that the part of Albany Road running through Kojonup town be called High Street, as was the main street of Fremantle, and this it was called for many years. At the same time the three streets cutting through the old police reserve were named Elverd, Spencer and Van Zuilecom.

In January 1905 both of the town's hotels changed hands. R. C. Treasure took over the Commonwealth from the Dearle family and G. Howlett was reported to have bought the Royal and rented all the Cornwall's farming land for ten years. Yet, in October of the same year it was announced that D. Krakouer was proprietor of the Royal and that Howlett had sold his general store that was opposite the Royal to R. L. Richardson of Katanning. The highly-respected J. W. Anthony was made manager of the new store and a small room at the south end of the building was rented to Kojonup's first bank, the National Bank of Australasia. The branch manager was J. Boxall. It is said that for a time he slept on the premises, in the banking chamber. The first two accounts registered in 1906 were in the name of J. McHenry Clark, but he was not destined to be a client for long.

In May 1908 a tragedy occurred at Glen Lossie (and resurrected amongst superstitious district patriarchs whispers of the property's half-forgotten curse). It happened that McHenry Clark was doing some business in his home while nearby his son-in-law was cleaning a gun. The older man is said to have asked Fitch to check something he had written and in so doing the gun in the younger man's hand went off and McHenry Clark was killed almost instantly. On 2 May it was recorded in the Kojonup Road Board Minute Book:

that all members meet at the office, Sunday May 3rd at 12-30 p.m. and walk to Glen Lossie and head the funeral from the house to the Katanning Road. Also that J. J. Treasure arrange with the secretary to have the Board represented at the funeral in Fremantle on Tuesday and a wreath be placed on the grave.[15]

Before this tragedy many other changes had occurred in the district. Another city businessman who had become interested in the district was J. C. G. Foulkes. He had bought the property south of the town known as 'Maybenup' and was making many improvements to it. His brother, W. J. Foulkes, had settled in the Muradup area and later shifted to a property at Marlyup; his wife was an active member of the Church of England in the district. In 1905, C. P. Reilly resumed the business of A. Mowan. The following year Margaret Norrish took over the Royal and six months later her daughter married John Cornwall, the son of the original owner.

In 1905 J. B. Harrison came from South Australia to escape the severe drought there. He had been used to wheat country but was weary of never having sufficient rain and decided to look for sheep land. He settled for some country north of the town which he was shown by one of Margaret Norrish's sons, who was a land guide for the district. It was called 'Coban Soak' and was said to have been named after an old kangaroo hunter who camped there for some years.

Early in 1906 the three oldest Harrison boys came to join their father. They had brought a horse and cart with them and were amazed on reaching Albany to learn that they would have to pay a sum of money to take the articles ashore. Fortunately they were able to wire their father for the money as they had very little cash with them. Once the matter was settled they hurried to Kojonup in the vehicle and spent their first night in the district sleeping in McHenry Clark's shed. Later in the year Mrs Harrison and the rest of the family followed.

At this stage the Coban Soak area (later called 'Boscabel') had not been surveyed. There was an intelligent Aborigine, Bobby Edgell, who badly wanted to have a Homestead block around the soak but it was made a reserve so that all could have the use of the water, and Edgell took the adjacent block. (Edgell once told Charlie Elverd that he was born under a huge red gum that grew near the property known as Glen Lossie and it would seem that this apportioned him to the Coban Soak area rather than to the Kojonup area. This same big red gum was sometimes referred to in Road Board Minutes when a landmark was required.

When the Harrisons arranged for the surveyor Bowler and his young assistant Fred Cox to survey their land they also surveyed Edgell's land and the Road Board gave permission for a road to the holding to be surveyed in October 1906. Edgell however never continued with his block and it was eventually taken over by a policeman, Tom O'Connor.

The surveyors were with the Harrisons about four days and the family took very great care not to incorporate any poison land in their selection. The first summer an 800-yard dam was excavated with a homemade wheelbarrow. Everyone gave a hand. The children ran themselves to a standstill going up and down the ever-growing slope. During the excavation one of the little fellows had a birthday and as a present the ingenious Mrs Harrison made him a little apron from a sugar bag, featuring a huge pocket in the centre front in which he could carry the clods. He was delighted with it and the envy of all the others.

Until this dam was filled the Harrisons had to cart all their water from Coban Soak. The first year they cropped twenty-five acres and it yielded between nine and ten bushels per acre. The family led a lonely life for the first few years with very few celebrations. About a week before Christmas the older boys would take some time off from their chores to go duck-shooting to provide a change of diet, but many times the festival would pass with little attention. However, the one holiday that was never overlooked was the day of the Kojonup Show. It was the highlight of their year.

In 1906 another block in the Jingalup Estate was settled, and the Ashe family had as neighbours three hard-working Swedish brothers, Edwin, Oscar and Eric Ericson. They built their dwelling on the edge of Murrin Brook and as well as carting contracts and the usual farming pursuits they cultivated an extensive vegetable plot that was admired by all.

In the same year a young man named F. G. Furniss selected a block much further south of the Jingalup settlers. He called it 'Mobrup' and the name was soon used to refer to most of the land in that part of Kojonup. Three years earlier he had selected another block further south but it was at his Mobrup holding that he finally put down roots. He came from Victoria and had arrived in Western Australia at the age of twenty with William Armstrong, Archie Holmes and Tom Hammeston, all of whom settled in the southern part of the state.

A year later, a second settler arrived and settled north-east of Mobrup. He was A. H. McKenney. He too had been born in Victoria but had come to Western Australia as a lad, with his parents. At first he worked around the south-west in timber mills and for relatives. Later he branched out into brumby-hunting and spent many hours in the saddle around the Tone River area. It was on one of these expeditions that he camped at a pool on the Towerlup River and felt an urge to settle. He was only nineteen when he first applied for a 160 acre Homestead block. Two years later he arrived at the site in a spring cart and only 2s. in his pocket, but with plenty of ambition and determination.

The days of these two settlers passed in very much the same way. Extra money was obtained from hunting kangaroos and possums for skins, countless horses were caught and broken in, contract work such as mallet bark stripping and carting was obtained and in between times they cleared and fenced their holdings. They were some of the fortunate few who did not have any poison problems. It was gradually being realized that there was a practically poison-free belt which extended from Mt Barker to Kulikup.

The McKenneys acquired vast lease holdings on the coast and it became the custom for the family to drove their cattle south for the summer. The journey took about a week on horseback, with the nights spent at the same specially selected camping spots each year. Other families in the area would join them and many happy memories linger of sing-songs around campfires, to the accompaniment of mouth organs and accordions.

Throughout the district shooting had become a widespread popular sport. In October 1905, after an exciting shooting match at which L. Treasure and E. Bagg were the winners, a unique dinner was held at the Commonwealth Hotel to celebrate. Included in the advertised menu were baked murphies, pickled eels' feet and mustard, cockroach pie, blackboy bardies, fully grown, whiskered and full flavoured and Treasure's snake juice to follow, as well as 'settle 'em powders'.

Settlers continued to make inquiries about the available land in the district. In 1906, the Italian Consul visited the area and hinted that it was being considered as the principal site for farmer settlers from northern Italy. Some Italians had already settled in the vicinity. Peter Paini was one of the first twenty clients to open an account with the Kojonup branch of the National Bank. Soon more Italians were to arrive and start their working lives in their new country by clearing, chopping and burning thousands of acres on contract for more moneyed settlers.

Included in the Italian Consul's party was M. F. Cavanagh, a Perth architect. The group was shown over the district by land guide Joe Norrish. Cavanagh was attracted to some land twenty miles west of Kojonup in the area known as Qualeup. He secured an initial holding of 4000 acres and arranged for it to be developed by contractors. Later he increased the acreage to 11,000 by purchasing adjoining land from Margaret Norrish and Goodall, Clayton and Ryall.

The district's most ardent champion, Henry Ranford, continued to recommend it for settlement and was behind most of the inquiries that were coming forward. He once likened 'Kojonup to "Sweet Auburn", loveliest village of the plain'.[16] As officer-in-charge of the Government's information bureau he was certainly in an ideal position to get results. At the end of 1906 he arrived in the district with five men—Ross, Wilson, Parker, Grech and Camillero—all of whom were keen to take up land, and in addition Ranford had been commissioned to select 5000 acres for another three men.

He had little time to fraternize with old friends in the district as he had to return hastily to Fremantle to meet thirty-six immigrants who were also prospective settlers. As one reporter said, 'the story of settlement around Kojonup during the past few months reads like romance'.[17]

Early in 1907 Maley Chipper who had a livery stable in Katanning drove out three 'new chums' from Katanning and dumped them on their selection with a few stores and a tent. The land on the Katanning Road had been chosen by one of the men, George Perkins. He had now returned with his brothers Jim and Tom to take up farming. Years later Tom recalled:

> On the Saturday after we arrived here George said, "Well, what about going to the town? We want some stores.' I said, 'Righto. Lead on Macduff.' He told us it was five or six miles out. On the road in, he pointed out the places to be seen. There was Bignell's about half way and the Dearle's on the opposite side. They had the old 'Cooliarrup' property now part of 'Doreenup'. Then we came to the top of the hill and although I knew by the distance we had walked that we must be there I said, 'And whose place is this?' George said, 'This is Kojonup.' My reply was more forcible than polite. I just said, 'When's the next b—— train out of it?'[18]

Tom Perkins wanted to learn how to develop a property so he went with two men, called Le Lievre and Bywater, to fence another settler's land, an A. Bastow, who had taken up a big area west of Kojonup. He learnt how to fence and made a little money on the side. This was most necessary if the Perkins' own land was to be developed. To gain capital they went in for all kinds of contracts—cutting axe tracks, forming roads, gravelling, putting in culverts or stone crossings and building, including the brickwork of the first Church of England and Richardson's new store. Whenever possible they bought up adjoining land as it became available.

Le Lievre was one of the new settlers who were congregating around the fine pools of water in the Cherry Tree Pool area. In that vicinity too was a Charles Cornish who had been batching there for some years. Originally Cornish had come to the goldfields, swimming his team ashore at Esperance. When he arrived in Katanning inquiring about land the land guide, (Mr) Peg Farmer, took him to Bald Rock. (This is thought to be about 1903.) Once when he was out looking for horses he came across Father Chmelicek's hut. The old priest came out saying, 'Welcome stranger, come and share my possum'.

In time Mrs Cornish and the family followed from the goldfields and as there was no closer school, Dick Cornish rode his horse eight miles into the Kojonup school. After having lived in the bustling goldfields Mrs Cornish found the isolation and the deprivation very trying. The children used to say, 'I wish all the trees were people'. They eventually sold the property to the Pratt family and later established a successful carrying business in Katanning. Crossing the creeks in this area was a major problem in winter and once when Cornish was giving a lift to one of the Norrish children he was amused to hear the little fellow repeat something he had no doubt heard adults in the family say many times: 'I wish whoever made this bloody creek had made a bloody bridge to go with it.'

Also settled in this area were the Sollys. They came from Broken Hill and lived in Katanning for two years until a seven-roomed house had been built on the farm. The family was large and a school was badly wanted. On making enquiries they learnt that they would have to supply a schoolroom and ensure an attendance of twenty. As the Le Lievres had left their cottage to live in Katanning this was turned into a schoolhouse and nearby settlers like the Carsons were canvassed for pupils. The teacher, Miss Dauaher, boarded with the Solly family.

Solly engaged in dam sinking for the Government and was away from the farm a great deal so he employed men to clear and fence. When the first clearing fire was put through, the York Road poison came up just like a forest, six and eight feet high, and many valuable animals were lost. After four years the property was sold to a Mr

Cummins who had only two children so the little school was closed. He only stayed for two years and then the land passed into the hands of the Davies family.

Another newcomer to this area was N. B. O'Halloran who came in 1908 to take up land selected the year before by his brother. It consisted of 300 acres of virgin land near the Beaufort River, bounded on the east by the 'Big Pool'. To the district's knowledge the Big Pool has never been bottomed but about 1912 an old Aboriginal, George Dinah, who was then between seventy and eighty, claimed to have seen it dry. There was hardly any poison on the river flats and the O'Hallorans were soon running 300 sheep.

West of Kojonup, settlers continued to arrive. The Javens family settled in the Orchid Valley area about this time in the neighbourhood of the Foley's highly esteemed property. During 1906 L. H. Lee and J. W. Hewson were taken on a tour of the Jingalup area by F. Van Zuilecom in his buggy and pair. They chose their respective blocks and then walked to Katanning to catch a train back to their families in Perth. When they returned the Lees and Mrs Hewson and children were able to travel on the newly-laid railway between Katanning and Kojonup, where they were met by James and Charles Hewson who had journeyed south in a recently purchased horse and cart. Lee gained permission to use Irving's homestead and sheds and eventually bought the forty acres on which they were built.

All these settlers, like many everywhere in the state, had reason to be grateful to the Agricultural Bank which enabled them to develop their land by degrees. For instance, L. H. Lee was granted on 10 March 1910:

> £60 for 40 acres of clearing to rung country.
> £25/13/9 for ringbarking 411 acres.
> £48 for 120 chains of fencing, (netting and four wires).
> £10/10/0 for 35 chains of fencing, (7 wires).
> £10 for 200 acres of poison grubbing.
> £35/5/0 for sinking a dam of 500 yards.[19]

Another person attracted to Jingalup Estate was A. J. Fisher who went in for horse-breeding in a big way, bringing from South Australia twenty-two mares and a stallion. They were grazed on the land between the Balgarup and Tone Rivers and from time to time mobs would be rounded up and broken in. As many as sixty to one hundred would be driven to a big horse sale held annually in Katanning.

The Boscabel district began to expand about 1910 when four families arrived together. They were Mr and Mrs Hunt with their two daughters and husbands, G. Hunter and E. Benn together with the latter's brother R. Benn and his wife. This group of settlers co-operated in a remarkable way until they were all able to fend for themselves. Later other families such as the Kellys settled into the district and the Harrison boys who were fast growing up went into farming for themselves. One of them, Claude, married the first schoolteacher of the little area, a Miss Thomson, whose parents had come from England to settle at Nornalup, and who was sent to open the Boscabel school in June 1914.

Whenever enough children could be mustered the early settlers tried to obtain educational facilities. At Marlyup about 1905 a Homestead block was taken up by a Mr Lange. His wife conducted lessons in her home for her own children. In 1906 an official school was established in a building on the Lange property and nine children were enrolled: Les, Marie and Spencer Lange, Mary, Patrick and Margaret Norrish, Anna Burchell, Elworthy Flanagan and Stephen Blackmore. Later two acres of land on the opposite side of the road were presented to the Government by Mr and Mrs Thomas Norrish (grandson of Richard) and a new schoolroom built.

With the widespread settlement, increased demands were made of the clergy of all denominations to provide services in outlying areas. Up until the 1900s the Anglican and Roman Catholic Churches were the only ones to hold regular services in the Kojonup district. In 1906 the Reverend James Pollard, Methodist minister of Katanning, preached in Kojonup in response to the many requests of his flock who had recently settled in the area, and henceforth that denomination tried to conduct services at regular intervals. The settler A. Liddell was an ordained Methodist minister and whenever possible he held services, in a voluntary capacity, in a hall or private home such as Haggerty's, Harrison's or Ness's. In 1909 the first Methodist missionary Harry Weaver arrived in the district and a small one-room manse was provided for him, then about 1922 the town acquired its first Methodist church. Despite the best intentions and efforts of their committee members it was not until 1911 that the foundation stone of the first St Mary's church was laid by the Anglican Church and until 1913 that the first portion of the Roman Catholic church, St Bernard's, was completed. As in many other districts the Bush Brothers of the Anglican Church, stationed at Williams, for many years visited the district and held services at isolated little centres, leaving behind them many tales of their courtesy and Christian dedication.

A glimpse of the very busy lives led by settlers during the first decade of the new century is derived from the terse daily diaries kept by various members of the Warburton family at Balgarup.[20] The pages are crammed with references to people, the weather, farm activities and social events, and reveal something of the passing parade of the times. The chores seem never-ending: poison grubbing, burning off, fencing, picking up stones, chopping suckers, cutting down wattle bushes for extra sheep feed, carting manure for the vegetable garden, planting fruit trees, ploughing the orchard, digging around trees, hoeing the vines, pruning, shooting parrots, blacksmithing, carpentering, tailing lambs, weaning foals, picking and packing fruit, stooking hay, cutting chaff, harvesting, repairing and painting the three wagons, carting mallet bark, gilgie fishing, making wine, shearing and winding and pressing wool, and hunting wild horses.

In return for the industry the rich soil of the property gave of its bounty. The diary reveals the sale of a wide range of produce: animals (sheep, horses, cattle, geese, fowls), meat (beef, mutton, pork), fruit (peaches, quinces, grapes, apples, figs, pears), vegetables (carrots, turnips, potatoes), boxes of eggs, a box of honey and, in December 1910, forty-seven bales of wool after a tedious month of shearing.

Twice in September 1900 snow was recorded, and slight snow again in June 1910. On 26 November of that year a terrific storm hit the farm and the occupants feared for the safety of the house. The pithy comments of the boys (George, Rex and Angus) when left in charge of the diary are very descriptive; for example they summed up a day of enforced idleness due to bad weather as 'Wet as the devil'.

The pages are scattered with familiar names such as Tunney (buying chaff), Van Zuilecom (visiting), Delaney (borrowing the header) but in March 1909 it was recorded 'a new settler called in' and in June 1910, 'went to Ashe's to buy four pigs for 12/6 each'. More and more new names creep in as the years pass: Foulkes, A. J. Fisher, Eastman, Silverthorn, Cox, Webb, Holly, Goodall, Halden, Knowles, and the hawkers Boor, Sunda and Hernan Singh.

In the first few agricultural shows of the twentieth century there was still a preponderance of old names in the prize lists, but gradually other names were included: Bilney, Young, and J., C. and G. Ladyman, Carson, Dennis brothers, Yates, Holmes, Weaber, Hornby, Wigglesworth, Perkins, House and Webb. By 1903 there were 700 people at the show and 750 entries were received. In this year competition ran high between the Kojonup and Carrolup schools, but the honours were evenly divided and peace was declared. A great favourite of the children each year was 'Pink Top' the vendor from Perth who sold lemonade. People would travel for miles for the shows and looked forward to seeing friends at them, from year to year. In 1912 there was great disappointment that the newly-opened Boyup Brook railway line had not operated on the day so that many friends and relations from that area could have attended.

The early shows were followed by a dinner at one of the hotels and many visiting Members of Parliament who it was thought had not come up to scratch during the year were openly criticized. In fact, the tone of the speeches was often more political than agricultural. On the other hand the M.P.s were tough old fellows well able to defend themselves, if not with the finesse of their modern counterparts, with straight from the shoulder retorts. Thomas Norrish in 1901, when proposing the toast to Parliamentarians, said, 'There had not been sufficient work and too much wrangling'[21] and the 'Federal tariff was sticking in the throats of everybody'.[22] A. Y. Hassell, M.L.A., when defending his role, admitted that the Government had no sympathy with the agriculturalists and as he represented the latter he was not going to support the present Government. He had specially come to the show so as not to be present at a forthcoming division. (A voice was heard to say 'Quite wrong'.)

At the 1903 show dinner the same politician recommended a motor transport service to the diners. The Hon. C. A. Piesse was quick on his feet and advised them:

> to accept nothing but a railway. He had heard of motor power being used but he would strongly urge them not to be made an experimental community for the Government to practice on with motors. Above all things he said, do not let the James Government take up your road with motors, for such machines would not submit to the rule of the road to Kojonup.[23]

The pioneering story for all the new settlers is much the same as those mentioned as examples. Few were exempt from hardship. As they, in their own special ways, conquered their land and developed their properties, or established themselves in the town, other problems beyond the confines of their fences arose. The need was great for better roads, medical facilities, educational opportunities, improved outlets for produce and more efficient mail services. It could be said, therefore, that the history of each settler is interwoven with the growth of the Kojonup Road Board, as it developed from the small, simple organization of 1871 to the much more complex and businesslike body it is today.

REFERENCES

[1] Extracts from Balgarup Diaries, 31 July 1900 (in possession of D. Crabbe, Kojonup).

[2] Police Occurrence Book, 418, 21 June 1900 (held in Battye Library, Perth).

[3] *Great Southern Herald*, 18 June 1904, p. 2.

[4] *Ibid*. 14 October 1905, p. 3.

[5] Magazine printed by *Morning Herald*, 2 May 1905, p. 73.

[6] *Great Southern Herald*, 11 April 1903, p. 3.

[7] *Ibid*. 5 October 1901, p. 3.

[8] *Ibid*.

[9] Police Occurrence Book, 418, 18 December 1902 (Battye Library).

[10] Teachers' Journal, 23 February 1903 (held by K.J.H.S.).

[11] *Great Southern Herald*, 2 September 1905, p. 2.

[12] *Ibid*. 4 April 1903, p. 3.

[13] *Ibid*.

[14] *Ibid*. 6 January 1906, p. 3.

[15] K.R.B. Minute Book, 2 May 1908.

[16] *Great Southern Herald*, 26 November 1904, p. 3.

[17] *Ibid*.

[18] Tom Perkins, Reminiscences (held in K.H.S.Recs.).

[19] Anthony Barker 'The History of Jingalup', p. 46 (Teachers' Higher Certificate, 1959; held in Rooney Library, Education Dept., Perth).

[20] Balgarup Diaries.

[21] *Albany Advertiser*, 12 November 1901, p. 2.

[22] *Ibid*.

[23] *Ibid*. 11 November 1903, p. 2.

12

The Growth of the Road Board

A PLACE OF ITS OWN

Before the turn of the century the Road Board had transferred its meetings to the Agricultural Hall, but it was not as successful an innovation as had been anticipated. At a special meeting on 26 January 1900 the chairman, J. J. Treasure, indignantly pointed out that several times in the past they had not been able to enter the building. In fact at the present meeting the members, W. T. Jones, A. Egerton-Warburton, L. F. Van Zuilecom, J. R. Norrish, J. Cornwall, himself and the secretary J. M. Flanagan had entered through the window! In addition to this inconvenience the hall was in a 'very dirty, disgraceful state'.[1] Van Zuilecom mentioned that when he was chairman of the building committee about three years before, the hall had been handed over to the Kojonup Road Board as it was the only public body in existence at the time. It was therefore decided to make R. Forsythe the caretaker until a management committee was appointed. Meanwhile, the first move was to buy two strong locks for the doors.

The newly-formed management committee determined to make some changes in the hall: to lengthen it by twenty feet, erect a stage, add a ladies' room as well as a room to be used as a Road Board office. A carpenter was given the contract to the value of £230. However he went to Katanning, ostensibly to obtain material for the proposed stage arch, and never returned! Fortunately he had only drawn £14 but a great deal of confusion resulted. The stone masons had completed their work and had not been paid and material was lying unused on the site. Finally, on 8 February 1903, it was arranged for J. J. and W. G. Mouritz and W. Jacobs to finish the alterations.

By April 1903, the hall was completed and the Road Board arranged with the committee to rent a room for £12 per year. With new surroundings came many new and progressive ideas but as so often happens in life the old had to make way for the new. In April 1904, the Board's first chairman, L. F. Van Zuilecom, did not seek re-election and a special mention was made in the minutes of the meeting of the great service he had given to the district and the Board since 1871.

Step by step, the members tried to establish the Road Board on a more businesslike basis. In April 1905 it was resolved to procure a seal and one hundred by-laws. In January 1906 it was decided that the meetings be held regularly on the second Saturday of each month, according to the by-laws. The following month a ratepayers' roll was drawn up by members. It was also decided to pay the secretary £6 for each meeting held. At the April meeting members were informed by the Western Australian Bank that, as requested, the Board's account had been transferred to the Kojonup branch of the National Bank. (There was a debit of £13.) Then in February 1907 J. M. Flanagan resigned as secretary and nine applications were received for the position. Those to apply were T. Phillips, C. H. Bailye, J. Gordon, R. C. Lange, A. J. Magrath, A. Bilston, A. J. Backhouse, J. W. Norrish and W. H. Kennett. Four ballots were held before A. J. Magrath was appointed.

Meetings continued in the room in the Agricultural Hall as usual, but members were beginning to realize that for a number of reasons a more central position would be preferable. In April 1907 the secretary wrote to the Lands Department requesting that when the police paddock was cut up a block be granted to the Board on which they could build their own offices. By the end of the year it was decided to give the hall committee three months notice and to hold all future meetings at A. J. Magrath's office in the main street, for which he was to be paid £1 a month. While the Board made arrangements to build their own office permission was given to Magrath to have erected in front of his building the most essential bridle posts and a flagstaff.

In August 1908, at a ratepayers' meeting which twenty-four attended, it was proposed by J. R. Tunney and seconded by J. J. Treasure, 'that plans and specifications and an amount of £250 on basis of pound for pound be adopted on building a Road Board Office at Kojonup on town block 122',[2] and this was carried. By August 1909, the architect Austin Bastow, a property owner in the district, had received three tenders and J. W. Rebond's tender of £254 was accepted. The new office was opened on 11 December 1909 at 7.30 p.m. by Arnold Piesse. Drinks and sandwiches were served and a meeting followed at which it was decided to insure the building for £250 and to have the telephone installed.

In the new year it was stipulated that office hours would be between ten and twelve in the morning and two and four in the afternoon, on

Tuesday and Friday. Additional improvements were made as they were found necessary. By April a picket fence and gate had been built and arrangements were under way to have installed a generator and fittings costing £11 to provide lighting. Five years later a tool shed was erected at the rear and a verandah attached to the front.

At last, Kojonup Road Board had a place to call its own and one which basically answered all its needs.

RATING

Such luxuries had to be financed. At the same time as building operations were in progress Kojonup members were very concerned with their increased running costs. Hardly a month went by without a new group of settlers applying for a road to be cleared or some other amenity. The Board's personal jurisdiction was spreading in all directions. The Board had no choice but to extend its operations to satisfy demands.

In 1902, R. Spencer and W. Jeffery asked for a road from the 170 mile peg on the Albany Road to the Broomehill boundary. In February 1904 the clearing of a road from Marlyup to Bilney's property 'Rocky Creek' was granted, and in August a road for the Haggerty and Yates families was dealt with by members, and Jack Lambe was given a contract to slab up Graham's Well.

By December 1904 it was decided that a rate would have to be struck and it was made ½d. in the £1. In the new year, the annual grant of £550 was condemned as totally inadequate, owing to the large increase in settlement and the amount of traffic on the roads, caused by the development of the mallet bark industry. The Government was requested to provide an additional £300 for making new roads and repairing old ones.

In March 1906 a stiff reprimand was received from the Under-Secretary for Works, stating that unless the Board was prepared to levy the minimum rate suggested, 1½d. in the £1, the Board would have to rely on its own resources for its income. After a couple of meetings at which proposals were passed only to be rescinded at the next meeting, it was decided in September 1906 that a rate of 1d. in the £1 would be struck on unimproved value of all land in the Board's district, for the year ending June 1907. In 1908, first class land was assessed at 10s. per acre; second class land at 6s. 3d. per acre and third class land at 3s. 9d. per acre. Pastoral leases were £1 on 1000 acres and poison leases were assessed as third class land.

34 Albert Bell, Methodist clergyman, and Boscabel residents Benn, Hunter and Hunt

35 Some of the district's first motor transport outside the Royal Hotel, 1927, when the Minister for Lands and Agriculture, the Hon. M .F. Troy, toured the district

Kojonup Road Board Offices: 36   Above left. Stage I, the functional meeting room at rear of the Agricultural Hall, built 1897, later converted to a private home and finally demolished

37   Above right. Stage 2, the offices built on Albany Road in 1909; now part of the Kojonup Women's Club

38   Stage 3, Kojonup Memorial Hall completed 1926. Righthand section was used by the Road Board, lefthand section now houses the Kojonup State Library

39   Stage 4, modern headquarters of the Kojonup Shire Council, 1971

The Road Board members were extremely reluctant to commence rating property owners greatly. From personal experience they knew that owning big stretches of land was not synonymous with possessing plenty of cash. The Minute Books covering these years record countless suggestions and attempts to get around this problem of rating.

As early as February 1905 the idea of dividing the district into wards was raised but rejected as too premature. However, at a ratepayers' meeting two months later there was some support for it. No more was done about it until September 1906 when it was decided to send the Road Board plan to the Lands Department so that the district could be marked into wards. Meanwhile, defaulters of cart and carriage licences were being religiously checked as a means of raising more finance and in a few weeks sixty-four dog licences were collected and the money promptly banked. (One hundred brass licence plates were purchased at 9d. each in 1906 for the vehicles.) Progress in establishing the wards was very slow and it was not until August 1909 that it was decided to have a special meeting on Saturday 28 August at 2.30 p.m., at the close of which all members would resign and nominate for re-election in wards. As a result of this meeting the following were elected, the names of the wards being derived from a well-known landmark in the area.

Namarillup	O. Bignell, J. Cornwall
Ongerup	R. Krakouer, G. F. Swiney
Muradupp [sic]	J. J. Treasure, H. Troode
Kojonup	W. T. Jones
Balgarup	A. E. Warburton, and later at an extra-ordinary meeting, J. R. Tunney[3]

With wards now established and represented on the Board, in March 1907 it was considered only fair that the annual grant should be divided proportionately between them, and Kojonup received £60, Namarillup £35, Balgarup £35, Ongerup £20 and Muradup £20.

In July 1911, a big change in rating was introduced, but only after the matter was discussed at great length. Henceforth, the Kojonup town ward was rated at 9d. in the £1, on annual rates, and the other wards were rated 1d. in the £1 on unimproved values. As a comparison, in his annual report for the year 1968-69 the president of the Kojonup Shire Council, L. N. Collins, stated that the general rate was 2 to 4 cents in the $1; the differential rate in the Kojonup townsite was .5 cents; and of the total revenue 44.22 per cent was raised by rates, the amount being $123,094, while 18.84 per cent, totalling $52,333, was received as grants.

INCREASED DEMANDS

No longer could Road Board members merely concern themselves with roads and matters close to their own gates. The Government realized this and a correspondence teacher was available to give direction to members, if required. Annual Road Board conferences were held and in 1906 the venue was actually at distant Cue, the representatives being supplied by the Government with ticket orders to cover the cost of the trip. The chairman J. McHenry Clark and W. T. Jones were appointed to attend. Nor did members try to stifle progress. On the contrary, they continually urged that land lying idle be opened to the public and not be tied up by big companies. Nevertheless, the new settlers did not let members rest on their laurels and at every meeting the members had some new project or demand to consider.

The 'Mooredup' folk were particularly enterprising. In August 1905, the secretary of their cricket club asked for ten acres to be set apart at the reserve for a recreation ground. The Board was quite agreeable but were not impressed with the rumour that some people were using the pool for swimming. It was decided to place a notice there prohibiting bathing! The name of this area, 'Mooredup', was considered confusing and the Lands Department contemplated changing it. 'Balgarup' and 'Pardellup' were mooted but it was finally decided only to alter the spelling to 'Muradup'.

Following the lead of the Muradup settlers, in 1906 the Nookenellup cricket club also applied for a recreation ground at Carlecatup on the Broomehill Road.

In December of the same year the Cherry Tree Pool people were agitating for a bridge on the Jackaneedup, three miles north from the Katanning Road. (The origin of the name of this area is not certain. Some say it comes from the red quandongs which grow there while others claim it is derived from an old settler called Frenchie who grew cherries there.)

Once the railway arrived the members were urged to demand improvements such as a responsible person in charge and a ramp for landing goods. Later, in 1913, C. K. Ross (the new owner of 'Glen Lossie') and W. T. Jones were pressing for an enlarged platform to facilitate the landing of the machinery which was then coming into the district, and a sheep race and yards. A goods shed was wanted over the line and platform and a light was felt to be necessary for when the trains arrived at night.

When Sir John Forrest and party were expected, in 1908, a Road Board deputation was arranged to meet them in the parlour of the Royal Hotel to discuss a special grant of £200 for constructing roads to the railway line and also a grant of £150 towards the proposed Road Board office. After dealing with such matters (and, it is implied, not before) the chairman was to invite the party to luncheon.

On this visit to the southern districts Sir John Forrest was also the guest at a picnic gathering with the go-ahead Muradup settlers, who took the opportunity to request Sir John to assist them financially in building an Agricultural Hall. This ambitious project was soon under way and in February 1909 the Muradup Hall committee was given permission by the Kojonup Road Board to use clay and water at the reserve to make the bricks.

In April, J. W. Hewson requested permission to clear a road to his boundary off the Towerlup Road. In 1910 one of the new Coban Soak settlers, Courtney, asked for assistance in obtaining a mail run to Coban Soak and the Collie Road. Another settler nearby called Murby offered to clear a portion of the Collie Road at the usual cost of 1s. per chain. (The wife of this same Murby was to become re-nowned throughout the state when she lived to the grand old age of 107 years, dying on 18 February 1968.) In February 1912, O'Halloran, Cornish and Carson waited on the Board concerning the surveying of a new road in their area. In the same year A. Egerton-Warburton requested the survey of a road at Ryans Brook.

For many of the new settlers far from their birthplace the mail was of utmost importance and the Road Board was continually being pressed to have the postal facilities improved. In April 1903 an interview with W. Cornwall on the subject opened with the statement: 'It's a rotten and most unsatisfactory service.'[4] It was claimed in 1907 that there had been no permanent postal official for over three years. In 1911 complaints were still being made and it was suggested that the post office be converted into a school quarters and a new post office be built in a more central position. In February 1912 the Road Board entertained Sir John and Lady Forrest again, this time at the Commonwealth Hotel. He was later shown over the post office and its defects enumerated, the inconvenient location and hours it was opened being particularly stressed. Sir John promised to have all requests considered.

Also for the convenience of the public and by popular demand, the Road Board urged in 1911 that the police station be connected to the telephone.

Another of its projects was traffic regulations. In 1909 it instituted by-laws relating to carrying lights on all vehicles, something which it had been endeavouring to come to agreement about for a considerable time. In August 1912 by-laws regulating the new intriguing motor traffic were approved. Two years later it was decided that the small brass plates for licensing traps be replaced by the more modern enamel ones. In January 1915 permission was sought by the Perth Auto Club to run a motor race through the town during the coming Easter.

The provision of street lighting was another problem to be tackled. In 1908 G. Appelbee was paid 15s. per month to light the street lamps. In September 1914 the Board was in a quandary regarding the type of lighting to have in the town and it was suggested that the gas lamp from Perth and the one from G. F. Logie be lit that night and all who could be present inspect them, following which tenders would be considered. The result of this very practical solution was the acceptance of Logie's offer of twelve lamps at £2 5s. 0d. each, erected on posts. In 1918 Logie was asked to run the lights until 11 p.m. on week nights and 12 midnight on Saturday. Twice ratepayers' meetings were held to consider purchasing the plant from Logie, but both times the idea was rejected. Up until the State Electricity Commission was connected to Kojonup in 1962, the provision of light for the town was a constant worry for the Board. In the year ending June 1969, $1439.13 was spent by the Shire on street lighting.

Among the many other matters which the members of the early Road Board were called upon to consider was the approval of Kojonup's first sub-division, part of location 3, by H. V. Piesse; the request of Father M. Reidy of the Roman Catholic Church in Katanning to hold mass in the Road Board office on the second Sunday of each month; the planting of fifty ornamental trees in the main street and the donating of another fifty to residents; the entertainment of a group of American boys visiting the town; and the perennial problem concerning the medical needs of residents.

THE HEALTH OF THE DISTRICT

In 1907 when it was hinted that a Board of Health should be established it was barely considered and the Road Board supervisor was simply asked to act as sanitary inspector. Kojonup had no hospital or doctor and many residents depended on the facilities at Katanning. In return for this service the Board was approached to assist in the maintenance of the hospital there, and A. Gee was appointed to represent the Board on the Katanning hospital committee. In August 1910 his daughter, Miss Gee, ran a concert with some of the Kojonup children to aid the Katanning hospital fund and the Road Board donated £3.

But Kojonup citizens were dissatisfied and in August 1911 they requested a public meeting to consider the matter of a resident medical officer. Forty people were present at this meeting. C. P. Reilly (he had taken over Mowan's business) proposed that a committee be formed. This was seconded by L. M. Ashe. Those appointed were J. Jeffery, C. A. Simms, O. Bignell, J. A. Carrol, J. W. Anthony, W. Larsen, J. M. Flanagan, L. M. Ashe, C. K. Ross, C. P. Reilly, J. Harrison and W. H. Haggerty, with secretary Magrath. This committee had varying success. At a meeting called in September there was not even a quorum. Initial enthusiasm was waning. A guarantors' list amounting to £126 1s. 0d. was recorded in September and sometime afterwards a Dr Baker was practising in the town.

J. E. Jones recalls Dr Baker lancing a callous from his hand in return for Jones' riding one of the doctor's horses at a race meeting. The operation was conducted at the doctor's residence, the old Noonan house, now renovated. The patient was given a nip of brandy and told to look out the window while the cut was made.

Dr Baker was still in the town in March 1914 as he made a complaint to the Road Board concerning straying stock on the roads. However, in June of the same year another public meeting was held which was attended by twenty-six residents and it was again decided to call for applications for a resident medical officer. An amount of £482 was guaranteed at this meeting. Yet in August 1916 a doctor was still unobtainable and at a special meeting at which a health inspector Dow was present, it was proposed that the Kojonup Road Board be gazetted as the health authority for the district, with Magrath as the local inspector. It was not until 1919, after a generous donation by the Kojonup Agricultural Society, that the committee whose secretary was then J. W. Anthony was able to go ahead and make concrete plans for building a hospital on the old Kojonup show grounds. Public support was obtained and the hospital was finally opened on 15 October 1922 with Miss E. Cartwright as the first matron and the first board of management consisting of R. Krakouer, president, J. E. H. Robinson, Mrs F. W. Bilney, Mrs J. G. Finlay and J. W. Anthony as secretary. Later in the same year Dr K. F. Abernethy commenced practice in the district, living for a time in the humble little Agricultural Hall which had been redesigned as a private residence, until his own dwelling opposite the hospital was built. Actually, there had been two applicants for the practice, both equally qualified, and the committee was in a dilemma as to whom to choose. The decision was finally made in a typically Australian fashion—by tossing a coin. The Kojonup district had no reason ever to doubt that it was the wrong choice. Until his death in 1959, Dr Abernethy gave his services to the community unstintingly and conscientiously.

THE RAILWAY

Since the turn of the century the residents of Kojonup had become more and more concerned over the enormous disadvantages of the town not being directly in touch with a railway line. Probably spurred on by the comments of the parliamentarians at the last agricultural show, a Road Board meeting was held on 14 February 1903 and it was decided to form a progress league and agitate for a railway line between the South-West and Great Southern lines. The first 'railway meeting' was held in the almost completely altered Agricultural Hall, on 21 March, and sixty interested people attended. It was regarded as urgent that the railway line be constructed from Katanning as soon as possible, and a petition was composed to be taken around the district for everyone to sign. This was to be the first of countless meetings and agitations on the subject.

Within a month another big meeting of one hundred people was held at Katanning sponsored by that Road Board in conjunction with both the Kojonup and Katanning Progress Leagues. One of the most enthusiastic supporters of the line at this meeting, and until its ultimate construction, was Henry Ranford.

Despite numerous other meetings and a great deal of talking throughout the district and extensive press coverage, by 22 October 1904 nothing definite had been achieved and it was arranged to send a deputation to the Premier to try to gain Government approval for the proposed line. As a result in November 1904 the Minister for Lands, the Hon. J. M. Drew M.L.C., visited Kojonup accompanied by his wife, with Henry Ranford, the Hon. Wesley Maley and several other gentlemen. In fact three drays departed from Katanning for the visit. Kojonup was reached at 10.30 p.m. 'and the whole company sat down with readiness to the excellent supper prepared by Host Cornwall'.[5] There was, however, one flaw, which horrified the Minister of

Lands—condensed milk was supplied! It looked as if the whole grand tour was going to be a dismal failure before it even began, but the irrepressible Ranford was equal to all emergencies and arranged for fresh milk to be obtained for the Minister at breakfast from a neighbour, Archibald. The party set out next morning at 9 a.m. with J. J. Treasure as guide and headed for Muradup, visits being made to Mrs Treasure, the Larsens and the Haggertys where one of the sons was quoted as telling the Minister that 'he was very well satisfied with the land but would not have gone so far had it not been for the promise of the railway'.[6]

> Eenyellup, the hospitable home of Mr L. F. Van Zuilecom, J.P., was reached shortly after 1 p.m. Here preparations for the Ministerial visit had been made on a lavish scale and full justice was done to the excellent viands provided. . . . The party was loath to leave this cool retreat which one of the number likened to the ideal country house so often read about and so seldom seen.[7]

From here the party travelled to the 'fine homestead of Augustus E. Warburton'[8] where afternoon tea was served by the daughters of the house after which the property was inspected, particularly the orchard of 1500 new apple and peach trees planted in the last two years by the owner and a small crop of Algerian oats which was estimated to return over fifty bushels to the acre.

The party returned to Kojonup about seven o'clock to find 'a great number of people assembled to meet the Minister who was cheered as he drove into the town'.[9] Then followed a banquet at the Agricultural Hall for over a hundred people, including some ladies, one from each family. Numerous speeches were made and an atmosphere of gaiety, triumph and hope reigned. The Minister said:

> The drive through the Kojonup district had been a revelation to him, and he considered two thirds of that traversed on Wednesday, was first class land. . . . The large amount of grass everywhere was amazing and it was a great pity that there was so little stock to feed on it. In his opinion there was a great future for Kojonup.[10]

One of the speeches most enjoyed was that made by the popular charmer, Henry Ranford, who had married into the district. How the crowd loved his comments:

> Kojonup was a beautiful place, and one for which he had much love. Its cooks were the best he knew and its girls the prettiest. In fact he didn't understand how a man could keep single in Kojonup.

A bachelor should be given a leather medal, and sent out of the country. (Laughter).[11]

The evening concluded with everyone convinced that in no time the line from Katanning would soon be under way.

However, twelve months later nothing concrete had resulted and when another Minister visited the Kojonup Show and said that a survey in connection with the line would be carried out as soon as possible the Kojonup residents took it with a grain of salt. Imagine the delight when survey operations were commenced before the month was out! But it was the last straw for Kojonup people when in February 1906 it was heard that the surveyor J. F. Wilson who had been working out the route of the line had been instructed to abandon the present line, as it had been decided that the route would be south of the Katanning Road instead of north, and the fifteen miles already surveyed was 'so much waste of time'.[12]

Confidence returned when tenders were called in May 1906, although there was some disgust on learning that the successful tenderer was the Public Works Department itself. When the labourers employed in unloading the rails from trucks in the Katanning yard struck for higher pay, in July 1906, there was a general feeling that the whole project was destined to be dogged with trouble to the bitter end. On the contrary, from that month the work progressed smoothly and by the following March a pleasant picnic was held at the four mile to celebrate the end of the construction. The workers all subscribed a small amount and the Kojonup ladies purchased and prepared the provisions. A train lent for the occasion left Kojonup at 10 a.m. and returned at 6 p.m. During the day games, races and tugs-of-war were organized.

The railway line from Katanning to Kojonup was constructed by 'the light railway system'. 'Branch lines built under this system were to be graded as closely as possible to the natural surface of the country across which they ran'.[13] The thirty-three mile line with sidings at Punchimirup and Carlecatup and the Kojonup terminus cost £17,197 5s. 0d. When train services were inaugurated the journey took two and a half hours in a 'G' class locomotive with a speed restriction of 15 m.p.h. Originally, the train left Katanning on Saturday and Wednesday at 11.30 a.m. and returned from Kojonup at 2.30 p.m. for a fare of 6s. 6d. each way.

As the Government did not seem to be initiating an official opening ceremony a Kojonup committee decided it would have to take arrangements in hand before the season broke and the farmers were all too busy ploughing the ground to attend. The Katanning inhabitants were very anxious not to be overlooked in any plans for festivities and on the great day, Wednesday 10 April, they closed their business houses at 11 a.m. and everyone who was free boarded the train for the journey across to Kojonup.

The circuitous route followed by the line opened up many delightful vistas and country unfamiliar to most of the travellers. Just before Kojonup the 'iron horse', hauling its chattering, high-spirited load, passed over the grassy acres of historic Warkelup where half a century before Richard Norrish had brought his family in their old cart, pulled by the mediocre Dobbin, to begin a new life. On reaching the destination the train's passengers 'found not so much as an old soap box'[14] and amid great merriment they scrambled down as best they could. There were plenty of buggies and wagonettes assembled to conduct them to the Agricultural Hall, where another of Kojonup's famed banquets awaited. Approximately one hundred guests were present, presided over by the chairman of the Road Board, J. McHenry Clark, flanked by F. H. and C. A. Piesse, the traditional champions of the railways.

The committee felt slighted because no Government Minister had travelled from Perth for the occasion and F. H. Piesse had to make suitable apologies. As was customary, every imaginable toast was drunk, preceded and followed by interminable displays of oratory from as many of the men present who could find an excuse to be on their feet.

But the railway issue was not dead, particularly as far as the Muradup settlers were concerned. Soon agitation was under way to extend the line to the west to connect with Boyup Brook and so link the two main southern railways—the South-West line and the Great Southern line. This was finally accomplished and the line handed over for public traffic in May 1912, over nine years after the Road Board had first decided to push for railway access between the two major southern tracks.

ROAD BOARD STAFF AND EQUIPMENT

Tendering was still the main method used for road works in the Kojonup district at the turn of the century, but its attraction as a means of getting a little extra money was diminishing owing to the increased development contracts offering, the booming mallet bark industry, and later the attractive returns for possum skins. (A good hunter could

snare three dozen a day. Charlie Elverd once made £145 in two weeks.)
Mostly, new settlers were only interested in doing road works that
were close to their own holdings. Their prime aim was to develop their
properties in order to qualify for further bank loans.

An idea of the small proceeds from road work may be derived
from the efforts of the Larsen family in 1905. For seventeen and a
half hours, providing his own horse and dray, H. Larsen received
£13 2s. 6d|; assisting him R. M. and H. E. Larsen received £7 each
and W. Larsen was paid £3 18s. 0d. for forming twelve chains of road.

In April 1908 the Road Board decided to appoint the trusty Robert
Forsythe as a dayman. In return for his labour and the supplying of
his own horse and cart he received 10s. 6d. a day. At the beginning of
1909 the idea of employing a man per week and the Board buying its
own horse was carried, only to be rescinded at the following meeting.
In June, Robert Forsythe was appointed foreman-dayman at 11s. per
day for 'himself, horse and dray',[15] when required. At the same time,
the secretary was made supervisor as well and was to receive 10 per
cent on all local money collected in addition to his salary, 'owing to
the Board's area being increased and being made into wards'.[16]

About this time, J. J. Treasure's son, Levi, had his first experience
of road work in a contract team run by Bill McVicker and Ted Linke.
They had the contract to do fourteen miles on the Blackwood Road.
Levi was responsible for bringing the gravel to the road. It was long
tiring work, from daylight to dark, after which the men would return
to their camp to prepare their own meals. Long before sun-up the
horses had to be taken some distance to Narlingup dam for their first
drink of the day.

In 1920 Levi became a permanent member of the Road Board,
taking over Rube Bilston's job at working the grader. For this he was
paid foreman's wages of 9s. a day. Horrie Walker was the other
permanent man, receiving 8s. a day to drive and be responsible, even
on weekends, for the team of four horses.

In 1923 the work gang was at Wahkinup, working on the Foley Road
and the secretary-supervisor set out to inspect the work in his T-model
Ford but became hopelessly bushed and could not locate the men. As
a result it was decided to appoint L. E. Treasure as works' supervisor
and this he remained until his retirement in 1956.

In July 1912 A. J. Magrath was engaged on a yearly basis at £150
per annum, with no commission. Two years later he asked for a raise
of £50 per year and it was granted, instantaneously and unanimously.
This emphasized the high esteem in which he was held by the whole

Board. They were not usually all of one mind. As the field of adminis-
tration broadened and became more complex members necessarily
had to rely more and more on the secretary, and rarely were his
decisions and advice not found to be commendable.

Magrath's popularity was not confined to the Road Board members.
He was well liked by all the town as he was so approachable and
willing to listen to an individual's problems and to assist where ever
he could. He was an agent for Henry Wills of Albany and would
arrange finance for farmers in return for the sale of their wool. For
those who had only a limited education he would fill out forms and
instruct them in matters such as taxation. There was no end to his
willingness. Naturally, in return the local men would offer to buy him
a drink or two at the very convenient pub just across the road. Often
he did much of his business in that quarter.

In April 1916 the Road Board launched out and bought its first
major plant. Time and again it had been considered but tossed aside.
A brand new tip dray was purchased from Mouritz Bros. for £23 15s. 0d.
and it was resolved to build a stable and chaff house for a horse that
was to be bought. The secretary was instructed to purchase all the
material and have the work done by daywork.

In 1918 a 'road-making' machine was acquired but not long after the
Board appeared to be having financial troubles. Nevertheless, on
Saturday 5 April 1919, at a ratepayers' annual meeting there were no
complaints and a vote of thanks was moved for the past services of the
chairman, members and secretary. Yet a week later it was recorded in
the Minute Book:

> Resolved, next meeting to be called by the Chairman when he has
> gained the necessary information respecting matters requiring his
> attention.[17]

What followed is a mystery. The Minute Books throw little light on
the tragedy.

It would seem that Magrath had been extremely worried over the
state of the Board's finances. From all accounts, he had been drinking
more than was wise, and the minutes preceding April certainly indicate
a state of befuddlement; words are frequently misspelt or omitted and
the writing often trails off the line.

Albert Elverd recalls passing Magrath as he stood in the doorway of
his office and Magrath told Albert that there was a letter there for
him. Albert replied that he would collect it shortly. Less than ten
minutes later a loud report was heard and when Albert returned,

preceded just a few minutes by Wooldridge, it was to see Magrath dead on the floor of his office, from a self-inflicted bullet wound.

In the minutes of the Road Board meeting of 3 May 1919, at which J. Delaney presided and the members Anthony, Bignell, Kennett, Haggerty, Bilney, Simms, Cussons and Jones were present, it was recorded:

> Before proceeding with the business of this meeting the Chairman referred to the death of the late Secretary, A. J. Magrath who had done good work for the Board and the District in the past and he felt sure all regretted his loss.[18]

C. P. Reilly was engaged as acting-secretary and remained as secretary until 1921 when he was succeeded by J. G. Finlay, who was typical of the many men who were returning to civilian life from the tremendous carnage of the 1914-18 war.

REFERENCES

[1] K.R.B. Minute Book, 26 January 1900.
[2] *Ibid*. 15 August 1908.
[3] *Ibid*. 18 September 1909.
[4] *Great Southern Herald*, 4 April 1903, p. 3.
[5] *Ibid*. 26 November 1904, p. 3.
[6] *Ibid*.
[7] *Ibid*.
[8] *Ibid*.
[9] *Ibid*.
[10] *Ibid*.
[11] *Ibid*.
[12] *Ibid*. 3 February 1906.
[13] A. Gunzburg, 'Kojonup Railway', 22 May 1968 (copy in K.H.S.Recs.).
[14] *Great Southern Herald*, 13 April 1907.
[15] K.R.B. Minute Book, 12 June 1909.
[16] *Ibid*.
[17] *Ibid*. 12 April 1919.
[18] *Ibid*. 3 May 1919.

13

War and its Aftermath

The first mention of the 1914-18 war in the Minute Books of the Road Board was on 12 September 1914 when it was proposed to have a public meeting the following Saturday at 4 p.m. in the Board office, to discuss ways and means to raise money for the war patriotic fund. At this meeting a committee of three was formed of W. T. Jones, J. Wood and A. J. Magrath. It was decided to approach Mrs C. K. Ross and Mrs J. M. Flanagan to arrange a ladies' meeting in support of the Red Cross. During the war the people of Kojonup were to be brought in touch with much that was new to them; for example, in April 1915 the Road Board donated £1 to the City of Perth's purchase of a 100 h.p. Gnome Vickers Gunbus biplane, to be presented to the Home (British) Government from Western Australia.

The intense loyalty felt in Kojonup was demonstrated in October 1916, when A. Thomson, M.L.A., visited the town to address a meeting on the Federal Government's first referendum on conscription. Patriotic enthusiasm carried unanimously the proposition that:

> This meeting of Kojonup citizens pledge themselves to support to the utmost of their ability the Referendum proposals of the Federal Government, as we believe they are necessary for the speedy successful termination of the war.[1]

The men of Kojonup had no need for conscription to draw them physically into the war. They were typical of thousands of Australian men who spontaneously volunteered and left behind them the close-knit little centre that had been practically their whole world up to their departure for the unspeakable horrors of the 1914-18 battlefields. The years of chasing and riding brumbies in the bush, of stalking and shooting wild game, of grinning and bearing hard times, of improvising, of competing on horseback at local shows, of gambling at race meetings and, most of all, the mateship engendered in the small isolated communities, all worked in moulding that unique soldier 'the Digger'.

One such young man was Levi Treasure. He had been born into a family of horse-lovers. He had known and ridden horses as soon as he could walk. At the age of fifteen he had joined the local Mounted Volunteers, when he was barely strong enough to hold the heavy rifles that were used at training. The commander of this Katanning-Kojonup company was H. V. Piesse and the lieutenants of the Kojonup troops were John Norrish and J. E. Jones, who trained the men once a month. An annual camp was held at the Carrolup Hall and, once, an unforgettable camp was held at Tammin which the famous Lord Kitchener attended.

On 8 September 1914 Levi, Roy Hart, Alf and Frank Ainsworth all set off together to enlist in Katanning. A lack of suitable mounts in the army gave those like Levi who had their own horse a distinct advantage. Of the eight young men from Kojonup who passed for the Light Horse Regiment only the five who had a horse each were taken immediately. The others had to wait for the next call-up. Those to be accepted were the Ainsworth brothers, Levi, F. Middleton and Fred Norrish. Soon Levi and his horse 'the Swank' set sail for the Middle East. (In the meantime the army, just as in Boer War times, began making enquiries in the district about the purchase of horses.) Over thirty of Kojonup's sons never returned, but died on foreign soil in France, Gallipoli or the Middle East.

As the war progressed the citizens of the town had a wooden plaque made, on which was listed the names of all those of the district on active service. It was placed on the wall outside the Road Board office and whenever news was received of one being killed a small disc was placed beside the name. This plaque now hangs in the foyer of the Memorial Hall.

In October 1917 a patriotic sports meeting was held by the Kojonup branch of the Katanning Returned Soldiers and Sailors Provident Association, in conjunction with the Kojonup Agricultural Society. It was a great success 'with a big sprinkling of khaki as many of the boys from the district had asked for leave to come down'.[2] Fifteen car loads had also travelled from Katanning. At a concert and dance held that night in the Theatre Royal (a tin hall which the Cornwalls had built on the south side of the Royal Hotel) the audience was addressed by Lieutenant Quilty who said that the 'Great Southern District held the proud record of having sent more men to the front, in proportion to its population than any other district in Western Australia'.[3] Later, a forceful recruiting speech was delivered by a Sergeant Lamb. Altogether, the patriotic fund benefitted by £200 from the takings of the day.

On 8 November 1918, the Kojonup schoolteacher recorded: 'persistent rumours of Armistice. Town deluded before and taking it quietly'.[4] One of the false celebrations could have been the patriotic sports meeting held just two days before by the Committee of Repatriation in conjunction with the Agricultural Society. Apart from the attractions for the children such as a merry-go-round and swinging boats visitors paid for the privilege of 'hitting the Kaiser'.[5] Included in the sporting events was a returned soldiers' race, which was won by H. Bagg, and a horse competition entitled 'Beheading the Turk',[6] which was won by T. H. Fleay.

By the twelfth it was known for sure that the war was over and the pupils, after being addressed by A. J. Magrath, were permitted to go home. The next day news arrived by car from Perth of extended holidays and celebrations so the school remained closed. On Friday it was decided it was useless opening the school for just one day so the children had yet another unexpected holiday. They were not to forget their exceptional good fortune on the occasion of the Armistice!

Slowly, the local boys drifted back to take up the thread of their lives again in the district. Steve Blackmore was the first of them to return with a decoration, the Military Medal, awarded for valour as a stretcher bearer.[7] Others like Thomas Rogers, who had lost his leg, had to face a life of adjusting and compensating. On the whole, the returned men brought a new vigour, outlook and impetus to the local scene, and many little country towns like Kojonup were to benefit immeasurably from the returned servicemen. In addition, the Government's soldier settlement scheme was to be instrumental in bringing new blood into the community. It is thought that at least sixty Kojonup ex-servicemen received some kind of assistance from the Government under this scheme. Notable in Kojonup's case was the arrival of the young ex-officer, Arnold Potts, to take up a soldier farm in the Marlyup area. He had been awarded the Military Cross in France and had been mentioned in despatches on four occasions. He was soon to prove an invaluable member of the district.

The first move of these keen 'old Aussies' was to form a Returned Servicemen's Association (the R.S.A., but later changed to the R.S.L.). The inaugural meeting was held in 1919 at the Royal Hotel with about seventy present. The office-bearers elected were Jack Finlay, Arthur Liddell, J. W. Hain and Jim O'Sullivan. These men, overwhelmed by their own good fortune, wanted most of all to establish some substantial monument to their fallen comrades and, with this in mind, land on

211

the corner of the highway and Broomehill Road was purchased from the publican, Albert Sims, for £35.

It was suggested that an obelisk be erected there, inscribed with the names of all from the district who had died in the war. To raise the necessary funds various functions and raffles were held. Then some bright spark hit on the idea of running silent movies and this they did most successfully for almost two years.

They were shown in the Theatre Royal and Miss Ivy Krakouer and Miss F. Doig (later Mrs Levi Treasure) took turns to collect the door money and play the piano. The films and projector were managed by two pairs, Arnold Potts and J. E. H. Robinson (the resident Agricultural Bank inspector), or Levi Treasure and Tom Davis (a Boer War veteran who was farming on the Collie Road). Sometimes, the local police constable had to be present to turn disappointed customers away when there was a full house.

The inadequacies of the existing public buildings were quite obvious and when it was suggested that the money raised might be better spent on a large public hall in Kojonup which would meet the requirements of the district for many years to come, it was enthusiastically supported by the returned men especially when the idea of incorporating in the building a Hall of Honour, in memory of the fallen, was included.

Consequently a deputation of J. E. H. Robinson and Arthur Liddell waited on the Road Board at their meeting on 7 September 1921 to submit the idea and explain that they were prepared to hand over £300 they had collected to decorate the Hall of Honour. The Road Board members were sympathetic but finances were not abundant just then and they would not promise anything.

However the germ of the idea had been planted and it began to grow. It was to continue to develop for five years. During that time, the decisions made and rescinded, the special meetings, general meetings and committee meetings held, the discussions and arguments recorded are manifold. The patience of those concerned, who saw the project to its ultimate successful conclusion, is deserving of the highest praise. In particular, J. G. Finlay and W. C. Cussons at all times did their utmost to forward the idea. As Finlay was an officer-bearer with both the R.S.L. and the Road Board, he was in a favourable position to guide the whole scheme over all obstacles. Cussons, a settler in the Boscabel area, considered the town had insufficient amenities for the wives and children of farmers when they visited the town and had to wait for any length of time. He saw the reading room and the open fireplaces with a welcoming fire on a cold day as not luxuries but essentials that should be provided by the town.

Outstanding though was the selflessness, co-operation and energy of the R.S.L. members. They were not prepared to just sit back and let the town leaders battle with the idea alone. They supported it generously and agreeably all the way.

The original plan was found to be too costly and features such as a billiard room, cool inviting verandahs and attractive floor tiles in the foyer had to be abandoned. To make the sceptical outcentres more conversant with the project various members of the Road Board and the R.S.L. visited functions held at different places to explain it all and were well received. Then, almost out of the blue, a referendum was demanded on the whole matter by the requisite number of rate-payers.

Therefore, on 15 November 1924, a referendum was held, 'on the question of borrowing £4500 for the purpose of erecting Local Government Memorial Buildings at Kojonup'. The results of the poll at the various booths were:[8]

	Yes	No
Boscabel	24	0
Muradup	64	50
Marleup	35	3
Jingalup	56	14
Cherry Tree Pool	14	28
Lumeah	24	40
Qualeup	18	18
Kojonup	287	16
Absentee votes	61	11
	583	180

The official return commented:

'close on 300 voters exercised their right to vote on the subject, whereas at an ordinary Road Board Election if a third of that number voted, it would be rather amazing'.[9]

An architect, F. J. Coote of Kendenup, was engaged to draw up plans and specifications and the building was placed in the hands of A. Thomson of Katanning. All the preliminary expenses were paid by the R.S.L. In fact if it had not been for their finance it is doubtful if the plan would have got off the ground. In return for their invaluable support J. G. Finlay was asked to lay the foundation stone on

11 November 1925 on a site which had been purchased from W. T. Jones for £225.

A Memorial Hall Comforts committee was formed by Mesdames Cussons, Ferguson, Church, Finlay and Honner to advise on the furnishings and act as a social committee in conjunction with the Road Board. When the plans had been modified to meet the costs the floor was thought by some not to be suitable for dancing so Mrs W. T. Jones took over the task of raising the extra money to have the original specifications for the floor followed. This amounted to £72. Arrangements were put in hand to buy a player piano, special crockery for the supper room, new office equipment, stage scenery and a drop curtain. The members of the Australian Natives' Association donated an Australian flag, the people of Jingalup donated a Union Jack and a barometer, and others donated lamps for the ladies' room and chessmen for the reading room.

Delays causing alterations of decisions were continuous and frustrating but eventually, on Friday 20 August 1926, the building was officially opened by Major-General Sir J. J. Talbot-Hobbs, C.M.G., K.C.M.C., V.D. It was a proud day for Kojonup and one that is still vividly remembered by many residents. Everyone for miles around converged on the town. Sir Talbot-Hobbs, the Reverend C. L. Riley, O.B.E., and D. N. Benson (secretary of the R.S.L. Executive) were met in Katanning by Captain A. A. Potts (president) and Lieutenant J. G. Finlay (secretary) of the Kojonup sub-branch of the R.S.L. and together with Mr A. Thomson, M.L.A., motored to Kojonup. They were given a luncheon in the Theatre Royal at which thirty-five returned men were present.

In the afternoon a ceremony was first held outside the hall. The schoolchildren, under the supervision of the headmaster, M. Anderson, sang several hymns, and after the unveiling of the Scroll of Honour, Trumpeter S. O. Harrison sounded the Last Post and Reveille.

The official party then moved into the hall and Sir Talbot-Hobbs was presented with a bouquet by the shy little daughter of Mr and Mrs T. Larsen. The chairman of the Kojonup Road Board, W. C. Cussons, welcomed the official guests and introduced Sir Talbot-Hobbs to the large audience. Appropriately the R.S.L. had the last word, when Captain Potts on their behalf handed over to the Road Board their final contribution: a cheque for £100, the movie picture plant and furnishings for the Hall of Honour, valued at £750.[10]

Still the day did not end. Official guests adjourned to the Theatre Royal for a civic banquet while busy volunteer workers hastily prepared the Memorial Hall for its first ball. Seven hundred people bought tickets to it and the dancing went on into the early hours of the morning just as it had done at the less sophisticated dances held in the past at the tin hall, the Agricultural Hall, the local pubs and at the very first jigs in the old barracks.

Prior to the opening of the Memorial Hall there had been a change of secretaries. In May 1926, J. G. Finlay had resigned to take over the Elder Smith agency from Richardson and Co. of Kojonup. It was with extreme regret that the Board accepted the resignation. When Finlay asked for a retiring allowance of one month's salary for each year of service the members were more than willing and, in addition, it was moved that ten weeks leave on full pay be granted to the secretary in return for his zealous services. (It was stated that he had only taken his annual leave once, since he became secretary.)

When the news of this unheard-of munificence reached the ears of a section of the ratepayers there was an uproar. Nothing like it had been heard before in the district. To many of the old settlers who had been brought up to expect Road Board commitments to be niggardly met, this new bountifulness was highly questionable. As a result, a special meeting of ratepayers was held on 19 June 1926, at which it was revealed that Finlay was to be given £216. A division was held on the motion that the Board pay Finlay the amount and, according to the scrutineers, twenty-eight voted in favour of the motion and twenty-six against. The meeting was adjourned but the matter was by no means settled.

In retrospect, this whole controversy seems to symbolize the parting of the ways of a new order and the old. The infusing of new blood and new attitudes into the district since the Armistice had created a new social order which regarded the district's traditional timeworn thinking as obsolete. The conversion was not made without a fight, and early in its life the new Memorial Hall was to be the scene of one of Kojonup's most tempestuous ratepayers' meetings.

On 21 August, the day after the opening of the Hall, an annual ratepayers' meeting was held which approximately 300 people attended. At this meeting the gratuity to be paid to Finlay was again raised. Once more a division was taken. This time over 90 per cent were against the motion and pandemonium broke loose. The chairman hastily adjourned the meeting and the members left the table amid great excitement. The new secretary C. B. Vincent remained seated with the books in front of him and was soon surrounded. Although there was no violence, amid great confusion he was escorted by the police to the Road Board office, with the books. The old-stager, R. Krakouer, is said to have commented that in all his experience he had never seen such scenes in Kojonup before.[11]

Another ratepayers' meeting was held on 4 September which 200 attended and a compromise was finally reached whereby Finlay was to receive a total of £100. The meeting concluded with the passing of a motion of confidence in the Road Board and peace reigned once more.

Early in 1933 C. B. Vincent left the town and for two years his place was taken by J. V. Burston. Then in June 1935, L. V. MacBride began his long association with the district, remaining as secretary of the Road Board until his retirement in April 1962. He witnessed the Board's progress through the cautious last years of the thirties, the trying years of the 1939-45 war and the affluent and changing post-war era. He was the last of the general factotums. Often he was expected to do his own typing, work out estimates, draw up legal documents, cover the fields of health inspector, traffic inspector and vermin board, all on a shoestring and with out-of-date equipment. One of his biggest headaches was the petrol rationing during the 1939-45 war. He can recall a citizen, when the undertaker was given ration tickets to collect a corpse, complaining because 'they were supposed to be only for seasonal work'![12]

While in office he assisted in establishing in the district many of the public services which are taken so much for granted today: the State Electricity System, the Comprehensive Water Scheme, the school bus organization and a favourite project of his—the State Library. He was the last of the secretaries of the Kojonup Road Board and the first shire clerk when the district became the Shire of Kojonup in 1961. Before his retirement the district's local government body made yet another shift—from the cramped Memorial Hall quarters to the original section of the modern and efficient office block from which it functions today, overlooking the busy highway with which, in 1971, it has been intrinsically linked for one hundred years.

REFERENCES

[1] K.R.B. Minute Book, 7 October 1916.
[2] *Great Southern Herald*, 27 October 1917.

[3] *Ibid.*
[4] Teachers' Journal, 8 November 1918 (held by K.J.H.S.).
[5] *Great Southern Herald*, 9 November 1918.
[6] *Ibid.*
[7] *Ibid.* 18 September 1918.
[8] K.R.B. Minute Book, 15 November 1924.
[9] *Ibid.*
[10] *Great Southern Herald*, 25 August 1926.
[11] K.R.B. Minute Book, from typed loose sheet dated 21 August 1926.
[12] Personal conversation with L. V. MacBride, 7 August 1969.

14

Between Wars

During the period between the two world wars Kojonup continued to attract new settlers from the east and overseas. All wards of the Road Board shared in this development and at every meeting decisions had to be made on providing axe tracks to some new settler's selection. Simultaneously, the old properties more than once changed hands.

For a time the original acres so favoured by Commander Bruce were farmed by a Mr Silverthorn who was a goldfields associate of one of that industry's most flamboyant promoters, Claude de Bernales, who eventually became the owner of the property. In 1924 de Bernales sold it, under an agreement, to D. A. Robertson. Owing to severe financial difficulties Robertson had to relinquish his ownership, remaining as manager for de Bernales. In so doing, the modest public-spirited Robertson became a highly respected member of the district, the avenue of prunus trees in Spring Street being a living memorial to his generous interest in the town.

Part of Van Zuilecom's property 'Eeniellup' was sold by the aging Louis to J. Silverthorn in 1910 but the memory of it remained vividly with the onetime homesick schoolgirl, Blanche Van Zuilecom, and in 1926 she and her husband John Egerton-Warburton succeeded in re-buying it so that her descendants are able to continue to farm it to the present day.

In 1928 another historic property was transferred—'Balgarup', where Kojonup's poison scourge had first hit the headlines, was bought by Major Gilbert Lewis of South Australia. In the same year Richard Norrish's original 'Warkelup' holding was surrendered to another newcomer, L. D. Forrest.

The experiences of each of the district's settlers, new and old, as they strove to make their way, is a story deserving of admiration. For every tale told hundreds could be substituted; for every one of success there is one of hardship.

Generally, there was an optimistic air prevailing in the farming communities in the twenties; credit was available, prices were buoyant, mechanization was just around the corner.

However one new problem that future generations of farmers had to face was the rapidly increasing numbers of rabbits. As early as 1894 it is officially recorded that rabbits were seen in Western Australia. In 1902 a small item in the *Great Southern Herald* gave a tip for preparing phosphorus to poison rabbits but it was no doubt thought quite an irrelevant piece of information by many readers. By 1920 Kojonup Road Board had its own vermin board and meetings were regularly held after the Road Board meeting. It is claimed that Carrie McDonald, at Boscabel, caught the first rabbit in the district in a possum trap in 1917. The reports of rabbit sightings increased year by year and many times were accompanied by doubtful statements that only one rabbit had been shot and there were no more; or that it was a full-grown doe and had never had any young! A few cautious farmers like the methodical R. Stevenson were among the first to apply for rabbit poison and to take every precaution to keep them in check, but still the reports kept being received, particularly along the rivers and creeks. It was to be a costly and persistent business for the conscientious man to keep production up and the rabbit numbers down.

In 1927, the Boyup Brook farmer P. D. Forrest is recognized as having discovered *dwalganup* subterranean clover. With the coming of subterranean clovers, together with artificial fertilizers, it looked as if the prosperous future that had been prophesied for Kojonup for so many years had finally arrived.

As early as 1923 a representative of the fertilizer company, C.S.B.P. & Farmers Ltd, Tom Gemmel, had travelled the South-West area by train and hired horse and sulky, advising on the use of superphosphate for topdressing pastures. Prior to this, individual farmers had experimented with various fertilizers including one known as Thomas's, an imported phosphate, and another which was mainly blood and bone. On 15 May 1913, the Warburtons of Balgarup recorded in their diary: 'Brought out 2 tons of Mount Lyell'.[1] Then on 24 May was written: 'Rex took 13 cases fruit to Kojonup, brought back 3 tons super. Got super from McGrath and Sharland'.[2]

One of the first farmers in the district to see the great possibilities in pasture improvement was V. D. Pailthorpe. At first he farmed in the Boscabel area but later took up what is now the 'Chapel Estate'. Here, as early as 1925, he topdressed some paddocks annually with 93 lbs per acre of Florida or Mt Lyell superphosphate. By 1928 he had sown 500 acres to subterranean clover and in 1928 he gave them two dressings of 93 lbs of superphosphate, one in March and the other in July, and it was recorded in the *Producers' Review* that 'on few properties in Western Australia can such good stands of subterranean clover be found'.[3] Yet some farmers for a long time were inclined to scoff, saying it was the same as throwing money away.

As late as May 1930 the *Western Mail* had a full page story on the development and high carrying capacity of the Kojonup areas and some of the claims are more than comparable with achievements today while at the same time indicating that the then current optimism had not yet been curtailed by menacing events elsewhere.

W. B. Haggerty of Muradup stated that he sowed a small patch with subterranean clover in 1908 although he did not know it at the time, having ordered 'white Dutch clover'.[4] In 1930 he had 1000 acres sown to it and considered he carried two sheep to the acre, all the year round, on topdressed established clover, with no hand feeding.

E. Johnston of 'Half Moon', west of Kojonup, had 1150 acres sown and 'the growth the clover was making was really remarkable and evoked exclamations of surprise from the district farmers'[5] in an inspecting party.

A. W. Partridge, who became regarded as Kojonup's best ambassador and who personally furthered the fortunes of the district with might and main at every opportunity, was then running the 'bottom hotel' and he took the party to see his property 'Priory Park', at a distance of eight miles north of Kojonup. Here he had 700 acres under subterranean clover (the mid-winter variety) sown at the rate of 3 lbs to the acre with 1 cwt of superphosphate.

At R. Stevenson's 'Crossburn', originally J. M. Flanagan's property, of 4500 acres 2400 acres had been cleared and topdressed and 2500 pure-bred Bungaree sheep were shorn and averaged 10 lbs of wool.

At Major Lewis's Balgarup property, of the 4300 acres, 1700 had been cleared and 1000 of these sown to clover. 'On a 200 acre paddock of natural pastures on which clover was scratched with superphosphate last year, more than two sheep to the acre have been carried all the year around.'[6]

G. M. Webb considered that on his 600 acres of clover land, with the assistance of clover hay, he could carry three sheep to the acre all the year applying as he did two dressings, totalling 90 lbs of superphosphate, each year.

Unfortunately, with their lush feed the farmers were also observing the coming of the red mite, the first awareness of it being in 1925.

This, together with the rabbit infiltration, looked like being their biggest problems in the future—so they thought!

Most of this expansion was achieved with horses. The tractor and lorry did not supplant the horse completely for a good many years. Some iron wheel tractors were being introduced but there was a lot of criticism of them as their wheels slipped and ploughed up the ground. After a stock sale in May 1926, a very successful motor tractor demonstration was given in John Delaney's paddock ploughing 'fairly hard ground with a four furrow plough'.[7] (At this same sale the white-bearded Delaney had been presented with an easy chair by the Road Board, in recognition of his long association with that body.)

Well into the thirties horses were still being used and P. P. Thorn recalls carting 200 tons of fertilizer from Carlecatup siding with a 10 ton wagon and a dozen horses, in that decade. Leaving home at midnight he would arrive at the siding about sunrise and the horses would enjoy a nose-bag while he loaded up, a task taking 1½ hours. They would eventually reach home about midday. Someone would unload while he caught up on his sleep to be ready for the next load. As far as he was concerned it was a great relief to see the finish of the working horses. They required an enormous amount of attention at all times. When twenty draughthorses were being used to sow or strip, someone was needed almost all day to cut chaff to keep up to them. In addition precious time was lost feeding, watering and rubbing them down. On the other hand, for personal use the machine was becoming increasingly popular each year and in 1930 three hundred vehicles were licensed in the district. Squatter Jones's family is said to have owned the first car in the district, about 1911.

Briefly, this was the overall picture existing in Kojonup when in 1929-30 the world experienced an economic collapse and prices of most primary products plunged downwards. For at least the first half of the thirties an economic depression throughout Australia brought all thought of prosperity and all hope of expansion to a full stop. In 1927 W. H. Penny who was the current owner of 'Glen Lossie' was proud to admit to an average price of 33½ pence per pound for forty bales. Two years later E. Johnston sold his twenty-eight bales for an inclusive price of twelve pence per pound; and early in the new year of 1930, the unhappy D. A. Robertson topped a sale in Perth with the inadequate price of 15½ pence per pound.

The full impact of the catastrophe seems not to have been immediately felt by the Kojonup Road Board members. In March 1930 there was some concern because rates were not being paid but the impression is given that it was thought to be only a temporary cessation. Then news was received from the Main Road Board which had been constituted in 1926 that owing to the prevailing financial situation it was difficult to say when funds would be available for main road works and that maintenance money might also be held up because of the financial depression.

In July the grave widespread nature of the slump had still not fully hit home. Three single men were dismissed and the scale of wages of the married labourers was reduced, but it was unanimously agreed to retain the salary and conditions of the secretary and supervisor at the existing rate. However, the next month the axe fell for them too and their salaries were reduced by £1 a month. Twelve months later both the secretary and supervisor had their salaries cut another 15s. per week and the driver and grader man had their weekly wage reduced from £4 to £3 16s. 0d. each. Four months later the secretary and supervisor were faced with yet another reduction. Nevertheless, compared with some they were well off. Many were unemployed and sustenance work was being found for fifteen married men from out of the district. Single men existed as best they could, the lucky ones working for farmers for just their keep.

All unnecessary expenditure, even to the provision of afternoon tea on Board days, was suspended and in June 1932 it was decided not to embark on any new work unless absolutely necessary. The rates outstanding at that stage were £2148, the largest for many years.

As for the farmers and their families, many are the tales that can be recalled of the grim days of the depression. Some lost their farms and others saved theirs by relying on their poultry, a cow and the despised rabbit for subsistence and by rigidly limiting all other demands. Long after, grateful farmers remembered the generous credit given to them by R. L. Richardson for essential luxuries such as sugar, tea and flour. Those who had been able to hold on to a flock recovered a little earlier as wool was the first of the primary products to firm (about 1934). However farmers were only just getting back on their feet and reconsidering an expansion policy as another crisis loomed. In 1939 the outbreak of war was announced and austerity conditions were reinstated as the Australian nation became involved more and more deeply in the world conflict.

It was not until after this 1939-45 war that the Kojonup district can really be said to have made rapid gigantic strides. As in the aftermath of the 1914-18 war, the servicemen returning to the district, or coming to it for the first time as soldier settlers, brought a new vigorous outlook to the district and were instrumental in bringing into production thousands of acres of virgin land. The advanced technical and scientific knowledge available increased the production of the established properties to a degree beyond the wildest dreams of the most sanguine of the early pioneers, while rising wool prices enabled many to enjoy a prosperity never before experienced.

Kojonup became known as a sound wool growing district; and in 1967 the sheep population of the shire passed the one million mark. For the year ending 31 March 1969, of the total area of 700,628 acres only 22.1 per cent was uncleared and of the cleared land 415,584 acres were under pasture. For the same period, the 337 holdings had a wool clip totalling 13,712,833 lbs from 1,291,987 sheep and lambs. In addition 11,213 beef cattle were grazed and 1,452,039 bushels of oats, 95,028 bushels of wheat, 475,696 bushels of 2 row barley and 19,073 bushels of 6 row barley had been produced.[8]

Yet such advancement was not attained without many trials. The wholesale use of clovers and superphosphate was thought to be linked with an increasing sheep infertility and loss of lambs. By the persistent efforts of the Kojonup Road Board, and in particular of the chairman at the time N. B. O'Halloran, in 1948 the property Glen Lossie was established by the C.S.I.R.O. as an experimental station. However, unfortunately for Kojonup even the Commonwealth was to be only a temporary proprietor and it withdrew in 1966 leaving Glen Lossie the dubious record of seventeen owners since it was first granted!

In conclusion, the message to be learnt from the history of Kojonup must surely be that 'no man is an island'. Time and again throughout the years of settlement, people and events miles away have changed the direction of its development. Nor can it be said that the Kojonup countryside has given willingly of its secrets and its bounty.

Amid all this change the Spring water, sadly salty now, has continued to trickle from under its guardian granite slab in the boulder-strewn valley. On the rise above, its companion since 1845, the little stone barracks, still surveys the passing parade of generations of Kojonup residents, the faster tempo of the Albany Road traffic, the rise of grander, modern dwellings and the dilapidation and sometimes demolition of familiar, outworn ones with which it shared countless memories. Through the wise forethought of the Kojonup Shire Council it will not share the same fate. Instead, under the respectful management of the Kojonup Historical Society into whose care it has been entrusted, it will continue to watch over the town and stand as a memorial to the pioneers of the past.

REFERENCES

[1] Balgarup Diaries, 15 May 1913 (in possession of D. Crabbe, Kojonup).
[2] *Ibid*. 24 May 1913.
[3] Pascoe, article no. 8, *Producers' Review*, 20 April 1929.
[4] *Western Mail*, 22 May 1930, p. 30.
[5] *Ibid*.
[6] *Ibid*.
[7] *Great Southern Herald*, 19 May 1926, p. 4.
[8] Statistics supplied at the annual general meeting of electors in respect of the financial year ending 30 June 1969 (held by Kojonup Shire Council).

Appendix I

EXTRACT FROM T. E. H. APLIN 'YORK ROAD POISON AND BOX POISON', *JOURNAL OF THE DEPARTMENT OF AGRICULTURE*, MAY 1967, VOL. 8, NO. 5

York Road Poison
(*Gastrolobium calycinum* Benth.)

York Road poison derives its common name from the fact that in the early years of settlement many stock died from eating this plant while being driven along the road from Perth to York. Stock losses due to accidental grazing of this species are still not uncommon and the presence of even a single bush in a paddock can cause heavy losses.

The three main forms of York Road poison are the typical form, the broad-leaved form and the narrow-leaved form. . . . The amount of mono-fluoroacetic acid present in these toxic plants varies from season to season, from locality to locality or even from plant to plant within the one locality. . . . As with other plants containing mono-fluoroacetic acid as their toxic principle, both York Road poison and box poison are most toxic when actively growing, for example, with the appearance of new shoots or suckers or when in the flowering or fruiting stage. Other factors such as the fluoride availability in soils and the acidity or alkalinity of soils have a bearing on the amount of poison present in the plant.

York Road poison and box poison are usually considered to be least toxic when they are dormant—usually in late summer, provided the weather is dry.

Appendix 2

Year	Chairman	Secretary
1871	L. Van Zuilecom	John Tunney, junior
1872	L. Van Zuilecom	John Tunney, junior
1873	L. Van Zuilecom	John Tunney, junior
1874	L. Van Zuilecom	L. Van Zuilecom (from 1 January 1874)
1875	L. Van Zuilecom	L. Van Zuilecom
1876	L. Van Zuilecom	—
1877	—	L. Van Zuilecom
1878	—	L. Van Zuilecom
1879	—	—
1880	—	—
1881	R. Loton	R. Loton
1882	—	R. Loton
1883	Joseph Spencer	——
1884	Joseph Spencer	Thomas Phillips
1885	Joseph Spencer	Thomas Phillips
1886	Joseph Spencer	Thomas Phillips
1887	Joseph Spencer	Thomas Phillips
1888	Joseph Spencer	Thomas Phillips
1889	—	—
1890	—	—
1891	J. G. Garritty	Thomas Phillips
1892	W. H. Graham	Thomas Phillips

The whole Board resigned, and on 30 September 1892 the following were elected:

Year	Chairman	Secretary
1892	J. J. Treasure	Thomas Phillips
1893	J. J. Treasure	Thomas Phillips
1894	J. J. Treasure	Thomas Phillips
1895	—	Thomas Phillips
1896	—	Thomas Phillips
1897	—	J. M. Flanagan
1898	—	J. M. Flanagan
1899	—	J. M. Flanagan
1900	J. J. Treasure	J. M. Flanagan

1901	J. K. Tunney	J. M. Flanagan
1902	J. J. Treasure	J. M. Flanagan
1903	J. J. Treasure	J. M. Flanagan
1904	J. J. Treasure	J. M. Flanagan

(Rating in the Road District first instituted in 1904)

1905	J. J. Treasure	J. M. Flanagan
1905-6	J. McHenry Clark	J. M. Flanagan
1906-7	J. McHenry Clark	J. M. Flanagan (to March 1907)
		A. J. Magrath (from March 1907)
1907-8	J. J. Treasure	A. J. Magrath
1908-9	O. Bignell	A. J. Magrath
1909-10	R. Krakouer	A. J. Magrath
1910-11	R. Krakouer	A. J. Magrath
1911-12	O. Bignell	A. J. Magrath
1912-13	R. Krakouer	A. J. Magrath
1913-14	R. Krakouer	A. J. Magrath
1914-15	R. Krakouer	A. J. Magrath
1915-16	R. Krakouer	A. J. Magrath
1916-17	O. Bignell	A. J. Magrath
1917-18	O. Bignell	A. J. Magrath
1918-19	J. Delaney	A. J. Magrath
1919-20	J. Delaney	C. P. Reilly
1920-21	J. Delaney	C. P. Reilly
1921-22	J. Delaney	J. G. Finlay
1922-23	J. Delaney	J. G. Finlay
1923-24	J. Delaney	J. G. Finlay
1924-25	F. T. Hill	J. G. Finlay
1925-26	W. C. Cussons	J. G. Finlay
1926-27	W. C. Cussons	J. G. Finlay
	F. T. Hill	C. B. Vincent (from 13 July 1926)
1927-28	H. L. Roche	C. B. Vincent
1928-29	R. F. Honner	C. B. Vincent
1929-30	R. F. Honner	C. B. Vincent
1930-31	J. Delaney	C. B. Vincent
1931-32	R. F. Honner	C. B. Vincent
1932-33	R. F. Honner	C. B. Vincent (to 25 February 1933)
		Miss E. M. Robinson (to March 1933—Acting)

		J. V. Burston (from March 1933)
1933-34	R. F. Honner	J. V. Burston
1934-35	R. F. Honner	J. V. Burston
1935-36	R. F. Honner	L. V. MacBride (from 5 June 1935)
1936-37	R. F. Honner	L. V. MacBride
1937-38	R. F. Honner	L. V. MacBride
1938-39	R. F. Honner (until deceased)	
	R. Benn (from June 1938)	L. V. MacBride
1939-40	R. Benn	L. V. MacBride
1940-41	R. Benn	L. V. MacBride
1941-42	R. Benn	L. V. MacBride
1942-43	R. Benn	L. V. MacBride
1943-44	R. Benn	L. V. MacBride
1944-45	R. Benn	L. V. MacBride
1945-46	R. Benn	L. V. MacBride
1946-47	N. B. O'Halloran (from 14 May 1946)	L. V. MacBride
1947-48	N. B. O'Halloran	L. V. MacBride
1948-49	J. F. Cavanagh	L. V. MacBride
1949-50	J. F. Cavanagh	L. V. MacBride
1950-51	J. F. Cavanagh	L. V. MacBride
1951-52	E. C. Jones	L. V. MacBride
1952-53	E. C. Jones	L. V. MacBride
1953-54	E. C. Jones	L. V. MacBride
1954-55	D. B. O'Halloran	L. V. MacBride
1955-56	D. B. O'Halloran	L. V. MacBride
1956-57	G. N. Lewis	L. V. MacBride
1957-58	G. N. Lewis	L. V. MacBride
1958-59	G. N. Lewis	L. V. MacBride
1959-60	G. O. Harrison	L. V. MacBride
1960-61	G. O. Harrison	L. V. MacBride

KOJONUP SHIRE COUNCIL: 1961-62 TO 1970-71

Year	President	Shire Clerk
1961-62	Cr G. O. Harrison	L. V. MacBride (to April 1962)

		M. J. Edmonds (from April 1962)
1962-63	Cr G. O. Harrison	M. J. Edmonds
1963-64	Cr W. H. C. Stretch	M. J. Edmonds
1964-65	Cr W. H. C. Stretch	M. J. Edmonds
1965-66	Cr W. H. C. Stretch	M. J. Edmonds (to January 1966) R. L. Leggo (from February 1966)
1966-67	Cr W. H. C. Stretch	R. L. Leggo
1967-68	Cr W. H. C. Stretch	R. L. Leggo
1968-69	Cr W. H. C. Stretch	R. L. Leggo
1969-70	Cr L. N. Collins	R. L. Leggo (to 20 March 1970) D. G. Ferris (from 4 May 1970)
1970-71	Cr L. N. Collins	D. G. Ferris

Appendix 3

Councillor	*Ward*
S. Crook	Balgarup
L. N. Collins (President)	Balgarup
W. A. McKenney	Ongerup
Mrs M. W. L. Lewis	Ongerup
F. J. B. Timms	Muradup
B. H. Brockman	Muradup
D. B. O'Halloran	Namarillup
D. A. Crouch	Namarillup
P. D. Lee	Town
F. W. Kelly	Town

Appendix 4

Unit	Name	Area	Year
48th Battalion	E. Armstrong	France	1917
51st ,,	J. V. Ashe	,,	,,
44th ,,	W. Bateman	,,	,,
11th ,,	H. Bick	Gallipoli	1915
,, ,,	J. Brentnall	France	1917
10th Light Horse	L. A. Cockrane	Middle East	,,
51st Battalion	L. A. Cole	France	1918
48th ,,	A. Dreamer	,,	,,
44th ,,	J. N. Elliott	,,	1917
51st ,,	H. H. Ferguson	,,	1918
11th ,,	F. T. Gare	,,	1917
,, ,,	J. Gare	,,	,,
51st ,,	C. W. Grover	France	,,
,, ,,	L. J. Grover	unknown	,,
11th ,,	W. G. Halden	,,	1916
44th ,,	J. Hart	,,	1917
11th ,,	V. B. Javens	,,	,,
44th ,,	C. C. Larsen	,,	,,
48th ,,	A. Little	,,	,,
,, ,,	P. Loney	,,	1916
51st ,,	A. J. McEwan	,,	,,
10th Light Horse	R. R. J. Norrish	Middle East	1918
,, ,, ,,	F. E. Norrish	,, ,,	1916
48th Battalion	R. H. Oliver	France	1917
A.R.T.	S. Parsons	,,	,,
44th Battalion	H. Rose	,,	1918
11th ,,	G. Stent	Gallipoli	1915
10th Light Horse	J. J. Thornett	,,	,,
,, ,, ,,	W. V. Weaber	Middle East	1918
11th Battalion	R. L. White	France	1917
,, ,,	G. Worthington	,,	,,

KOJONUP MEN WHO DIED IN THE 1939-45 WAR*

Unit	Name	Area	Year
11th Battalion	J. Baker	Middle East	1941
48th ,,	H. E. Cooper	,, ,,	1942
51st ,,	C. J. Elvey	,, ,,	,,
R.A.A.F.	T. F. Eyre	Germany (missing)	1944
,,	I. L. Felgate	,, ,,	,,
48th	L. W. Flanagan	Middle East	1942
R.A.A.F.	H. Gaunt	Timor Sea (missing)	1943
,,	H. Gould	,, ,, ,,	1944
,,	A. W. Hain	Burma (missing)	,,
11th Battalion	E. Halford	N.W.	,,
4th Machine Gunners	F. W. Hall	P.O.W.	,,
R.A.A.F.	H. S. Jones	Germany (missing)	,,
3rd Machine Gunners	J. M. Ladyman	P.O.W.	,,
11th Battalion	A. Liddell	Greece	1940
R.A.A.F.	R. C. Lindsey	Germany (missing)	1944
S.P.O.	N. Merfield	New Guinea (missing)	1944
W.R.A.N.S.	G. Parker	Australia	1944
48th Battalion	N. L. Purse	Middle East	1942
R.A.A.F.	C. D. Robertson	Timor Sea (missing)	1945
16th Battalion	F. Sanderson	Middle East	1942
32nd ,,	J. Schorer	,, ,,	,,
16th ,,	C. M. W. Smith	,, ,,	,,
R.A.A.F.	P. Sturges	Germany (missing)	1944
3rd Machine Gunners	S. Warren	P.O.W.	,,

* Collected and supplied by Levi Treasure.

Index

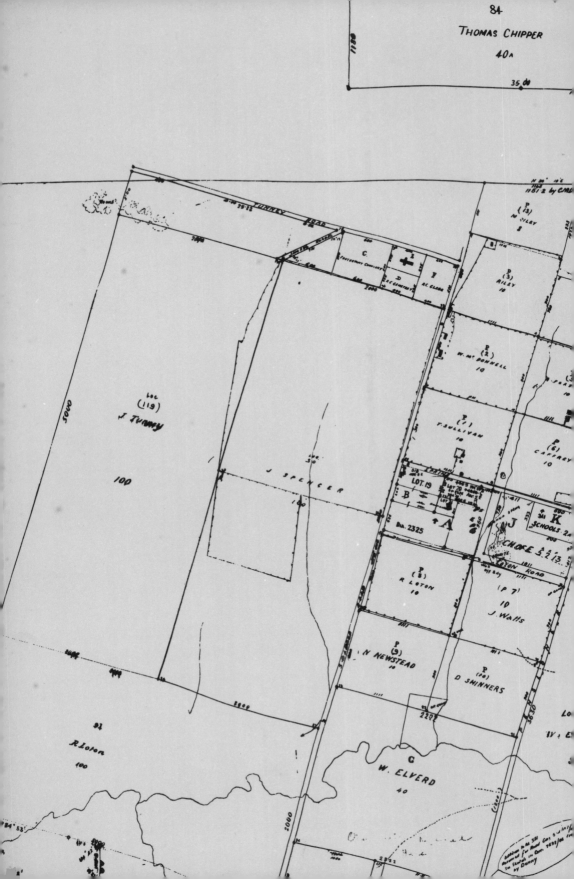